# The *Hiawatha* Story

T0345904

# The *Hiawatha* Story

JIM SCRIBBINS

University of Minnesota Press
Minneapolis | London

## THE FESLER–LAMPERT MINNESOTA HERITAGE BOOK SERIES

This series reprints significant books that enhance our understanding and appreciation of Minnesota and the Upper Midwest. It is supported by the generous assistance of the John K. and Elsie Lampert Fesler Fund and the interest and contribution of Elizabeth P. Fesler and the late David R. Fesler.

Appreciation and thanks are extended to the railroad employees, railfans, editorial staff, and all the other persons who helped to make this book possible.

Published by the University of Minnesota Press
111 Third Avenue South, Suite 290
Minneapolis, MN 55401-2520
http://www.upress.umn.edu

Library of Congress Cataloging-in-Publication Data

The Hiawatha story / Jim Scribbins. – 1st University of Minnesota Press ed.
p. cm. – (The Fesler-Lampert Minnesota heritage book series)
Originally published: Milwaukee : Kalmbach, 1970.
Includes index.
ISBN 978-0-8166-5003-3 (pbk : alk. paper)
1. Chicago, Milwaukee, St. Paul, and Pacific Railroad Company.
2. Hiawatha (Express train).
TF25.C5S37 2007
385'.220973--dc22

2007007491

Printed in Canada on acid-free paper

The University of Minnesota is an equal-opportunity educator and employer.

15 14 13 12 11 10          10 9 8 7 6 5 4 3 2

# CONTENTS

**6 INTRODUCTION**

**8 SPEED**

**10 ENTER THE HI**
"Speedlined" became the adjective

**28 FROM TIP TOP TAP TO BEAVER TAIL**
The train that netted $700,000 in a year

**40 RIBBED CARS AND 4-6-4'S**
What was unprecedented became astounding

**64 100 HITS 100**
A few figures for skeptics to mull over

**72 DIESELS, WAR, AND S.R.O.**
In an all-out war, all-out Hi's

**84 FAMOUS 15**
The locomotive that sold the steam-powered Milwaukee Road on diesels

**90 SKYTOPS AND SUPER DOMES**
More diesels and enough new cars to make a 2½-mile Hi

**116 YELLOW PAINT AND RED INK**
For President Crippen, "an unhappy task"

**128 NORTH WOODS HIAWATHA**
The Hi that was the fisherman's friend

**140 MIDWEST HIAWATHA**
"The audacity to challenge entrenchments"

**156 OLYMPIAN HIAWATHA**
To fill a void, "a perfect train"

**188 CHIPPEWA-HIAWATHA**
Where aging Pacifics dimmed their headlights for deer

**202 EPILOGUE**

**204 WAY OF THE HIAWATHAS**

**224 LOCOMOTIVES**

**258 ROLLING STOCK**

**266 INDEX**

# INTRODUCTION

I MUST HAVE BEEN 10 or 11 years old when I discovered what was to become my favorite place for train-watching. Not that I had missed much on the Milwaukee railroad scene. Our house was only a half block from the Northern Division main line and, if I wished or the weather ordained, I could view the railroad traffic from our living-room window.

At night, in bed, I would hear the Mallet articulated pusher which ruled the grade separating our neighborhood.

It would lose its footing, and cinders would cascade onto the house roof as it fought for traction. The passenger trains were plentiful and in groups, which made them something special to be saluted from a reserved close-up seat on the Harley-Davidson shipping platform.

To a 10-year-old it seemed as though the beautiful open-platform observation car of the *Copper Country Limited*, the red cars of the Soo Line, and the loud-talking new Mikados with the huge initials U.S.R.A. on their tender

Al Kalmbach was planning the first issue of a new magazine called TRAINS at his home a few miles away when the Milwaukee Road photographer captured a familiar scene on film at Wauwatosa, Wis., a Milwaukee suburb. Forget for a moment that the great Hudsons now are scrapped, that the distinctive frame depot has long since been demolished, that the passenger train itself is on the wane. The date is April 30, 1940, and the Milwaukee's Twin Cities *Hiawathas* are the toast of Midwest railroading, in all the world the fastest things on wheels behind a steam locomotive. Yes, the hometown railroad has hit the big time. — *Milwaukee Road.*

flanks would go on forever. The "tin lizzies" could not possibly affect the trains.

Here at the foot of 32nd Street was enough railroading to surely go on forever, and with some to spare. As I got closer to the end of the street the view opened out. A 20- or 30-foot bluff furnished a place to sit and see the whole mile valley of railroad at work.

Nearest to me was the Merrill Park suburban station, the main line, and then a giant's ladder of short ready tracks for engines ready to go as called. Beyond were the coaling stage, sand and water facilities, two almost complete circle roundhouses, a brace of special-purpose shop buildings, foundry and miscellaneous, and, more dim in the distance, assorted large and small freight yards.

What a stage and what a backdrop! And things could happen and often did. A constant parade of new ideas in railroading could be viewed. For a while the *Pioneer Limited* was pulled by standard Pacifics brightly painted orange and red. A couple of doodlebugs used flash steam instead of the usual internal combustion. Various schemes of compounding were tried in the constant fight to make the steam locomotive more efficient. One by one the electric locomotives for the Puget Sound electrification stopped on their way West for public showing and mechanical adjustment. The Twenties in turn were ushered out by

bigger and faster steam locomotives and improved rolling stock.

But the biggest story played on the Merrill Park stage was that of the *Hiawathas*. The atmosphere at the engine terminal and shops that spring of 1935 was supersaturated with suppressed excitement. The prospect of a race for the Chicago-Twin Cities business created unusual team spirit.

The story of the *Hiawathas* has needed telling. It is the story of mid-20th century railroad passenger service in microcosm. Detailed behind-the-scenes study of the *Hiawathas* shows the traffic pattern of the Milwaukee Road during a critical period, but also gives us the answer to what other similarly situated railroads did during the same years.

This book is that story, told by Jim Scribbins, whose service in the Milwaukee Road passenger department spans much of the same period as the famous streamliners. Jim's writing for TRAINS Magazine has primed his typewriter for one of the most exciting railroad sagas of the times. The *Hiawathas* came and they largely have gone. What happened in between is, every bit of it, between the covers of this book.

*A. C. Kalmbach*

Milwaukee, Wis.
December 1969

# SPEED

K4'S whipping the *Detroit* and *Chicago Arrows* across the Fort Wayne Division in record time. The Great Steel Fleet rolling incessantly behind magnificent Hudsons . . . Toledo, Collinwood, Buffalo . . . mile after mile, night after night, averaging better than 60 miles an hour. Or closer to Chicago: rebuilt 2900's on the *400*, "Setting the Pace for the World"; brave little *Electroliners*; shovel-nosed units bringing home the bacon with the world's fastest, the *Morning Zephyr*, No. 21.

Or men: Harry Mayell notching his splendid GG1 away from a speed restriction. Or Engineer McGhee and Fireman Roop calling signals to each other above the clatter of their J making child's play of streaking four cars of *Powhatan Arrow* across tidewater Virginia.

All this, and so much more, was what speed on railways was for others. For me it will always be most vividly illustrated by Milwaukee Road No. 100 when the E7's on the head end were permitted free rein to 100 miles per hour.

The voice on the p.a. ("*The Hiawatha is now arriving on the eastbound track, way down near the highway for Portage, Madison, and Watertown, alongside the shelter for . . .*") is muffled by the approaching speedster. Its air horns sound a couple of off-note chords — E7's slide by, brake shoes sparking, bell ringing. Porters in the vestibules

8

of the two head coaches beckon, for time is precious. Before a seat is reached, one hundred folks from the "Valley" have been loaded and an almost imperceptible motion starts the train.

The roar of 4000 horses digging in echoes back. Though it is uphill much of the way, the first 7 miles is negotiated in only 6 minutes 45 seconds from the dead stop. Over the top, No. 100 seems to leave the rails and glide gently in space . . .

Keeonk keeonk *onk* kee — onk. "Marchowsky's" crossing, and the homes of Mauston flash by, almost blurred; a slight bounce at the double street crossing at the edge of the depot platform, and again, the sensation of being just above the rails, not on them. A moderate lurch on the curve east of town, then down the speedway with occasional bits of gravel hitting the coach floor. *Moving now.* The 10.6 miles to Lyndon are clocked in 6 minutes 25 seconds. *Averaging 99.2.* More gravel. The EMD's horn continually emits its raucous warning in advance of sandy little side roads. Suddenly — no advance indication — the brakes take hold . . . speed drops from near 100 to about 70 — there's a bit of a jolt and the left edge of the coach elevates appreciably on the first of the series of curves along the Dells.

In seconds the brakes release, the *Hi* is free. But not for long. A second, more severe application accompanied by the echo of steel pressing steel reduces speed to 40 through the reverse curve and across the high bridge: Wisconsin Dells. Off the span, the impatience of two pairs of V-12's becomes known.

Within a mile speed is back in the 80's *and increasing.*

Again the train is like the wind, rushing violently along, overtaking and passing every vehicle on the parallel highway.

Eight miles to go.

*"Portage will be next in about five minutes. Change for Madison."*

Three miles out; speed still in the 90's. Now only 8000 feet left . . . the roar ahead subsides, the fleet Indian swoops beneath the highway overpass, brakes take hold on the long curve. Remarkably smooth brakes, no rough stuff, nothing spilled.

Thirty-five at the west end of the platform.

Twenty passing the operator's bay.

*"Keep back, folks. Let 'em off, please."*

The run described is the cumulative impression of many rides between New Lisbon and Portage, Wis. Reductions in the maximum speed limit make such timings no longer possible. The piece is reprinted from May 1961 TRAINS Magazine.

E. A. Behr.

9

# ENTER THE HI

"Speedlined" became the adjective

FROM 12:30 to 1 p.m. on May 29, 1935, radio station WLS in Chicago, Ill., broadcast a program which originated not in its studios but beneath the trainshed of Chicago Union Station. The radiocast included a performance by one of WLS's western musical groups and speeches by Mayor Edward J. Kelly and Milwaukee Road President Henry A. Scandrett. The significant part of the program was the christening by Jeannie Dixon, daughter of the general passenger agent of the CMStP&P, of a strange-looking, attention-drawing conveyance. Listeners then heard a bell ringing and muted exhaust puffs . . . and the *Hiawatha* was an accomplished fact.

Although this departure of No. 101 was heralded, it was not actually the beginning of *Hiawatha* service, for eastbound counterpart No. 100 had steamed out of Minneapolis one-half hour earlier, after a ceremony which included the presence of the mayor and a christening with water from fabled Minnehaha Falls by agent C. H. Crouse.

What events had led to these occasions?

In 1934, when North America was fascinated by minuscule "egg-shaped," "motor-driven" trains introduced by the Union Pacific and the Burlington, the individualistic Chicago, Milwaukee, St. Paul & Pacific Railroad undertook in its Milwaukee Shops the construction of full-size lightweight passenger coaches of radically improved design. Coach 4000, rebuilt from the sleeper *Great Falls*, was a compromise design utilizing its original clerestory roof and riveted-steel underframe but employing welded smooth sides identical to those of the fully streamlined cars which were to follow. The 4000 was carried on six-wheel trucks and actually weighed more than many standard CMStP&P coaches.

Early in May completely new coach 4400, equipped with four-wheel trucks and weighing 35 per cent less than conventional coaches, was turned out. It facilitated high-speed operation at economical maintenance costs. The space allotment per individual passenger was increased from 6½ to 10½ square feet, with 48½-inch seat centers. The car provided the passenger with a reclining seat, air conditioning, wider-than-usual luggage racks that stretched the full length of the main passenger compartment, larger toilets with adjoining smoking lounges for both men and women, roomier vestibules, and a quietness and smoothness of ride never achieved before.

Marshall Field & Company had assisted in the interior design of the cars. The basics were flesh-colored ceilings, brown walls, and Durite green asphalt tile floors. For all practical purposes, the design of the coaches and trucks was the result of the imagination of

Moments after splitting the air at a steady 112.5 mph for 14 miles on May 15, 1935, the highly polished streamlined prow of No. 2 was admired by dozens of townspeople at New Lisbon, Wis. The first complete consist of *Hiawatha* equipment, shown here occupying track normally used by "Valley" trains to Woodruff, had been wyed for the return leg to Milwaukee of the first true high-speed test run of the train and locomotive. — *Milwaukee Road*.

On July 20, 1934, Hudson 6402 proved the feasibility of high-speed operation between Chicago and Milwaukee by taking a revenue train up to 103.5 mph during a special test. Undoubtedly the men in white shirts have come down to the Milwaukee depot from the shops to inspect the 4-6-4 after her momentous run with Second 27 — which covered the 85 miles in 67 minutes 35 seconds. — *Rail Photo Service*.

This may be the only photograph taken of a *Hiawatha* Atlantic before shrouding was applied. The entire front end was lagged and jacketed to keep down the temperature inside the shrouding. Note the saddle-shaped sandbox just to the rear of the steam dome. — *Alco Products*.

Karl F. Nystrom. Nystrom had come from his native Sweden to the Grand Trunk Railway in Canada, then had moved on to the Chicago, Milwaukee & St. Paul in 1922 as an engineer of car design. On the Milwaukee he rose to the position of chief mechanical officer. Subsequent improvement in the Milwaukee's car design, and notably in truck design, can be accredited almost entirely to this man. He was perhaps the outstanding authority on trucks west of the Atlantic. In 1941 he was awarded an honorary Doctor of Engineering degree by Marquette University in Milwaukee, Wis.

Mass production commenced with coach 4401. The interior design of this car and the 39 that followed was somewhat different, resulting in a seating capacity of 48 in the body of the car, 10 in the men's smoking room, and 5 in the ladies' smoking room compared with 40, 9, and 5 respectively in the 4000 and the 4400. The 4400 had lights above the aisle, an arrangement which was eliminated from subsequent cars. At the same time, dormitory cars for use on the *Olympian* also were constructed to this design. These cars contained a main room with 36 reclining seats, a smoking room with 20 reclining seats, and a section sleeping space for 16 dining-car crew members.*

In 1934, car 4400 went to Chicago for the second year of the Century of Progress Exposition. It was the only full-size preview of the forthcoming streamlined era at the fair. The new cars rolled from Milwaukee Shops into service on the *Olympian, Pioneer Limited, Day Express, Fast Mail, Arrow, Southwest Limited,* and *Sioux,* and on unnamed trains in Illinois, Wisconsin, and Michigan.

There were other hints of what was to come. On July 15, 1934, Chicago & North Western and Milwaukee Road, in a jointly timed endeavor, inaugurated trains between Chicago and Milwaukee on a 90-minute schedule for the 85 miles. One C&NW train in each direction and two northbound and three southbound CMStP&P trains made this time — a reduction of 15 minutes from the best existing schedule. N. A. Ryan, assistant to the general manager of the Milwaukee, was largely responsible for the time reduction as well as the raising of the speed limit for passenger trains from 70 to 75 mph. He felt that even more improvements could be made, and was particularly anxious to capture for the Milwaukee some of the publicity being bestowed on the owners of the new diesel streamliners.

*Throughout the careers of the *Hiawathas,* the Milwaukee built additional head-end, dormitory, dining, and parlor-cafe cars to streamlined design. These never saw *Hiawatha* service and consequently are not a part of this narrative.

Arrangements were made on the CMStP&P for a really fast run from Chicago to Milwaukee with train 29, the 90-minute morning train. On Friday, July 20, No. 29 operated as Second 27 in order to gain free rein. Few if any passengers attached any significance to the presence of business car *Wisconsin* on the markers end, and not until they found themselves in Milwaukee considerably ahead of their anticipated arrival time did they realize that an unusual event had taken place. The run was to be as close to normal operation as possible, and no special preparations were made except to give Hudson 6402 (Baldwin 1929) a thorough lubrication and to station sectionmen at grade crossings to flag approaching motorists. Techny, Ill., 20 miles out, was achieved in 21 minutes; then engineman William Dempsey let his F-6 4-6-4 out, passing Wadsworth (43 miles) in 35 minutes, and Sturtevant (62 miles) in 48 minutes. Rounding a 1-degree curve at 102 mph produced "little discomfort" on the *Wisconsin.* The high point of the trip was the 103.5 mph maximum speed achieved between Oakwood and Lake, Wis. The remaining 7 miles of running to Milwaukee was subdued by comparison.

Although a 75-minute timing had been sought, the 85 miles was negotiated in 67 minutes 35 seconds — a start-to-stop average of 75.5 mph. The train was composed of five conventional cars weighing 388.5 tons; the weight of the 6402 (including tender) was 653,650 pounds. The locomotive trailing truck, the tender trucks, and all car trucks were roller-bearing equipped. The average of 89.92 mph for 68.9 miles was regarded as a new world record, surpassing the time of a June 1932 test train operated by England's Great Western Railway that, although it averaged 81.6 mph start to stop, did not exceed a cruising speed of 92 mph. Moreover, officials thought that Second 27 could have done better had the road not desired to avoid any undue risk on a train carrying revenue passengers.

In August the cat was out of the bag. Burlington, North Western, and Milwaukee Road each announced that it would make substantial reductions in running time for day trains between Chicago and St. Paul from approximately 10 to 6½ hours over routes varying from 407 to 431 miles. It was not uncommon to be able to drive from the Twin Cities to Chicago at a 50 mph average speed, and buses were making considerable inroads on rail passenger traffic. Furthermore, keeping the time of the important passenger trains shorter than that of the new 11-hour time freights over the same route was desirable. The Q, however, went even further. It announced that it would use trains of the "*Zephyr* type," and demonstrated its intentions by

The American Locomotive Company was a highly imaginative concern indeed in 1935. To herald the arrival of the radically new streamlined A's, the firm ran this series of advertisements in *Railway Age*. Certainly no other set of four locomotives received the publicity the Milwaukee Road high-steppers did. — *Alco Products*.

14

AMERICAN LOCOMOTIVE COMPANY

30 CHURCH STREET · NEW YORK · N·Y·

# BREAKING THROUGH!

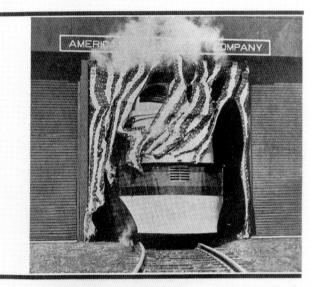

April 30, 1935

At 3 P. M. at Schenectady, N. Y., steam again broke through into a new era in railway passenger traffic.

AMERICAN LOCOMOTIVE COMPANY

ALCO

30 CHURCH STREET · NEW YORK · N·Y·

15

Coach 4000, rebuilt from the sleeper *Great Falls*, was the result of the Milwaukee's first attempt to build a car that would counter the appeal of the articulated *Zephyrs* being delivered to the Burlington. — *Milwaukee Road.*

Another view of the May 15, 1935, test train that achieved unprecedented high speeds between Milwaukee and New Lisbon reveals a dynamometer car coupled between Atlantic No. 2 and the first *Hiawatha* consist. Railroaders and New Lisbon townspeople alike peek underneath the shrouding to see "what makes her go." — *Milwaukee Road.*

In all its glory — from fast-stepping Atlantic to Beaver Tail parlor — a complete *Hiawatha* consist pauses somewhere near Chicago for a preinaugural portrait. An exhibition tour of Milwaukee Road cities also preceded revenue service of the two seven-car sets of equipment, which entered the timetable as trains 100 and 101. — *Milwaukee Road.*

Days-old cinder-dusted snow covered the landscape on a cold, gray February 22, 1936, as the new *Hiawatha*, still meeting the challenge of its first winter, roared under the Sangamon Street viaduct moments after leaving Chicago's Union Station. A man on the overpass, three men in a box car, and a street crossing guard, as well as pioneer rail photographer Alfred W. Johnson, all paused to observe the display of erupting exhaust and billowing smoke, and the grand sweep of the gray, orange, and maroon streamliner into the horizon. — *Alfred W. Johnson.*

"Here She Comes" and "There She Goes" are photographer Alfred W. Johnson's titles for these views of No. 101 raising the dust through Wisconsin Dells, Wis., on September 24, 1935. The train left Portage — 17 miles behind the Beaver Tail's markers — on a schedule that called for a start-to-stop average speed of 71.8 mph to the next stop, New Lisbon — another 26 miles up the double-track main line. — *Alfred W. Johnson.*

operating the *Zephyr* from Chicago to St. Paul in 6 hours 4 minutes, including six 1-minute stops.

The North Western, because it merely upgraded conventional locomotives and cars, was able to jump the gun on the competition by inaugurating its *400* on January 2, 1935; but the next day, to keep in the headlines, the Milwaukee reduced the time of its 90-minute trains on the Chicago & Milwaukee subdivision to 85 minutes.

A week later came the revelation that in the fall of 1934 Milwaukee Road had ordered from the American Locomotive Company two streamlined steam locomotives with many new features enabling sustained high-speed operation faster than any previous steam locomotive, and that special rear cars for the projected Chicago-Minneapolis streamliner were nearing completion. By the end of January the time of two of the Milwaukee-to-Chicago expresses had been reduced to 80 minutes, equaling the time of the C&NW *400*, and providing the highest start-to-stop average speeds between metropolitan centers in the United States.

In February the company-coined term "Beaver Tail" was first used in reference to a photo of the parlor-observation cars fresh out of the shops and, significantly, lacking nameplates beneath their rear windows. In April the first mention of the new trains' name appeared, and the road clarified pronunciation by making it known that the accent was on *Hi*awatha, stressing the first syllable to sound the same as in the greeting "Hi."

Plans for the train had been well along before a definite name was decided on. Various suggestions were advanced: the passenger department favored *Flash* to signify speed; Operating Vice-President J. T. Gillick suggested *A-1* since that term was used in 1935 as "A-O.K." is now. Four Milwaukee employees, including Clarence E. Brophy of the mechanical engineer's office, suggested the name *Hiawatha*, which caught the favor of C. H. Bilty, the road's mechanical engineer. The two men began a campaign to promote their choice. Bilty was the chief link between the railroad and Alco, and since the name *Hiawatha* also had been suggested by Alco Vice-President J. B. Ennis, the builder helped advance it by referring to the two engines by that name in correspondence with Milwaukee officials. The legendary Indian was fleet of foot, as the train would be, and characters in Henry Wadsworth Longfellow's poem "The Song of Hiawatha" could be associated with the city of Winona (Wenonah), Minn., and with Minnehaha Falls in Minneapolis. By April the Hiawatha victory had been won. About that same time,

"speedlined" first appeared as an adjective pertaining to the train.

The matter of whether the railroad or the builder contributed the most to the design of the 4-4-2's which were to pull the train will never be resolved completely. Bilty's office decided that the Atlantics would not be painted black and ordered the pattern shop to make wooden models of the proposed locomotive covering and of the Beaver Tail. Apparently the road made inquiries of other builders too before choosing Alco. Years later, after the A's had been scrapped, a Milwaukee Road official offered the opinion that the mechanical aspects of the design, including the choice of wheel arrangement, had been primarily an Alco responsibility.

The road's decision for a steam-powered train was prompted by a number of reasons:

1. Steam was best suited to pull the full-size streamlined cars that were to be employed. Use of such cars in turn provided more passenger comfort than would a small, cramped articulated train.

2. The consist of the train could be varied in accordance with demand (and that turned out to be a valuable asset).

3. Existing facilities could be used.

4. The *Hiawatha*, being a full-size train, required a power plant whose proportions were available only with steam.

5. Steam-locomotive design was considered to offer greater grade-crossing protection to crew and passengers.

6. Steam provided full horsepower at top speed.

7. The initial investment for steam was a quarter of that for diesel.

So at 3 p.m. on April 30, 1935, *Hiawatha* Atlantic No. 1, handled by a mock Indian engine crew, broke through paper bunting to emerge from the erecting shop at Schenectady, N. Y. Addresses by New York Governor Herbert Lehman, Alco President William Dickerman, and Milwaukee Road President Henry A. Scandrett; reading of a poem, "The Song of the Speedlined *Hiawatha*," by Mrs. Norman C. Naylor, wife of an Alco veep; and even the band music were incidental to the appearance of the Class A 4-4-2. The unusual contour and a liberal use of color contributed to No. 1's striking appearance. A black cowling extended from the recessed stack to the cab roof; the covering over the boiler above the running boards was light gray. Directly below the running boards was a maroon stripe, which rose to roof level along the front side of the cab and continued back along the tender. Another maroon stripe edged the bottom of the shroud, just above the centers of the drive wheels, and the bottom of the tender. The space between these two stripes was traditional Milwaukee orange. (Later the familiar Indian-silhouette-in-oval was added to the center of the tender side and a small bit of maroon was placed at the rear of the tank to blend into the center stripe of newer passenger cars.) The pilot was light gray, as were the cab and tender roofs. Huge stainless-steel wings, with the number on a red plate centered beneath the recessed headlight, wrapped the front of the cowling and extended back beyond the torchlike classification lamps. Midway on the boiler's flanks were HIAWATHA nameplates. Wheels, cylinders, and truck frames were brown, and all lettering was in gold.

The Milwaukee types (as the road described them) were the first streamlined steam locomotives designed as such from origin, the first locomotives in U. S. modern times for which speed alone was the governing design factor, and the first Atlantics built since 1914. They were intended, by the road's admission, to cruise at 100 mph and to reach 120 mph — plenty of reserve power if needed. All axles were equipped with roller bearings, and 300 pounds boiler pressure was used. Oil was chosen for fuel because it eliminated intermediate coaling stops, was cleaner, and afforded better fire control.

No. 1 arrived in Chicago on May 5, and No. 2 three days later. They came none too soon. CB&Q's first *Twin Cities Zephyr* had entered service on April 21, which meant that the *Hiawatha* had to battle two strongly entrenched rivals. The A's were given shake-down runs in freight service, with entirely satisfactory performance; but on passenger trial runs the wearing surfaces of the crossheads grew so hot that at high speeds their bronze liners melted. After approximately 400 miles of operation the piston rings had to be re-placed. The crosshead problem was solved by the use of pure tin liners, and Milwaukee Shops chemist L. E. Grant developed new piston packing rings that were good for 16,000 miles.

On May 8 No. 1 reached 90 mph with a 500-ton train. The big event, though, was a May 15 round trip between Milwaukee and New Lisbon with engine No. 2. Engineman Ed Donahue had a complete consist of *Hiawatha* equipment. The train, carefully timed to each milepost with stopwatches and chronometers, loafed along at 65 to 75 mph as far as Watertown "just to get the feel of things," then the decision was made for the remainder of the run to find out just how fast comfortable travel could be achieved. Ninety-one mph seemed like 45. At 100 mph a shout erupted from the mechanical department personnel doing the timing — 103.5 . . . 105 . . . 105.5 . . . 109, and still comfortable. Finally came 112.5, and the train rode like a dream. In the diner, a full glass of water held every drop.

The trip to New Lisbon had required 113 minutes for 136 miles, a start-to-stop average of 74.9 mph, and the 112.5 mph had been maintained without difficulty for 14 miles. According to Engineer Donahue, the faster he went the better the locomotive rode — al-though this was not necessarily a speed-test run. It seemed as though everyone between Milwaukee and New Lisbon had turned out to see the train pass, and at the terminal of the "Wisconsin Valley division," school was dismissed so that the pupils could witness the special event. Students, teachers, and townspeople were treated to a ride around the wye. On the return to Milwaukee a stop was made at the mainline terminal of Portage, where on-line and off-line pas-senger agents, who were aboard to obtain firsthand knowledge of the *Hi*, conducted local residents through the train. Between Portage and Milwaukee, brake tests were made, and on one of these tests the train was brought from 100 mph to a complete stop in 6600 feet. (In 1950, when service on the *Hi's* was only a cherished memory for the A's, the 4-4-2's were still used on brake tests conducted by the Milwaukee for the Association of American Railroads.) On May 20, No. 2 started an 11-car, 790-ton *Pioneer Limited* without slipping and worked to 85 mph.

Extensive exhibition of the new equipment preceded inaugura-tion of the *Hiawatha*: in the Twin Cities on May 17, 18, and 19; in Red Wing (where no stop was scheduled), Winona, and La Crosse on the 20th; in Madison and Janesville on the 21st and in Beloit and Rockford on the 22nd (these four cities were not along the route of the *Hi*); in Milwaukee° on the 23rd; and in Chicago on the 24th and 26th. Well over 138,000 persons took the opportunity to inspect the speedster. One set of equipment was used to take the Chicago Traf-fic Club to Milwaukee for a joint meeting with the Milwaukee Traffic Club, and on Saturday, May 25, a demonstration trip (by in-vitation, fare $1) was operated between Chicago and Rondout, Ill.

Most of the public attention naturally centered on the locomo-tives and cars, but the railroad gave the track structure what now would be described as an "upgrading" to convert 410 route-miles of line from a 70 mph to a 90 mph or better railroad. A good deal of heavier rail was laid (although not exclusively for the benefit of the *Hi*) and considerable work was done to allow authorized speeds of 90 mph on 1-degree curves. This was accomplished by raising the

---

*It was here after the exhibition had closed that the author saw his first train of *Hiawatha* equipment, simmering beneath the sparse illumination of the west end of the depot.

This is how the competition looked that faced and raced the Milwaukee's new *Hiawatha*. Chicago & North Western's *400*, getting a wheel through Milwaukee's lakefront parks behind a big Pacific, offered passengers upgraded conventional equipment and a 400-minute schedule between Chicago and the Twin Cities. The second edition of Chicago, Burlington & Quincy's *Twin Cities Zephyr*, shown at right wyeing into St. Paul from Minneapolis, was a lightweight articulated speedster that had helped put the word streamliner on the lips of Americans. — *Earl Ruhland (above); H. W. Pontin (right)*.

superelevation of the outer rail from 2½ to 3½ inches, and paying close attention to the alignment of the spiral, or easement curve, connecting the straight track with the curve itself so that passengers would experience no uncomfortable sensation entering or leaving a curve. Some curves, particularly between La Crosse and St. Paul, were — and still are — sharper than 1 degree, and these required lower speeds. This process was constantly refined until, in 1940, 1-degree curves were brought to a permissible maximum speed of 100 mph. Signaling also had to be changed to permit more warning and reaction time. In most cases this was easily achieved by removing alternate wayside signals to make blocks of 2 miles in length. Between Portage, Wis., and Hastings, Minn., the new trains had the added protection of cab signaling installed a few years earlier under Interstate Commerce Commission regulations.

The inaugural timetable indicated a 90 mph maximum for trains 100 and 101 "except where the schedule permits a higher speed," and actually set no maximum for the trains. Speed boards were located sufficiently in advance of curves to permit reductions in time to round the curves with brakes released. Speed tapes were placed on Nos. 1 and 2 and were checked daily; it was made clear that no speed violations would be tolerated. Some minor infractions were recorded at first, but one can guess at what was considered a "minor violation" on straightaways, since the road itself made it known that on regular runs in the early years speeds of over 100 mph were reached.

The original schedule prescribed these start-to-stop average speeds:

| Between | Train 101 | Train 100 |
| --- | --- | --- |
| Chicago-Milwaukee | 68 mph | 68 mph |
| Milwaukee-Portage | 66.4 mph | 67.2 mph |
| Portage-New Lisbon | 71.8 mph | 73.9 mph |
| New Lisbon-La Crosse | 67.7 mph | 69 mph |
| La Crosse-Winona | 55.2 mph | 55.2 mph |
| Winona-St. Paul | 59.4 mph | 58.5 mph |

St. Paul (410 miles) was reached in 390 minutes from Chicago. Coincidentally, the over-all speed of 62 mph was precisely the same as that scheduled for the Silver Jubilee streamliner of Britain's London & North Eastern Railway between London & Newcastle.

Thus, on Wednesday, May 29, 1935, the *Hiawatha* became a reality.

This publicity photograph, taken from the Chicago & North Western overpass at Techny, Ill., shows the Milwaukee Road freight connection which utilizes C&NW trackage rights most of the way from Bensenville. The *Hiawatha* test train is Chicago bound. The contour of the top of the tender was designed to match the rooftops of the coaches. — *Milwaukee Road.*

# FROM TIP TOP TAP TO BEAVER TAIL

The train that netted $700,000 in a year

THE CARS of the *Hiawatha* followed construction patterns nearly identical to the 4400 coaches. The equipment weighed approximately one-third less than conventional standard cars but more than the ultralight articulated diesel trains then coming into use. Coaches and parlor cars were slightly over 78 feet long; the restaurant-buffet was approximately 5 feet shorter. All cars were the same exterior width as conventional rolling stock but were 4 inches wider inside. The tops of the roofs were 1 foot 4½ inches lower.

The head car of the new train was officially designated its restaurant-buffet "with Tip Top Tap room." The forward portion contained the first cocktail bar ever carried on a train in America (and possibly elsewhere for that matter). The back bar was against the forward bulkhead the full width of the car. The serving bar had a few feet of standing space in front of it and was edged with a chromium handrail at the top for patrons to steady themselves while drinking. Next came a booth, a circular table, and another booth on each side of the aisle seating four persons apiece. The Tip Top Tap room had no exterior windows. Recessed lighting above its curved wall panels was reflected from the light-colored ceiling to illuminate the lounge at all times. Furniture was of tubular metal design with cherry red leather upholstery and green composition tabletops. The floor covering was composition of a striped design. A bulkhead wall with swinging door separated this rolling oasis from the adjoining dining room, which was decorated in more subdued tones. Dark paneling extended to a meeting with the flesh-colored ceiling design approximately 1 foot above the windows, at which point semifrosted lighting fixtures circled the room. A coach-size window with aluminum frame was next to each of the six tables for four, and aluminum striping extended vertically on each side of the windows through the curved portion of the ceiling. Square tubular metal tables were topped with dark composition, and the chairs, also tubular, were upholstered in green leather. A bulkhead separated the dining area from the linen closets, pantry, and kitchen. Although there was a service door on the right side of the bar and one on the right side of the kitchen, the only entry for passengers was through the rear (kitchen) end from the following cars. Beverage and food service was continuous during the entire run of the train. Sandwiches, pie, and coffee also were served at coach seats by a dining-car waiter at normal mealtimes.

Following the tap-diner were three coaches, a parlor car, and the Beaver Tail (sometimes referred to as Beaver Tailed) parlor car. The straight parlor had the same basic interior as the coaches, with men's and women's smoking lounges, and 22 reclining, rotating seats

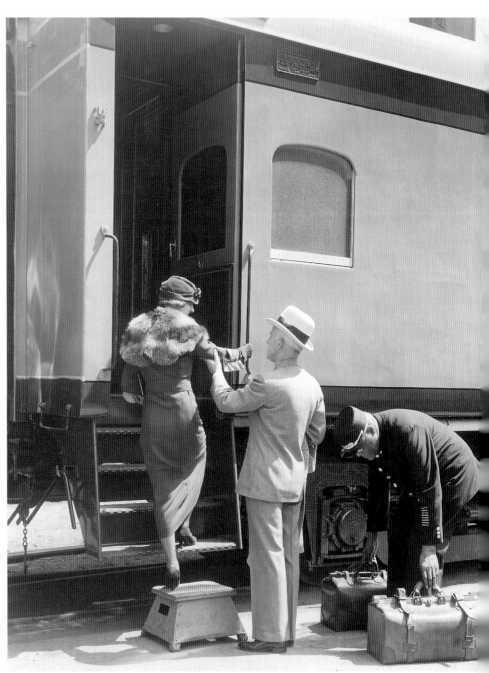

in the main section. The Beaver Tail contained both men's and women's lounges at the vestibule end and 20 reclining, rotating seats in the main portion. Behind these was a single seat of the same type on the left side opposite an emergency door for the flagman on the right. Over this rear section the ceiling was lower, and luggage racks were absent. Across the back, directly in front of the sloping Beaver Tail, were three slightly smaller chairs which neither reclined nor rotated. The Beaver Tail's windows were somewhat larger than the car's side windows, and were triangular or pie-shaped.

The exterior color combination of all the cars was not too different from the traditional Milwaukee scheme with its basic orange (the color design of the tenders was extended throughout the train). Roofs were light gray, touching a maroon board with gold lettering. Flanks were solid orange with another maroon stripe edging the bottom. Trucks and equipment beneath the carbody were brown. The roof and letterboard colors dipped slightly down the Beaver Tail's slope, which carried a backup air horn above its windows and a maroon and raised-gold *Hiawatha* name sign below. The underframe extended beyond the tail to afford anticlimb bumper protection. Standard electric markers were used. The basic welded construction of all the cars eliminated the usual protrusions, such as bolts. Only window frames and necessary safety appliances broke the smooth sides.

The *Hiawatha* was an immediate success, exceeding everyone's fondest hopes. In their first 11 days of operation, 100 and 101 carried 4968 passengers, averaging 222 northbound and 231 southbound. A fourth coach was added to the consist June 15, 1935, and a stop was inserted at Red Wing, Minn. A fifth coach (making an eight-car consist) entered regular service on August 3. Through July 31 in both directions the trains were on time except for one 30-minute delay arriving Minneapolis owing to a cloudburst.

By the middle of July the *400*, which had averaged 150 passengers per trip, found its patronage reduced to 130 to 140 per trip; and

Men's and women's smoking rooms were combined with washrooms and lavatories in the original 4400-series coaches which introduced the Milwaukee's "speedlining." Highly polished smooth sides reflect obvious pride in the *Hiawatha*. The porter's 40 years of service guarantee him a position on the top train. — *All photos, Milwaukee Road.*

Immediately behind the A was that wonderful rolling oasis, the Tip Top Tap restaurant car. In the windowless forward one-third of cars 5251 and 5252, passengers could stand at a genuine bar (complete with handrail for aid on those 90 mph curves) to quench their thirst and to remark on the fortunate course of events which found prohibition repealed preceding the speedliner's design. It was probably more prudent to down the stuff that made Milwaukee famous in one of the booths, where the bright walls and indirect lighting revealed how modern train travel could be. The dining room was more conservatively paneled in wood. The rear one-third of the cars contained the kitchen. Cars were later altered for midtrain use, then were rebuilt for mail-and-express service. — *All photos, Milwaukee Road.*

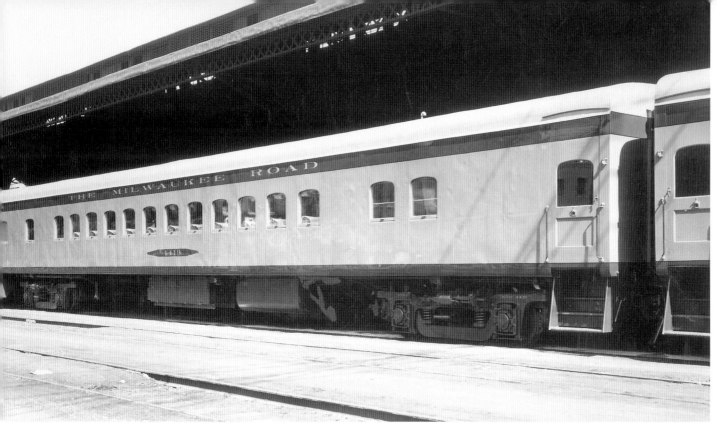

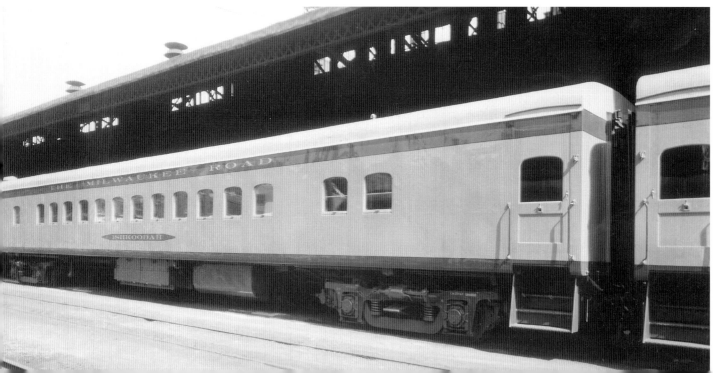

No exterior difference in appearance existed between coaches and straight parlors save for the naming rather than numbering of the first-class cars. Interiors too were identical except for the type of seats. The Beaver Tail cars had small rear windows above a substantial anticlimb bumper, and the air horn could be used during backup movements in and out of South Minneapolis and Western Avenue. The designers failed to use the observation to its ultimate: all seats faced the interior. The three seats across the tail were somewhat smaller, did not revolve or recline, and probably were not sold unless all other seats had been assigned. These original Beaver Tails eventually went on the *North Woods*, the *Midwest*, and the *Chippewa Hiawathas*. — All photos, Milwaukee Road.

35

the *Zephyr* (which had been placed on a two-round-trips-per-day basis on June 2) was averaging 78 out of a possible 88 passengers per trip. Ever since its first day, the *Hi* was pitted against what was probably the most rugged competition in the industry. One or two streamliners on other roads enjoyed more spectacular patronage and earnings, but these had their respective rail fields to themselves. The *Afternoon Hi* consistently remained near the top in those years.

In approximately six weeks of operation the original *Hiawatha* carried 16,564 passengers. Most of this business undoubtedly could be traced to the attractiveness of the trains themselves, which had every convenience and amenity then known; but some of it could be attributed to a general improvement in over-all train service offering direct Madison (the capital of Wisconsin)-Portage connections, and to a reduction in running time for the *Pioneer Limited*. Of considerable importance was the connection at New Lisbon with the day trains on the "Valley division." Much Valley business had found it convenient to ride the *400* to Adams and to use the highway from that point. But this business returned to the Milwaukee . . . and more.

On the Saturdays toward the end of June and for the Independence Day holiday, it was necessary to operate a Second 101 between Chicago and New Lisbon. From there it proceeded ahead of regular train 105 and arrived in Minocqua 30 minutes in advance of the normal schedule. The equipment was then deadheaded to La Crosse, Wis., whence it operated as Second 100 to Chicago on Sunday afternoons (at the time no day train ran on the Valley on Sundays). For this service, a solarium-parlor car, an air-conditioned diner, and air-conditioned coaches (possibly 4400's) were used. These were powered by Pacific 6160, an F-3 which had been converted to oil and classed as F-3-c. It was painted to resemble the Atlantics, with gray boiler jacket and orange cab edged with maroon. Sheet metal covered air reservoir and pumps to give a smoother appearance. Paint on the tender was identical to that on the A's. On a few occasions the 6160 pulled a regular *Hi* in the rare instance a 4-4-2 failed.

On July 28 a Second 100 was operated from Minneapolis for the first time. It carried a tour party and was headed by a Hudson instead of the 6160. During July the *Hi* carried 50 more passengers in each direction than in June. For three days of the Labor Day weekend two sections were operated in each direction; on the fourth day three sections ran to and two sections ran from Minneapolis.

Passenger Traffic Manager George B. Haynes stated that one-third of the business on the *Hiawatha* was entirely new and that the train was earning $3.65 per mile, an amazing profit. Moreover, the Tip Top Tap was contributing an additional $228 per trip. Parlor-car passengers were not transferring to the coaches, as they were on other roads with improved coach accommodations. In fact, the parlor cars were usually sold out three days in advance. An express car (streamlined) was added to increase revenue further, regularly resulting in a nine-car consist.

The *Hiawathas* attracted enormous crowds of onlookers. Throngs surrounded the engine during the stop at Milwaukee, for example, making it difficult for the fireman to mount the tank to take water. U. S. Highway 12-16, paralleling the CMStP&P much of the way between Wisconsin Dells and Tomah, Wis., was the daily location for hundreds of persons who turned out to witness the passage of both trains in rapid succession. Nos. 100 and 101 normally met between New Lisbon and Mauston. A back cover of one issue of the Milwaukee passenger timefolder described this gathering in detail. The Evanston (Ill.) *News-Index* published an account of the multitude that assembled at the Dempster Street crossing west of that city for the daily passages. The paper estimated that if all spectators along the route were placed end to end and flat, they would form a line from Chicago to a point approximately 75 miles beyond Minneapolis. The road published photos of endless people and automobiles lining paralleling roads to watch the speedliners.

On the afternoon of November 4, anyone familiar with goings-on at the north gate of Chicago's Union Station and at the Minneapolis depot prior to the departures of 101 and 100 would have noticed more than the usual alertness punctuated by running conversations on special phones. A gateman was in communication with his counterpart at the opposite terminal, and passengers were being counted as they walked to the platforms. No. 100 departed Minneapolis without incident, though. A few minutes later in Chicago came a brief excited gesture and a hurried, "She's it!" to General Passenger Agent W. B. Dixon, who stepped forward, introduced himself, and presented gifts and a scroll to Mrs. Carrie Johnson of South St. Paul, Minn. By careful calculation, Mrs. Johnson was the 100,000th person

On a hot Saturday afternoon in the summer of 1935, middle-aged F-3-c Pacific 6160 gallops through Brookfield, Wis., with Second 101. She has scampered up the hill from Elm Grove, and there'd better not be a Soo train blocking the diamond at Duplainville. — *Milwaukee Road*.

to ride the *Hiawatha*. She was guest of honor at a small en route ceremony, and all riders of 101 received souvenirs of the occasion.

From May 29, 1935, through the end of the year, the *Hiawatha* had been earning an average of $2.25 per mile and had managed to handle 138,866 riders. August was the busiest month, with 25,003 passengers; the greatest single day was, quite understandably, December 24, when 1866 passengers made trips in two sections in each direction.

The year 1936 continued with great success for the *Hi's*. For example, in Chicago at 9:30 a.m. on January 24 it looked as if 101 would depart that afternoon with approximately 250 passengers in its eight-car consist. Thirty minutes later the demand for tickets brought the decision to operate a second section with coaches, diner, and parlor to Milwaukee only. First 101 steamed out with 155 passengers, Second 101 with 178.

On February 29 came an announcement that an equipment trust had been requested which would include one 4-4-2 locomotive, express-taps, diners, coaches, and parlors at an estimated cost of $920,000. On March 31 (again by means of phone communication between terminal platforms) Mrs. William S. Anderson of Minneapolis was named the *Hi's* 200,000th passenger. She received a traveling case, and was guest of honor at an en route reception.

As the first year of *Hiawatha* operation drew to a close, chief executive Scandrett announced estimated earnings of $700,000 above operating expenses, interest, and depreciation. On May 29, 1936, the "River division" engineman about to latch out the throttle of No. 1 leaving Minneapolis was welcomed into the Chippewa tribe (Longfellow's legendary Hiawatha was a Chippewa). In the Windy City, Mohawks paddled up the Chicago River, removed their canoe, built a fire on the park strip edging the Union Station trainshed, and declared the engineman of train 101 one of their nation.

On June 5 the New Lisbon-Minocqua connecting trains were extended to Star Lake for the summer. The July public timefolder listed them as "The *Hiawatha*, North Woods Section," with numbers 200 and 201 replacing their previous designations of 105 and 106. During the July Fourth holiday, through Star Lake sections were operated three days and second Twin Cities sections two days with a total of 6000 passengers. Business in June was half again as much as it had been in June 1935; in July it was 45 per cent higher and in August 36 per cent higher than in the same months a year earlier. Atlantic No. 3, which had been received in May, was put to work on extra sections.

The ceremonies have been concluded in Chicago's Union Station. The train is filled with excited passengers, officials, and crew, and you can bet that all personnel at the Western Avenue roundhouse and coach yard have their eyes fixed on the speedster's passage. It's approximately 1:08 on the afternoon of May 29, 1935, and this is the first run of the *Hiawatha*. — *Howard Christiansen.*

# RIBBED CARS AND 4-6-4'S

### What was unprecedented became astounding

NEW EQUIPMENT for the *Hiawatha* was exhibited at Chicago, Milwaukee, scheduled intermediate stops, and the Twin Cities October 5-10, 1936, and entered regular service on the 11th — a totally new train (except for motive power) after only 16 months of service. Opportunely, the numberplates of the A's were such that the Two-Spot could be used advantageously to illustrate material pertaining to the consist of the second *Hi*.

The "*Hiawatha* of 1937" incorporated several notable improvements. Cor-Ten steel and aluminum alloys were employed to further reduce weight so that cars weighed 41 to 43 per cent less than standard equipment, and the new nine-car train weighed but 27 tons more than the seven-car train of 1935. The Tip Top Tap had proved so popular that it was placed in its own express-tap car at the head end. A 48-seat dining car was used (the largest single-unit diner on any road at the time), and a third parlor car, containing a drawing room for the first time, was added.

Exteriors were enhanced with retractable steps and wide diaphragms. Equipment carried beneath the carbody — air conditioning, batteries, water tanks — was enclosed in a shell to reduce wind resistance, to lower the center of gravity, and to improve looks. Cars had only one vestibule, which was at the forward (or women's) end,

a practice continued in subsequent equipment. For the first time the trademark of fluting, or ribbing, appeared on car sides above and below the windows, which were squared off in contrast to the convex-type window of the first train. Exterior colors were the same as on the first *Hi* but with slight modifications: the roof was silver instead of gray; a small silver stripe paralleled the top and bottom window lines; and a maroon wing centered below the windows displayed the car's number or name. (Throughout the *Hiawatha*'s existence, coaches, diners, and tap-lounge cars have carried only numbers. Through 1938, parlor cars received names only, but their postwar editions received both names and numbers.) The backup horn and buffer were omitted on the Beaver Tail, but more glass was added and the *Hiawatha* scroll was set off in a maroon wing.

A major change in the interior design of coaches and parlors was the inclusion of bulkheads separating the body of the car from the passageways at either end, eliminating the openness in the first train's cars. Special attention was given to improvement of lighting, ventilation, and air conditioning and to soundproofing. Automotive rather than home-type radios were installed in the Beaver Tail and (for the first time) in the tap, and were controlled by the crews. Vestibules and luggage racks were wider than on the first edition,

It's shortly after 1 p.m. on a summer day in 1941, and the Galewood (Ill.)-to-Sturtevant (Wis.) "patrol" (as way freights on CMStP&P are designated) has cleared the main track near Glenview and two of its trainmen fix their attention on the passage of the *Afternoon Hiawatha*, No. 101. Although the F-7's had been on the property nearly three years, the capable A's frequently were seen on 100 and 101. —TRAINS: *Linn H. Westcott.*

and coach porter service was introduced along with the new cars.

Bone-white ceilings, with recessed lighting in the tap and dining cars, were used throughout the train. The Tip Top Tap portion of the head car had no exterior windows except for one porthole on each side near the bar. It was still permissible to drink standing on the gray floor and firmly grasping the bar's handrail; or one could be seated at any of the 40 red leather chairs arranged booth style around rectangular or circular tables. Pink tinted mirrors hung where windows normally would have been cut into the blue walls. A service door to the bar area was on the right side of the car, but the only public entrance was through the rear from the train and past the conductor's office space. The added amenities of the 1937 *Hiawatha*, compared with the 1935 train, provided for the patrons' comfort and pleasure. Coach seats were redesigned and upholstered in velour; lighting was recessed into the luggage racks, which were unchanged in appearance from those of the 4400's. Light-colored veneer was used below the luggage racks on all walls.

Coach passengers entered the new dining car from the kitchen end. Walls of the rolling restaurant were imported silver-gray harewood veneer; carpeting was two-tone blue, and tables and chairs were chrome and aluminum. The tables had blue tops, the chairs were upholstered in coral rose velour, and place mats substituted for full tablecloths. Beverages were available with meals, and complete tap service was offered between 2 and 4 p.m. Off-the-tray snack service was continued in the coaches at mealtime.

Behind the diner was a 28-seat parlor car, followed by the drawing-room car which had its private accommodation at the rear between the body of the car and the men's room. The room seated five — in individual chair, double seat, and sofa — and, of course, had an adjoining private toilet annex. A full-size table could be installed in the room, and all seats in the three cars had small individual drop-leaf tables. Walls beneath the windows were African mahogany; they were avodire veneer between and above the windows, including the undersides of the luggage racks and complete end walls. The contour of the seats was different than previously. The interior of the rear car was considerably altered from that of its predecessor. Small toilet rooms replaced the smoking lounges at the forward end, and a new observation-lounge was built into the Beaver Tail. Separated from the 26-seat body by an avodire veneer bulkhead with large windows were four non-reclining seats arranged in pairs of two on each side, with a sofa for four across the tail. The room had the failing of virtually all observations in that its seats faced inside rather than toward the windows. The use of drapes eliminated the "bare wall" atmosphere of the first Beaver Tail. Seats in all the parlors were of turquoise and green plush; carpeting was blue. The normal consist of the new edition was express-tap, four coaches, diner, and the three parlors. The original train went into standby service.

Aided by its new outfitting, the *Hiawatha* continued to pile up records, netting $2.49 per mile during 1936 for an estimated total of 1 million dollars. *Railway Age* commented, "Probably the most outstanding record of all of the fast and streamlined trains is that of the *Hiawatha*, which since May 29, 1935, has averaged 723 passengers (both trains) per day." Business in January 1937 increased 35 per cent over that for January 1936 despite the re-equipping of the *Twin Cities Zephyrs* with expanded six-car trainsets on December 18, 1936. The gross income for the period between May 29, 1935, and May 29, 1937, exceeded 2.6 million dollars, and by its second birthday the *Hi* had sped well over a half million persons to their destinations. In August a new connecting train, No. 29, departed from Milwaukee behind 101 with Madison-bound passengers. In the first seven months of 1937, 39,436 more passengers traveled by *Hiawatha* than for the same period in 1936; and the speedliner was netting $2.62 per mile with no allotment for track and miscellaneous expenses charged against it. Increases in patronage were shown throughout 1937. Later it was figured that the *Hi* netted $2.63 each time a milepost was passed — and they skipped by every 57 seconds.

In February 1938 CMStP&P announced plans to acquire 55 passenger cars and 6 new locomotives (by this time No. 4, which turned out to be the last of the Atlantics, had been strutting its stuff for approximately 10 months), primarily for *Hiawatha* service.

For the third anniversary celebration of the *Hi* (at which time the passenger count was nearing 900,000), enginemen of the *400* and the *Twin Zephyrs* rode the A's as guests, and birthday cake and buttonhole bouquets were distributed to passengers.

Meanwhile, back at the shops and at Schenectady, the assembly lines had been busy. For three days the third set of equipment, accompanied by a brand-new F-7 Hudson, was exhibited in Chicago, Milwaukee, and the Twin Cities, with brief showings at scheduled intermediate stops; and on September 19, 1938, the "*Hiawatha* of 1939" entered service. The 1936 replacement of the first train had been unprecedented in rail history; this was even more astounding.

The normal consist of the *Hiawatha* that was "ahead of the time" was unchanged from that of the 1937 train. The 1939 train also carried an express-tap, four coaches, a diner, and three parlor cars. The appointments were considerably improved, both visibly and invisibly. The train was styled through the co-operative efforts of the Milwaukee's mechanical department and industrial designer Otto Kuhler, and several innovations in the trucks were the result of the continuing efforts of K. F. Nystrom. For the first time trucks had exclusively coil-spring suspension, in conjunction with hydraulic shock absorbers and sidesway stabilizing devices. The descriptive brochure of the new *Hi* featured the trucks in a photo and an explanation in layman's terms. Dozens of rubber mountings in the trucks, as well as in the couplings and buffer plates, served nearly to eliminate vibration and to ensure a smooth ride. Walls, floors, and ceilings were carefully treated with a plastic sound deadener. Air conditioning, as always of the steam-jet type, was improved.

Although the exterior continued the basic Milwaukee colors, its arrangement was quite different from that of its two predecessors. Five corrugations ran the full length of each car compared with two in the 1937 train; and there were two more broken ribs in the window area. Portholes were used in the tap room, which for the first time had windows at most of its tables, and in doors and toilets. Regular windows in the body of the cars were grouped in twos and threes by rounded outer edges and small circling aluminum bands. For the first time, a maroon stripe ran the length of the train through the window area, but the maroon bottom belt was eliminated. The most striking enhancements were the fresh stylings of the F-7 Hudsons and the Beaver Tails, both the work of Otto Kuhler.

In this writer's possibly prejudiced opinion, the Beaver Tails of 1939 were the outstanding observation cars on any set of *Hi's* or, for that matter, on any train to date. They certainly possessed the largest rear windows, and more important, they featured a sofa facing those huge expanses of glass. The exterior fins were complementary. What could be more tempting to the departing

No. 100 comes off the Wisconsin River bridge and passes the Wisconsin Dells depot at approximately 40 mph on September 24, 1941. Another curve and then the brakes will be released, enabling the fleet 4-4-2 to run like an arrow to Portage. — *Alfred W. Johnson.*

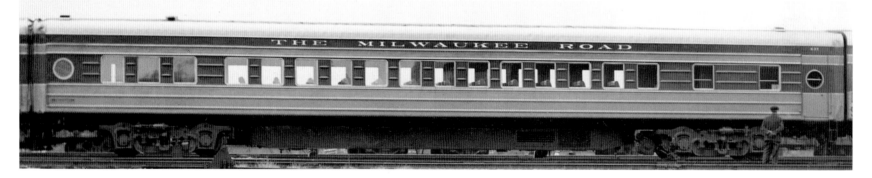

Alfred W. Johnson can be thanked for this rather remarkable sequence of the entire consist of *Hiawatha* 101 backing from the Western Avenue coach yard to Chicago Union Station on October 18, 1940. Otto Kuhler's finned treatment of this final series of Beaver Tail observation cars is strikingly illustrated. It is apparent that even prior to Interstate highways and jet airliners long consists were not always the rule. Today consists almost as short operate behind combinations of FP7's and E9's or FP/45's. These provide much more horsepower, but they don't move today's trains as fast as the 3 undoubtedly wheeled its train nearly three decades ago.

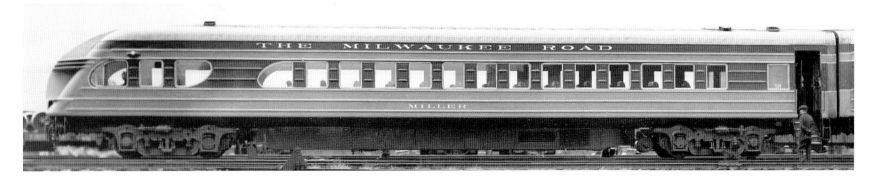

47

The second set of *Hiawatha* equipment provided full dining cars. Identical cars were built for the "electrified" *Olympian*.

Unlike smoking, imbibing was permitted in mixed company. The two portholes were for the convenience of the bartenders.

To the joy of nonsmokers, Milwaukee Road situated large smoking lounges — illustrated in this 1937-model car — adjacent to the washroom and lavatory areas. — *All photos these pages, Milwaukee Road.*

The décor was more sedate in the parlor cars, which contained solid luggage racks of bleached maple edged with chrome bars. The porter is placing the luggage in a special locker.

1937 coaches featured recessed lighting with air-conditioning ventilators beneath each lamp. — *All photos these pages, Milwaukee Road.*

Unlike many streamlined parlors, *Hiawatha* first-class cars always have been equipped with fully rotating and reclining seats. Small drop-leaf tables are an added amenity.

Coach passengers enjoyed a large amount of legroom between the widely spaced seats, and individual windows enhanced the view.

The mistake of too many curtains and inward-facing seats in the 1937 parlor cars was rectified a decade later.

Interiors of all the third series of *Hiawatha* cars were well executed. The superb rear sofa of the Beaver Tail was hard to equal anywhere. — *All photos these pages, Milwaukee Road.*

Dining-car windows of the 1939 trains were larger, permitting better viewing while partaking of *Hiawatha* steaks. Use of draperies enhanced the Indian motif.

Semicircular table area was adjacent to the bar in the forward end of the tap section of the tap-express cars.

This is the coach section of a dormitory car used on the *Olympian*; the third series of *Hiawatha* coaches were identical. There was more contrast to the wood than the photograph shows.

On train 100, 48-seat dining cars eased the task of serving early dinner to passengers detraining at Milwaukee and a later dinner to through passengers who wished to eat in the hour between Milwaukee and Chicago.

The fireman has thrown a couple of scoops of sand into the firebox of the A as it storms upgrade out of New Lisbon with train 100, which appears to be made up of eight cars this trip. After that rise is crested, No. 3 will undoubtedly be wheeling at the century mark down the speedway which consistently saw the top speeds achieved on the Milwaukee Road. — TRAINS: *Linn H. Westcott.*

With the maximum nine cars allotted to a 4-4-2, No. 2 whips the *Afternoon Hiawatha*, train 101, through the sparsely settled Chicago suburban area of 1936. Ahead lies the Deerfield-Lake portion of the "Chicago & Milwaukee" — territory which was carded for an *average* speed of 90 mph. — *Rail Photo Service: Vernon Seaver.*

Not even Lucius Beebe, despite his oft-published affection for "standard" trains such as the *Banner Blue, Detroit Arrow,* and *Twilight Limited* and his expressed revulsion for shrouded steam, could resist the *Hiawathas.* Train 101 was photographed near West Lake Forest. — *Lucius Beebe.*

passenger walking past the bumper post in Minneapolis or Chicago? (Later Mars red warning lights were installed.)

Inside the observation parlor, the seating capacity of the sofa shaded by the fins was amplified by seats for two on either side directly behind and also facing rear. Six center lounge seats unfortunately faced the aisle, but happily, another pair of double seats with their backs to the bulkhead again faced in the correct direction. The bulkhead between the smoking-observation section and the main portion of the car was graced with an Indian arrow design in its windows. Furniture in the observation room was of modern wood design, and parlor and coach seats were changed in design from previous styles.

Both parlors and coaches had aluminum leaf ceilings and virtually identical (except for larger seating capacity in the men's room of the coach) smoking lounges upholstered in green — leather for men and mohair for women. All window frames were walnut, and fluted black walnut filled the central windowposts of the groupings of windows. Window groups in the parlors were divided by drapes with an Indian motif, while those in the coaches were partitioned by normal wall color. Both of the straight parlors contained a drawing room with sofa, two chairs, and a toilet annex. The walls of the first-class cars were walnut below the lower window line and bleached maple above. Coach walls were entirely of bleached maple, as were bulkheads in all revenue cars. Both types of cars had solid luggage racks of bleached maple edged with walnut, and housed recessed lighting fixtures whose lenses were fitted with metal louvers to prevent glare. Carpeting in the parlors was a lively gray and brown. Coaches contained solid composition flooring. Passageways through-

This view from a hillside above Pewaukee Lake depicts well the top contours of an F-7 and its cars. The coal supply is down a bit, but there are enough black diamonds to reach New Lisbon. The engineer will apply brakes for the 70 mph curve into Hartland, Wis. — *E. Ruhland*.

(Far left) The image of the *Afternoon Hiawatha*'s F-7 blurs on the film of A. W. Johnson as the 4-6-4 crosses the canal drawbridge at Portage Junction, Wis. Mars warning light, plus dents in the pilot, had been added by September 1941.

57

No. 101's Beaver Tail is just clearing the subterranean depths of Chicago Union Station's platforms as Hudson 103 charges out of the Canal Street curve and from beneath the approach tracks of North Western Terminal. The 4-6-4 is getting a run for the climb to above-street elevation and will shower the photographer with soot and cinders. (Far right) Winter's chilly dampness is emphasized by the low-hanging exhaust as the finned solarium disappears beneath Milwaukee Avenue. — *Both photos, Alfred W. Johnson.*

58

out the train (past kitchen and smoking rooms) were walnut veneer below the windows and bleached maple above, and had protruding bleached maple "rubbing strips" to prevent marring of the walls by luggage. Vestibule interiors were orange with a maroon footboard and had the added convenience of movable safety hand bars which were swung parallel to the train when it was in motion to make a narrow aisle between interior doors and diaphragms. Seating was rust or green in alternating cars. Window shades were these two colors too; a coach or parlor with rust seats was equipped with green shades, and vice versa.

A colorful drape of Indian motif divided the public portion of the dining car into a cafe section housing the four tables nearest the kitchen, and a restaurant. In the cafe, chairs were green, the ceiling was apple green. Restaurant chairs were done in rust, and the canary-yellow ceiling reflected a soft glow when lights were turned on. A predominantly red carpet covered the floor in the entire car, and all tables were bracketed to the walls without legs. Tabletops were cream with brown stripes. Windows were larger than those in earlier diners, and their sides were edged with drapes containing the same crossed-arrow design. Lights were just below the curve of the ceiling in a continuously louvered fixture. All walls were of bleached maple.

Portholes of the Tip Top Tap were set off by the standard crossed-arrow drapes, and ceiling and lighting were identical to those of the diner. The floor was neutral brown. The tap room contained eight booth-type tables for four. Seats followed the modern wood design in the Beaver Tail with walnut booth dividers carrying bas-relief gun-metal sculpture depicting Indian lore. A smaller forward section adjacent to the bar, designated the cocktail lounge, contained four circular tables with semicircular cream leather seating parallel to the train. Its windowless walls were light coral, and tabletops were red and cream. The novelty of the car was built into the small bulkhead splitting cocktail and tap rooms, and consisted of a strip above the aisle displaying the names, in gold plastic, of the stations served by the train. It was lighted from behind, and an attendant would illuminate the proper station name as the journey progressed. Departing Chicago, "Milwaukee" would glow; leaving there, "Portage" would be displayed; and so on. Air conditioning was filtered throughout the train by a center aluminum duct above the aisle. The interior decorations, through their use of native woods, were considered to lend a softness of tone and color.

The following is a comparison of the three sets of *Hiawatha* equipment:

|  | **1935** | **1937** | **1939** |
|---|---|---|---|
| Cars | 7 | 9 | 9 |
| Weight, lbs. | 806,900 | 860,400 | 856,100 |
| Revenue seats | 238 | 291 | 300 |
| Nonrevenue seats | 138 | 173 | 199 |
| Total seating | 376 | 464 | 499 |

A record 1 million passengers were handled in the 40 months ending October 6. Dr. and Mrs. Lewis J. Pollock of Chicago were presented with traveling bags by Passenger Traffic Manager F. N. Hicks in commemoration of the event. The average rate of return up to August 1, 1938, excluding charges for track maintenance, taxes, solicitation, and miscellaneous items, was 108 per cent.

Busy holiday seasons for the *Hiawathas* no longer rated as news items because these were now considered normal. The big *Hi* news of the winter season took place on January 21, 1939, when Governor Harold Stassen of Minnesota, then 31 years old and the youngest chief executive of any state, donned the uniform he once wore as a Milwaukee sleeping-car and parlor-car conductor to collect first-class tickets on train 6 between Minneapolis and St. Paul. No. 6 wasn't the *Day Express*, but it was more first-class than ever, making its first run as the *Morning Hiawatha*. Again, Minneapolis was ahead of Chicago in initiating *Hiawatha* service, since No. 5 did not depart from the east (actually south) end of the route until 2 hours later, after dedication by Mayor Kelly and chief trustee Scandrett.

No. 6's schedule was made 5 minutes longer than No. 100's to allow extra time for cutting in a full RPO at St. Paul. Six made a positive (instead of conditional) stop at Red Wing, stopped at Sparta rather than at New Lisbon, and stopped at Columbus. Mainly because the schedule of local train 58 offered convenient co-ordination with that of the *Afternoon Hi* at New Lisbon, the eastbound *Morning* train was not burdened with the many stops that had to be included in the schedule of No. 5. The new westbound train made no fewer than 16 positive and 2 conditional halts between Chicago and St. Paul and, with some fine locomotive work, covered the distance in 7 hours 50 minutes. Both *Morning* trains carried head-end cars streamlined to the same exterior design as the newest passenger vehicles: No. 6 carried an RPO and 1 express car; No. 5 included these plus 2 additional expresses. Both carried a baggage-tap, 3

Trains are a bit off the card, since the depot clock in Milwaukee indicates 2:25 p.m. and Second No. 5 is just steaming out.
A Mars-lighted F-7 impatiently waits with No. 101. — *A. C. Kalmbach.*

Scarcely three months of age, F-7 No. 102 stands at the west end of the Milwaukee depot with its American Locomotive Company builder's plate clearly visible. The 4-6-4 is standing on the track adjacent to the turntable and apparently is not on a through train. — *Amos G. Hewitt.*

The great Hudson and its train are fresh out of the erecting shops. The date is August 23, 1938, and a special movement has been made to Brookfield, Wis., to break in and to photograph the new speedliner. — *Milwaukee Road.*

coaches, diner, drawing-room parlor, and Beaver Tail parlor. Both regularly drew Class F-7 Hudsons on the head end, although the *Afternoon Hi* continued to use Atlantics unless it consisted of more than 9 cars. The "*Hiawathas* of 1939," *Morning* and *Afternoon*, required 15 new coaches, 6 drawing-room parlors, 4 Beaver Tail parlors, 4 diners, 4 baggage-taps, and 2 RPO's. Express cars for 5 and 6 came from a group of cars built for all trains, and were not exclusively *Hiawatha* equipment.

Introduction of coal-burning *Hiawatha* power necessitated construction of a special coal chute at New Lisbon to enable the westbound trains to take more black diamonds during the station stop. Nos. 100-105, although they often were referred to as "Hiawatha Hudsons," were designed for all heavy high-speed passenger work on the Milwaukee, and were found with regularity on the *Pioneer Limited*, the *Olympian*, and sometimes on the *Arrow* to Omaha. The basic *Hiawatha* orange and gray colors were retained, but in redesigned arrangement. The shroud design was changed considerably across the nose. The black dome cowling was run down the front to enclose the headlight, which was lowered to sink partially into the silver wings. There was fine stainless-steel vertical grillwork in the cowling. Handrails curved gracefully from the "teardrop" classification lamps to the center of the wings beneath the headlight. C. H. Bilty stated that for reasons of weight the shrouding was not extended over the drivers (as had been the case with the A's) — thus, in his words, "fully exposing the life-giving elements of the steam locomotive." Running boards which terminated above the lead truck were orange, edged with maroon stripes that extended back to the cab door to help bring a transition to the maroon full center of the tender sides. The running-board orange flared to cover the shroud behind the firebox and the cab side beneath the windows, and continued across the tender. Black spread from the top casing across the entire cab roof and spilled around the large glass area of the cab windows. The top portion of the side of the coal bunker was black with THE MILWAUKEE ROAD lettered in gold. The top of the tank was silver. Rectangles above the pilot truck were black, and the pilot was edged in maroon. Drive and pony-truck wheels were gray-green; most other visible machinery beneath the shroud, as well as the tender trucks, was brown.

To this writer, the F-7's represented the ultimate in streamlined steam locomotive appearance. Walter Zackon, writing in the National Railway Historical Society *Bulletin*, called them "queens of steam."

Both the Atlantics and the Hudsons did well in subsequent months, maintaining an on-time standing of 93 per cent for all four trains. The 4-6-4's did so with up to 14-car consists. Patronage and revenue for the *Afternoon Hi's* was the heaviest.

An interesting sidelight on the problems that can confront a railroad is the following case from the Milwaukee's files: Chicago children, presumably from a school near the main line, acquired the dangerous after-school habit of throwing stones at trains and smashed a number of windows. Company police contacted the principal of the school whose students were suspected, and a few days later "that learned lady" requested from the railroad the largest photo of the *Hiawatha* the road could supply. Her idea was to stage a contest among the students to produce the best copy drawing of the train photo. Her aim was to make the pupils train-minded in a constructive way and to teach them that trains were to be admired rather than used as rolling targets. A girl and a boy, both eighth-grade students, tied for first place with their entries, and their prize was a trip to Milwaukee on the *Hiawatha*. They traveled on trains 5 and 6, were treated to lunch in the diner, and were given tours of the train (including the cab before departure) and the Milwaukee Shops. Afterward there was a remarkable decrease in vandalism along that portion of the Milwaukee.

The *Hi's* have never been snob trains with an exclusive clientele, as was, say, the New York Central's *20th Century Limited* in its prime. Yet they have managed to carry hundreds of notables, among whom were Crown Prince Frederick and Princess Ingrid of Denmark in April 1939, and Prince Bertil of Sweden nine years later. The speedliners have also received a consistently good press, in addition to the usual compliments extended to new equipment at inauguration.

In May 1939 commentator Nancy Grey of Milwaukee *Journal* radio station WTMJ in Milwaukee presented a program on the *Hiawatha* and interviewed an engineman, a conductor, and a chef from one of the trains. By the fourth anniversary of the *Afternoon Hi*, the train had carried 1,185,000 passengers, averaging 400 in each direction per day. In the diner of 101, CB&Q officials and *Twin Zephyr* conductor Lloyd W. Mathers were guests for lunch. Afterward Mathers rode as far as Milwaukee as guest conductor, accompanying the well-known Ernie Haddock, who was the *Hi's* C&M conductor at the time. The engine on this occasion was No. 1.

During the Christmas season, both *Morning* and *Afternoon*

trains comprised up to 14 cars, and both made their scheduled time. *Hi* 101 ran in four sections and 100 in three sections on December 22, and each train ran in two sections on the 23rd. Nos. 5 and 6 were given separate head-end sections the entire week preceding Christmas.

By fall 1939 gradual cuts had reduced the time of No. 5 by 30 minutes between Chicago and St. Paul without eliminating any of its stops; but the first improvement in running time for the *Hi's* as a whole came in January 1940, when Nos. 6, 100, and 101 were rescheduled at 6 hours 15 minutes between St. Paul and Chicago. This was to match the time of the *Zephyrs* (one was a 6-hour train), which had been reduced coincident with the opening of a new Q route through La Crosse that had removed the line from city streets. The general time reduction for the *Hi's* brought about a run for train 6 between Sparta and Portage of 78.3 miles in 58 minutes start to stop for an average of 81 mph. To the best knowledge of experts in the field,° this represented the fastest regularly scheduled opera-

---

*The distinguished French motive-power expert, Baron Gérard Vuillet, offers an absorbing account of the speed potential of the F-7 Hudsons in his book *Railway Reminiscences of Three Continents* [Thomas Nelson and Sons Ltd., 1968]: "The load of the *Hiawatha* was at first increased to 12 cars (550 tons) but with such a load it was found that 'the schedules were not fast enough to bring out the best performance of the engines.' After accelerating to 105 mph, a steam-chest pressure of 150 pounds per square inch, with 25 per cent cutoff, was sufficient for maintaining the required speed. With very little effort 120 mph was averaged for 4.5 miles on practically level track, the maximum speed being 125 mph. It was therefore proposed to increase the cruising speed of the *Hiawatha* from 90 to 105 mph, reducing the scheduled time for the 85.6 miles between Chicago and Milwaukee from 75 to 60 minutes. It may be mentioned that the fastest time made by a 4-4-2 between Milwaukee and Chicago was 59 minutes. However, a gentlemen's agreement existed between the three lines competing for the Chicago-Twin Cities traffic and, as the other two could not follow, the contemplated acceleration did not take place."

tion with steam power at any time anywhere in the world; and the record remained unbeaten as long as steam power was operated in high-speed service.

During 1940 the *Afternoon Hi's* bounded along as strong as ever, running as many as four sections in each direction on a single day, and averaging 187 passengers per train. The *Morning* trains in the first 19 months of operation averaged 104 passengers per train for a total of 277,533. Both trains ran consists as high as 15 cars and still maintained their 93 per cent on-time performance record.

On November 30, 1941, Hugh McManus, who had handled 101's first trip out of Chicago, retired at the age of 70 after 51 accident-free years of service. On his last turn at the throttle of train 101 he drew F-7 No. 102. During his *Hiawatha* career McManus had been pictured in Lionel catalogs in connection with the manufacturer's tinplate *Hiawatha* trainset, and now, on his final trip, Lionel presented him with one of its sets.

Christmas travel in 1940 was heavier than for the previous year, but not as many sections were operated, thanks to the greater pulling power of the F-7's. On December 22 passenger traffic was so heavy that people were standing on train 101 at Union Station, so two additional coaches were cut in at the Western Avenue coach yard, bringing the consist to 15 cars. The next day this problem was prevented by backing a 15-car train into the station.

A new high in monthly patronage of the *Afternoon* train was established with the carriage of 38,472 persons in August 1941. The previous record for a single month had been 36,508 in August 1937. The *Morning* trains carried 22,456 compared with 19,648 in August 1940.

# 100 HITS 100

A few figures for skeptics to mull over

THE *Hiawathas* and the great Atlantics and Hudsons that pulled them epitomized the streamlined steam age. In an era when it requires the novel technology of a Turbotrain or the physical plant underwriting a Metroliner to conquer the still magical 100 mph ground-speed barrier, it almost seems legendary that steam-powered *Hiawathas* regularly and effortlessly reached the century mark. As part of a series of articles entitled "Timing the Fast Ones," E. L. Thompson in the May 1939 issue of *Railroad Magazine* (© The Frank A. Munsey Co., 1939) detailed one such everyday, high-speed run of a *Hiawatha*. His account is reprinted here through the courtesy of *Railroad Magazine*. Mr. Thompson also had his stopwatch aboard Hudson No. 100 in January 1941 to record a 110 mph trip down the Milwaukee-Chicago speedway. This report, beginning on page 70, is reprinted from the May 1968 issue of TRAINS Magazine.

ONE of the fastest sustained timings in America is that of the westbound afternoon *Hiawatha* of the Chicago, Milwaukee, St. Paul & Pacific, which is allowed but 38 minutes for the 57.6 miles from Tower A-20, near Techny, Ill., to Lake, Wis., or at an average speed of 90.9 mph. This should be sufficient reason to tempt anyone interested in train timing to ride and check the train, and that was what lured me to Chicago in midwinter. This train is operated over the 411.5 miles from Chicago to St. Paul in 6½ hours, or at an average speed of 63.3 mph.

On that particular day, it was dispatched in but one section, consisting of nine streamlined cars, weighing approximately 430 tons. One of the new streamlined Hudson-type engines, No. 100, was on the head end, in charge of Engineer Stephens. I climbed aboard shortly before starting time, and utilized the few remaining moments for a brief chat with the engine crew. The maximum "allowed" speed is 100 mph for the *Hiawatha* and *Chippewa* trains; other trains are allowed 90 mph, so this should certainly give the Milwaukee the honor of permitting the fastest allowed speeds in America.

At 1 p.m., right to the advertised second, the wheels began to move. Due to restrictions, we left town slowly. And the new F-7 class engines were held to 50 mph for the first 9 miles to Mayfair. But I was immediately impressed with the wonderful action of the engine. The slightest movement on the throttle caused the locomotive to virtually surge ahead. And passing Mayfair, the engineer really settled down to serious business. I had previously stationed myself directly behind the engineer, in full view of the speedometer. And then, that indicator began to climb higher and higher. It reached

ILWAUKEE ROAD

Robert Klubertanz.

93 passing Northbrook and held this until the slowdown for the curve near Deerfield.

We were then on the fastest scheduled section of the run to Milwaukee as previously mentioned. We had to average about 91 to make our running time and we were off to a good start with a speed of 92 at Tower A-20. After a slight fall to Deerfield, we again began climbing and reached 96 at West Lake Forest. The crossing at Rondout calls for an 80 maximum, and the engineer obediently pinched her down. We had picked up 19 seconds on the schedule from Tower A-20 to Rondout. Again we started climbing, and after 92 by Wilson, the needle went to the "century" mark passing Gurnee and held there for about 1½ miles.

We were down to 93 by Wadsworth, but had still lost 1 second on the run from Rondout. Curves and a slight grade brought us down to 86 and then the crossing at Ranney meant another 80. We lost 8 seconds from Wadsworth. Thirteen seconds were picked up to Sturtevant, which was passed in a little less than 53 minutes from Chicago. Climbed back up again slowly and just past Caledonia hit the 100 mark again, only to fall to 97 by Oakwood. Near Tower A-68, we passed the eastbound morning *Hiawatha*. As we came over a slight crest near Lake, we were on 95, and the run from Tower A-20 to Lake had been made in 15 seconds under schedule. On the dip past Lake, we went to 100 for the third time, but the brakes quickly came on as we ran into the curves approaching Milwaukee, which after an easy run from Washington Street, was reached a little more than 2 minutes ahead of time, or at an average of over 69 for the 85 miles.

At Milwaukee we changed engineers and took water. We were 2 minutes late when finally getting under way. Then came more than 5 miles of restricted running and 9 minutes were consumed in this stretch. After passing Wauwatosa Engineer Knowlton widened on her. Several slow order curves were encountered, and just about the time we were rolling good, we would have to slow down. Several speeds of 90 were noted and the needle was up to 95 when the brakes came on for Watertown, which was passed through 2 miles under the restriction of 35. For the next 45 miles, the speeds kept fluctuating. Several curves and slight grades were encountered; the maximum was 92 reached several times and the minimum was 70. We had nearly recovered the 2 minutes as we passed East Rio a mere 7 seconds late. Arrival at Portage was a little over one-half minute early. We had covered the 92.9 miles in 78 minutes, or at

an over-all average speed of 71 mph. Here water was taken again.

For several years, the runs of the *Hiawatha* between Portage and New Lisbon have been classed as the fastest steam runs in America. (The run of the eastbound *Hiawatha* from Sparta to Portage now holds this honor.) The eastbound *Hiawatha* is allowed but 35 minutes for the 43.1 miles between New Lisbon and Portage, but our westbound timing is 37 minutes, this including station time at New Lisbon. The start from Portage was very good, and we were up to 60 in 4 minutes, 75 in 5, 85 in 6½, and 90 in 8 minutes.

A speed of 92 was reached and held until the slow orders near Wisconsin Dells. First there was a 70 curve, then more than a mile of 65 curves, and finally another 70. We then climbed steadily, passing Lyndon at 99 and reaching 100 just after that. A slight grade dropped the speed back to 89, but it was up to 98 when the brakes came on for Mauston. There was no increase from that point to New Lisbon, and a very easy stop was made. The time for this run had been 34 minutes 16 seconds, or at an average of about 76 mph, a remarkable figure considering the short distance. Here the North Woods section of the *Hiawatha* was standing just prior to its departure for Minocqua.

Acceleration was even more rapid from New Lisbon, and the mile-a-minute mark was reached in less than 3 minutes, 75 in another 1½ minutes, and 84 the next minute. In other words, we achieved 84 mph in a little over 5 minutes, from a dead stop. Just then the brakes came on for Camp Douglas, dropping the speed to 59. Climbed steadily to 91 and after passing Oakdale, got up to 93, only to drop back to 88 by Tomah. Then came a rapid slowdown, as we went on the single-track stretch at Tunnel City at 31. On the 2.7-mile stretch we again accelerated, and were back to 74 going on the double track at Raymore. The needle was on 93 approaching Camp McCoy, and after a slight fall to 91 by the station, it went to 95, only to slow up to 88 through Sparta. Went right back to 90 and held this speed for 14 miles, before falling off to 80 by West Salem. Back up to 90 and held this until slowing to 47 for the crossing at Medary and after a slight recovery were back to 40 by Grand Crossing and eased into La Crosse very slowly, nearly 1½ minutes ahead of time. We had covered the 59.8-mile stretch in slightly under 50 minutes, or at an average of 71.7.

I got down to walk around the engine while coal and water were taken. It was getting very cold as Engineer Hoard climbed aboard and told me that my fast speeds were over for the day.

Most of the remainder of the trip was made in the 70's, although we did once reach 89. We were away from La Crosse a half minute late and went on the single-track stretch that crosses the Mississippi River. "Old Man River" was completely frozen over, and by then the cab windows were getting all frosty as the steam and smoke coming back were freezing when they hit the glass. Visibility was at a minimum, but this did not seem to worry the engineer who said this was a frequent occurrence.

Speed stayed low until we went back on the double track at River Junction. We necessarily had consumed over 6 minutes for the 3.3 miles. From there to the CGW crossing near Winona, the speed hovered between 71 and 74. We dropped to 60 over the crossing and eased into Winona several minutes to the good. Some slow running followed through the town over the numerous grade crossings, but were up to 45 by Tower CK. Speed got to 67 quickly and then gradually eased up to 71 in the next 10 miles. After passing Weaver, we soared to 80 for about 3 miles but were then off to 71 by Kellogg. Another short run of 80 followed and then came down to 62 through Wabasha. All the time, we were following the frozen river and Engineer Hoard was content to roll along at around 70 except on a few straight stretches. Another 80 spurt was noted past Lake City, thence back down to 70, but up to 77 by Frontenac and went to 82 past there before slowing to 60 around a curve, then climbed back to 73 before the slowdown approaching Red Wing. Fifty was maintained for several miles before the slowdown for the stop.

We were away right on time for the last stretch of the run. Kept climbing and just past Island Siding touched 87. Between that point and Blackbird Junction, the two tracks are separated. Soon a yellow signal came into view, to be followed by a red signal. As we stopped, a flagman, who must have been nearly frozen by then, advised us that there was a broken rail about 15 car lengths ahead and to proceed with extreme caution. This we did, and from the time we made the stop until the rear car passed the broken rail we had used 4 minutes.

Went right to work and hit 89, before slowing to 80, but back to 85 by Blackbird Junction. Kept this up until coming to 40 through Hastings, which was passed 8 minutes late, thanks to the delay over the broken rail. The unfortunate part of the lateness was that we had long since passed the best running ground. But the engineer meant business and kept "driving" and after again crossing the

Mississippi River, at 35, we went to 60 for a while and then climbed slowly to 80.

From Hastings to Newport the tracks are again separated and are used jointly with the Burlington. Dropped to 59 at Newport, which was passed a little over 5¼ minutes late. Up to 80 again, but down to 60 at Oakland. Pushed up to 70 passing through St. Paul Yard, but soon had to come down to 50, which was held until the crossing stop just outside St. Paul. Eased into the Union Station at that point less than 2 minutes late. Despite the broken rail, the *Hiawatha* was practically on time — ample proof that the schedule is an easy one for locomotives. And we had covered the 411.5 miles from Chicago in just about 369 minutes of actual running time, or at an average of 66.9 mph.

There was little chance for running from there to Minneapolis, and since we left St. Paul only a minute late, there was no occasion for it. After passing Fordson Junction, we slid gradually up to 48 by Merriam Park and 50 by G Tower. Then dropped to 22 over the many street crossings, and with a very slow finish, stopped at Minneapolis 3 minutes to the good. A thermometer outside the station told me it was several degrees below zero.

The complete log of the trip follows:

### Log of the Hiawatha, February 2, 1939

Nine streamlined cars, approximately 430 tons; Hudson-type (F-7) engine No. 100, tractive effort 50,300 lbs., 84-inch drivers, 23½ x 30-inch cylinders, boiler pressure 300 lbs. Engineer W. E. Stephens, Chicago-Milwaukee; Engineer H. B. Knowlton, Milwaukee-La Crosse; Engineer A. C. Hoard, La Crosse-Minneapolis.

| Miles | | Stations | Speeds | Time | Schedule |
|---|---|---|---|---|---|
| 0.0 | Lv. | Chicago | | 1:00:00 p.m. | 1:00 p.m. |
| 2.9 | Pass | Western Avenue | 30 | 1:08:09 | |
| 5.4 | | Pacific Junction | 52 | 1:11:58 | 1:09 |
| 6.4 | | Healy | 52 | 1:12:58 | |
| 8.2 | | Grayland | 47 | 1:15:10 | |
| 9.0 | | Mayfair | 49 | 1:16:19 | |
| 10.2 | | Forest Glen | 67 | 1:17:41 | |
| 11.6 | | Edgebrook | 73 | 1:19:00 | |
| 14.3 | | Morton Grove | 85 | 1:21:08 | |
| 16.2 | | Golf | 87 | 1:22:19 | |
| 17.4 | | Glenview | 90 | 1:23:09 | |
| 20.2 | | Techny | 92 | 1:25:07 | |
| 20.3 | | Tower A-20 | 92 | 1:25:12 | 1:22 |
| 20.9 | | Northbrook | 93, 90 curve | 1:25:37 | |
| 23.9 | | Deerfield | 90 | 1:27:34 | |
| 28.0 | | West Lake Forest | 96, 98, 82 curve | 1:30:03 | |
| 32.3 | | Rondout | 80 | 1:32:51 | 1:30 |

| Miles | | Stations | Speeds | Time | Schedule |
|---|---|---|---|---|---|
| 36.8 | | Wilson | 92 | 1:36:08 | |
| 38.6 | | Gurnee | 100, 90 curve | 1:37:15 | |
| 42.9 | | Wadsworth | 93, 86 upgrade | 1:39:52 | 1:37 |
| 47.0 | | Russell | 86, 80 curve | 1:42:44 | |
| 51.6 | | Ranney | 80 | 1:46:00 | 1:43 |
| 52.6 | | Truesdell | 84 | 1:46:44 | |
| 57.5 | | Somers | 94 | 1:50:00 | |
| 61.8 | | Sturtevant | 89 | 1:52:47 | 1:50 |
| 66.0 | | Franksville | 93 | 1:55:31 | |
| 68.1 | | Tower A-68 | 93 | 1:56:54 | 1:54 |
| 69.4 | | Caledonia | 95, 100 | 1:57:41 | |
| 72.8 | | Oakwood | 97, 98 | 1:59:46 | |
| 77.9 | | Lake | 95, 100, 71 curve | 2:02:57 | 2:00 |
| 80.3 | | Powerton | 71, 60 curve, 40 | 2:04:46 | |
| 83.9 | | Washington Street | 31 | 2:08:52 | 2:09 |
| 85.0 | Ar. | Milwaukee | | 2:12:45 | 2:15 |
| | Lv. | Milwaukee | | 2:19:18 | 2:17 |
| 87.0 | Pass | Milwaukee Shops | 39, 44 | 2:23:33 | |
| 88.2 | | Grand Avenue | 34, 47, 44 | 2:25:19 | |
| 90.4 | | Wauwatosa | 47 | 2:28:27 | |
| 94.9 | | Elm Grove | 68, 70, 59 curve | 2:33:13 | |
| 99.2 | | Brookfield | 75, 84 | 2:37:15 | 2:34 |
| 101.9 | | Duplainville | 80 | 2:39:11 | |
| 105.3 | | Pewaukee | 91, 68 curve | 2:41:41 | |
| 109.9 | | Hartland | 70, 82 | 2:44:58 | 2:43 |
| 112.6 | | Nashotah | 76 | 2:47:05 | |
| 114.8 | | Okauchee | 87 | 2:48:40 | |
| 117.8 | | Oconomowoc | 90, 86, 90 | 2:50:39 | 2:48 |
| 123.5 | | Ixonia | 88, 95 | 2:54:31 | |
| 131.0 | | Watertown | 33 | 3:00:10 | 2:58 |
| 135.3 | | Richwood | 81, 88, 77 curve, 8 | 3:04:51 | |
| 140.6 | | Reeseville | 71 | 3:08:49 | |
| 145.9 | | Astico | 90, 92 | 3:12:44 | |
| 149.7 | | Columbus | 91 | 3:15:15 | |
| 153.3 | | Fall River | 86, 70 curve | 3:17:42 | |
| 159.1 | | Doylestown | 85 | 3:22:15 | |
| 162.5 | | East Rio | 91, 70 curve | 3:24:07 | 3:24 |
| 163.9 | | Rio | 76, 67 curve | 3:25:37 | |
| 168.9 | | Wyocena | 90, 92 | 3:29:36 | |
| 176.7 | | Portage Junction | 50 | 3:35:10 | |
| 177.9 | Ar. | Portage | | 3:37:24 | 3:38 |
| | Lv. | Portage | | 3:41:04 | 3:41 |
| 186.7 | Pass | Lewiston | 90 | 3:49:53 | |
| 188.5 | | Cheney | 92, 70 curve | 3:51:05 | |
| 194.8 | | Wisconsin Dells | 65 | 3:55:50 | |
| 203.4 | | Lyndon | 99, 100, 89, 98 | 4:02:22 | |
| 214.0 | | Mauston | 88, 89 | 4:09:06 | |
| 221.0 | Ar. | New Lisbon | | 4:15:20 | |
| | Lv. | New Lisbon | 84 | 4:17:40 | 4:18 |
| 227.0 | Pass | Camp Douglas | 59, 91 | 4:24:10 | |
| 233.3 | | Oakdale | 90, 93, 91, 93 | 4:29:00 | |
| 239.8 | | Tomah | 88, 31 switches | 4:33:18 | |
| 243.2 | | Tunnel City | 34, 45 tunnel | 4:36:24 | 4:36 |
| 245.9 | | Raymore | 74, 93 | 4:39:44 | |
| 251.4 | | Camp McCoy | 91, 95 | 4:44:00 | |
| 256.2 | | Sparta | 88, 90 | 4:46:41 | 4:46 |
| 262.8 | | Rockland | 90 | 4:51:13 | |

| Miles | | Stations | Speeds | Time | Schedule |
|---|---|---|---|---|---|
| 266.4 | | Bangor | 90 until slowing | 4:53:35 | |
| 271.0 | | West Salem | 80, 90 | 4:56:49 | |
| 278.0 | | Medary | 47, 57 | 5:02:15 | 5:04 |
| 279.6 | | Grand Crossing | 40 | 5:04:08 | |
| 280.8 | Ar. | La Crosse | | 5:07:35 | 5:09 |
| | Lv. | La Crosse | | 5:14:28 | 5:14 |
| 281.2 | Pass | West Wye Switch | 25, 48 | 5:16:15 | |
| 282.8 | | Bridge Switch | 39, 53 | 5:18:58 | |
| 284.1 | | River Junction | 36, 70 | 5:20:42 | |
| 288.2 | | Dresbach | 72 | 5:24:46 | |
| 289.9 | | Dakota | 71 | 5:26:16 | |
| 293.7 | | Donehower | 73 | 5:29:31 | |
| 298.5 | | Lamoille | 74, 71 | 5:33:31 | |
| 303.1 | | Homer | 74 | 5:37:19 | |
| 305.4 | | CGW Crossing | 60 | 5:39:28 | |
| 307.5 | Ar. | Winona | | 5:42:36 | |
| | Lv. | Winona | 32 town | 5:44:28 | 5:45 |
| 309.4 | Pass | Tower CK | 45 | 5:48:35 | |
| 313.6 | | Minnesota City | 67, 69 | 5:52:47 | |
| 323.7 | | Minneiska | 71 | 6:01:38 | |
| 326.9 | | Weaver | 71, 80 | 6:04:22 | |
| 334.4 | | Kellogg | 71, 80, 70 | 6:10:24 | |
| 340.5 | | Wabasha | 62 | 6:15:33 | 6:15 |
| 342.4 | | Reads Landing | 69, 70 | 6:17:19 | |
| 353.0 | | Lake City | 69, 80, 70 | 6:26:42 | |
| 359.3 | | Frontenac | 77, 82, 60 curve, 73 | 6:31:51 | |
| 369.9 | Ar. | Red Wing | | 6:41:40 | |
| | Lv. | Red Wing | | 6:42:40 | 6:43 |
| 372.0 | Pass | Island Siding | 71 | 6:45:45 | |
| | Ar. | Red Signal Indication | | 6:51:30 | |
| | Lv. | Red Signal Indication | | 6:51:55 | |
| | | Rear of train over broken rail | 89, 80 | 6:55:20 | |
| 384.5 | Pass | Blackbird Junction | 85 | 7:02:40 | |
| 390.3 | | Hastings | 40, 35 bridge | 7:06:58 | 6:59 |
| 391.5 | | St. Croix Tower | 31, 60, 80 | 7:08:43 | 7:01 |
| 403.4 | | Newport | 59, 80 | 7:20:20 | 7:15 |
| 407.9 | | Oakland | 60 | 7:24:12 | |
| 408.9 | | St. Paul Yard | 70, 50 until Xing | 7:25:16 | |
| 411.5 | Ar. | St. Paul | | 7:31:40 | 7:30 |
| | Lv. | St. Paul | | 7:34:00 | 7:33 |
| 412.4 | Pass | Chestnut Street | 30 | 7:37:15 | 7:35 |
| 413.3 | | Fordson Junction | 38, 45, 48 | 7:38:53 | 7:37 |
| 417.3 | | Merriam Park | 48 | 7:45:00 | 7:44 |
| 418.7 | | Tower G | 50, 22 | 7:47:18 | 7:47 |
| 420.5 | | South Minneapolis | 27 | 7:50:26 | 7:50 |
| 422.4 | Ar. | Minneapolis | | 7:57:02 | 8:00 |

NOTE: Speeds as shown represent speed at station, occasionally on slow order curves, and maximum and minimum between stations.

A new F-7 wheels an equally new consist of train 101 at an estimated 85 mph between Pewaukee and Hartland, Wis., in 1938. Note the enclosures for undercar equipment. — C. P. Fox.

REMEMBER the Milwaukee Road's 100 mph speed limits 25 years ago and the 75-minute timings of the *Hiawatha* between Milwaukee and Chicago? Today both of these are part of the past. The maximum speed permitted on the Milwaukee now is 90 mph and the best time on this stretch is 80 minutes (78 minutes westbound), including a stop at Glenview.°

But just prior to World War II, the eastbound schedule of the *Morning Hiawatha* allowed 75 minutes — and it was operated with steam. On a cold day in early 1941, that grand and glorious first engine of the Milwaukee's streamlined Hudsons, the 100, made this run in 69½ minutes, including a 45 or 50 mph slow order over a temporary detour south of Rondout. Except for this detour, net time would have been about 68 minutes for the 85 miles. This may not be the record, but it is easily the best timing chronicled by this correspondent. According to the mileposts (at high speeds this system, with each second representing 2½ to 3 mph, is not too reliable), maximum effort was 110 mph on two separate occasions. All mileposts from outside Milwaukee until the approach to Chicago were timed to the nearest second. Cecil J. Allen, of British rail-timing fame, would frown on this method; but here in the United States, railroads do not have quarter-mile posts, half-mile posts, and so on. To add a bit more controversy, the charts of the CMStP&P show the Milwaukee-Chicago mileage to be 85.5. The chief discrepancy lies between Kinnickinnic Draw and Kinnickinnic Lake — 5.0 miles in the working timetable and 5.5 on the charts. For years both Chicago & North Western and Milwaukee Road printed 85 even miles in their timetables, although the distance on North Western was shorter (84.4 miles) and on Milwaukee Road it was longer.

The accompanying figures tell the story of the January 14, 1941, run of No. 6. Note that the magic 100 mark was first touched at the third milepost past Tower A-68; and from a mile past Sturtevant, *31 consecutive miles were timed at 100 mph or better.* The slow order over the temporary detour interrupted this string of three-figure speeds, but starting again at Northbrook, 8 of the succeeding 11 miles were also covered in the 100's. Eleven miles out from Chicago Union Station, which was within city limits, a 35-second mile was posted — 103 mph. Possibly keeping in mind the slow order over the temporary detour, the engineer tried here to minimize the delay.

Although the line is free of any severe grades, several short pulls

---

*The railroad in 1968 reduced speed between Chicago and the Twin Cities to a maximum 79 mph, resulting in a best time of 86 minutes Milwaukee-Chicago.

## Up, Up . . . Past 100

Chicago, Milwaukee, St. Paul & Pacific train No. 6; Tuesday, January 14, 1941; nine cars, 430 tons. F-7 Hudson No. 100 — tractive effort, 50,300 pounds; drivers, 84 inches; cylinders, 23½ x 30 inches; boiler pressure, 300 pounds.

| Miles | Stations | Mph per milepost | Actual | Schedule |
|---|---|---|---|---|
| 0.0 | MILWAUKEE | | 1:38:03 p.m. | 1:35 p.m. |
| 1.1 | Washington Street | | 1:41:30 | 1:38 |
| 2.1 | Kinnickinnic Draw | 64-64-67-68 | 1:42:48 | |
| 7.1 | Lake | 75-78-88-92-92 | 1:48:24 | 1:44 |
| 12.2 | Oakwood | 97-97-97 | 1:51:56 | |
| 15.6 | Caledonia | 97 | 1:54:02 | |
| 16.9 | Tower A-68 | 90-97-100 | 1:54:50 | 1:52 |
| 19.0 | Franksville | 97-97-100-103 | 1:56:09 | |
| 23.2 | Sturtevant | 97-103-100-103 | 1:58:37 | 1:56 |
| 27.5 | Somers | 103-103-103-103-103 | 2:01:09 | |
| 32.4 | Truesdell | 100 | 2:04:01 | |
| 33.4 | Ranney | 103-100-100-100 | 2:04:37 | 2:03 |
| 38.0 | Russell, Ill. | 100-100-100-103-100 | 2:07:21 | |
| 42.1 | Wadsworth | 103-110-106-103 | 2:09:50 | 2:09 |
| 46.4 | Gurnee | 103-100 | 2:12:14 | |
| 48.2 | Wilson | 100-103-103-103 | 2:13:18 | |
| 52.7 | Rondout | 103-103-110-64 | 2:16:04 | 2:16 |
| 57.0 | West Lake Forest | 73-78-88 | 2:19:15 | |
| 61.1 | Deerfield | 88-90-97 | 2:22:07 | |
| 64.1 | Northbrook | 103 | 2:24:02 | |
| 64.7 | Tower A-20 | | 2:24:26 | 2:24 |
| 64.8 | Techny | 92-100-103 | 2:24:31 | |
| 67.6 | Glenview | 100 | 2:26:21 | |
| 68.8 | Golf | 100-100 | 2:27:06 | |
| 70.7 | Morton Grove | 97-97-103-103 | 2:28:05 | |
| 73.4 | Edgebrook | 97 | 2:29:44 | |
| 74.8 | Forest Glen | 72 | 2:30:44 | |
| 76.0 | Mayfair | 46 | 2:32:14 | |
| 76.8 | Grayland | 59-65 | 2:33:12 | |
| 78.6 | Healy | 56 | 2:34:55 | |
| 79.6 | Pacific Junction | | 2:35:58 | 2:37 |
| 82.1 | Western Avenue | | 2:39:11 | |
| 85.0 | CHICAGO | | 2:47:30 | 2:50 |

NOTES: Snowing hard from Rondout to Chicago. Slow order of about 45 or 50 mph over temporary detour between Mileposts 55 and 56 for grade-crossing-elimination work. No other delays, although the speeds at Mayfair and/or Grayland apparently were less than at present.

Even standing still for a builder's portrait, an F-7 4-6-4 hinted at built-in speed potential. — *American Locomotive Company*.

are worthy of mention. Coming out of Milwaukee, after crossing the Kinnickinnic River, there is a 2-mile grade of 0.67 per cent; then following a mile of level comes another 2 miles of 0.67 per cent. The latter is at Lake, the highest point between Milwaukee and Chicago (742 feet elevation). Still another 0.67 per cent pull lies just past Caledonia, but this is preceded by a downgrade on which momentum can be gathered. The only other grade to be considered is a short rise from Gurnee to Wilson (0.6 per cent), then the running ground is all more or less favorable. Milwaukee and Chicago elevations are both a shade over 590 feet.

Obviously, most of the line is adapted to fast running. In 1941, in the first 2 miles out of Milwaukee there were restrictions of 10 mph from the station, 30 mph on curves, 45 mph over the C&NW crossing, and 50 mph over the draw. Until the 70 mph restrictions over the crossings at Mayfair and Grayland were reached, the only slow order was found over the Elgin, Joliet & Eastern crossing at Rondout. (At different times since the inauguration of the *Hiawathas* in 1935, this crossing has had several restrictions and occasionally none; today it is 80 mph.) Between Pacific Junction and Chicago were continuous restrictions — from the 60 mph at the Junction to 15 mph going into Chicago.

On the westbound run the 57.6 miles from Tower A-20 to Lake required an average speed of 90.9 mph with the 38-minute timing. So far as is known, this is the fastest sustained timing ever printed in this country which could be and *was* maintained. The 38-minute time is 2 minutes less than the eastbound timing shown in the table on page 70.

For the benefit of skeptics, here are a few figures to mull over. The 33.7 miles from Franksville to Rondout were run in a shade under 20 minutes for an average speed of 101.01 mph. From Lake, outside of Milwaukee and at the top of the grade, to Edgebrook, outside of Chicago, took 41⅓ minutes for the 66.3 miles, an average speed of 95.04 mph, including the slow order south of Rondout. The entire run averaged 73.43 mph (or 73.86 using the 85.5 mileage). After deducting for the slow order (more time is not allowed owing to the rapid recovery), the average speeds are 75.00 mph for 85 miles and 75.44 for 85.5 miles.

Today only two railroads permit 100 mph speeds (over certain sections), and in general the running is not as fast as in prewar days. But the next time you think you have been traveling along at a good clip, remember what the steam engines were doing in regular everyday service with the *Hiawatha* a quarter-century ago.

# DIESELS, WAR, AND S.R.O.

In an all-out war, all-out Hi's

SEPTEMBER 20, 1941, will be inscribed forever in the history of the *Hi* for the arrival of the inevitable. That morning, No. 15, a 4000 h.p. product of Electro-Motive composed of two E-6 cab units, headed train 6 out of Minneapolis. It had come up from Chicago during the night on mail-and-express train 57. In November it was joined by No. 14, two needle-nose Alco 2000 h.p. cab units, which handled 101 to Minneapolis and returned on *Fast Mail* 56. C. H. Bilty remarked that there was no question of the speed capabilities of the A's and F-7's, but that the diesels were acquired as a matter of efficiency. The 14 and 15 could make a daily round trip between Chicago and Minneapolis, doubling the mileage of steam. Unknown at the moment, the diesels were to make available two more F-7's for use on the soon-to-come expanded wartime consists of other mainline trains. With all due respect to steam, No. 15 turned out to be one of the finest units of motive power to grace the Milwaukee's rails in modern times.

The color scheme of the E-6's was an obvious attempt to duplicate the design of the shrouded steamers. The upper two-thirds of the carbody was the same shade of gray as the boiler cover, and an orange stripe (to give a running-board effect) was drawn across the lower third with a small maroon line edging the bottom. On the 15 the orange band widened to circle the nose, which carried a large wing inscribed THE MILWAUKEE ROAD. No. 14 was considerably more colorful. Its orange belt was edged on the top and bottom by a thicker maroon stripe that was worked at the front into what would presently be described as "sculpture," to bring about a gray, maroon, and orange nose with a smaller stainless-steel wing and stainless-steel THE MILWAUKEE ROAD in individual letters on the maroon portion of the nose. The sculpture was touched off in yellow and extended from the cab roof across the center section of the windshield over the nose and encircled the Mars headlight. Alas, this scheme did not last, and in less than a year the 14 received the uninspiring arrangement of its brother. The 14 turned out to be the last power built by Alco for mainline *Hiawatha* service.

Despite the continuing success of the *Hiawatha* (it consistently ranked second in earnings in the country, exceeded only by the Southern Pacific's *Coast Daylight*, which had no comparable competition), the same economics that brought diesels to some of the *Hi*'s also caused revisions in the parlor-car assignments of the trains. By the summer of 1940 one drawing-room straight-parlor car had been removed from the consist of 100 and 101. During the next year Beaver Tails *Miller* and *Mitchell* were rebuilt to include a drawing

72

room. They were assigned permanently as the through parlors for trains 5 and 6, whose straight drawing room-parlors were operated only between Chicago and Milwaukee. Part of the parlor-car business may have been lost to the *400*, which had become a streamliner (with matching schedule) in September 1939 — serving the wealthy lakeshore area of Chicagoland through an Evanston stop — and always carried two full parlors and a parlor-bar-observation.

The January 1942 timefolder indicated restoration of the straight parlor to train 6 only, with no specific westbound counterpart; the August 1943 folder returned such a car to the consist of No. 5. The author does not recall seeing more than two parlors on any of the Twin Cities *Hi's* at this time, except for occasional special movements.

By this time, American entry into World War II had taken place. There was no time for fanfare; and with gas and tire rationing, and with greatly expanded military training, publicity wasn't needed to fill trains. The previous records of all streamliners fell like pins at an ABC tournament. Earnings and consists of the *Hi's* jumped, and 15-car consists were commonplace. Often a Second 5 was operated to handle head-end cars and local passengers (*i.e.*, between Milwaukee and Oconomowoc). New *Hiawatha* equipment entered service almost unnoticed.

Authorization to construct the cars had been received early in 1941. Because of the defense and war efforts, innumerable substitutions of material were made to leave prime items available for war work. This added to the weights of the finished cars and created construction difficulties for the road. For example, the usual reclining-back seats could not be obtained, and instead, a seat which tilted like a rocking chair was installed.

As for appearance, the wartime equipment was built with skirts below the carbody — the first and only such application on CMStP&P cars — that extended the full length of the car without any cutaway beside the trucks (although these skirts possibly were not as low as on cars of other railroads), lending a square shape. Fluting was carried over, but in a somewhat different pattern. The roof was silver-gray, and letterboard, window stripe, and skirt were maroon. The remainder of the side was done in orange, and trucks and visible underframe equipment were brown.

Liberal use was made of fluorescent lighting in all interiors, with cheerful results. Tubes were in a parallel continuous fixture beneath the luggage racks. Their glow shone directly down from the fixture and bounced off the nearly white undersides of the luggage

racks. Above the post between each window, and serving to break the continuity of the fluorescents, were individual gold stars mounted on a black plastic square to serve as night-lights. They produced a soft illumination sufficient for overnight travel, or for the four daily passages of the *Hi's* through the bore of Tunnel No. 1 at Tunnel City, Wis. As in previous equipment, no aisle lights were used in the body of the cars.

Considerable attention was given to interior finishings despite difficulties in obtaining materials. All walls were two-tone walnut, as were ceilings above the luggage racks. The center of the ceiling, above the aisle, was a continuous ventilation grille of metal painted an off-shade of purple. A paralleling belt of off-white, or cream, dropped from the ceiling down the bulkheads, filling the space between the aisle and the edge of the luggage racks. Seats were green with gold stitching worked in. The new diners featured Venetian blinds; coach windows had shades.

The coach floor plan was radically changed from that of previous *Hiawatha* cars. Individual smoking rooms for men and women were replaced by one large smoking room to be used by all at the blind end of the car. Instead of individual washrooms there were tiny toilet cubicles at the vestibule end on either side of the aisle. To help compensate for the absence of the previous ample-size washrooms for the ladies, a powder room was provided in a separate cubicle. On the men's side of the aisle that space was taken by well-needed shelves for extra luggage.

The Pittsburgh Plate Glass windows were hermetically sealed fog-proof double glass. Portholes were retained only in doors and toilets. Further-improved trucks were used (many persons were of the opinion that the 1942 coaches represented the finest of Nystrom's craftsmanship), along with Budd disc brakes, insulated draft gear, and Waukesha motor (rather than steam jet) air conditioning. Although 31 new cars emerged quietly from the Milwaukee Shops during the spring and summer of 1942, they did not represent a complete re-equipping of the *Hi's*. For one thing, no parlor cars were built. And only two diners and two full-length tap cars, along with the last two combines constructed by the Milwaukee, were used on the *Afternoon* train. The *Morning Hi* continued to use the 1939-style express-tap and diner. For both trains, skirts were welded to the Beaver Tail and regular parlors, as well as to diners and taps used on 5 and 6, to conform with the latest series. Much 1939 equipment and even some 1937 cars were fitted with skirts.

Though No. 14 was second to be delivered, the Otto Kuhler-styled Alco bore the lower number of the Milwaukee Road's two passenger diesels. Already it had been repainted when this publicity scene was taken. — *Milwaukee Road.*

It's 1 p.m. in St. Paul and the 7-foot drive wheels of F-7 104 are starting to roll train 100, the *Afternoon Hiawatha*, out of Union Depot. The year is 1942; the big 4-6-4 has already been modified with a Mars signal headlight high above the regular headlight, and wartime traffic increases have made additional coaches an everyday occurrence. On this day, for example, two earlier-series coaches are cut in behind the combine. Parlors at the rear of what appears to be a 13-car train show how the skirting introduced on the 1942 cars has been added to earlier equipment. — *Both photos, W. J. Pontin.*

Only four days old, 15 flashes through New Lisbon with the *Morning Hiawatha*. The westbound coal chute in the background of the top photo was installed specially to accommodate 4-6-4's on trains 5 and 101, which made station stops here. The bank at the left was cut away later to permit the laying of an eastbound passing track that enabled No. 58 to remain parked in the station while awaiting the arrival of passengers off train 100. Wartime traffic soon would be so heavy that coach passengers would have to stand in the aisles or sit on suitcases. — *Both photos, Alfred W. Johnson.*

In September 1942, coach 477 was repainted in a patriotic red, white, and blue livery and sent throughout the system to encourage the purchase of war bonds. Then it was frequently assigned to trains 100 and 101. — *Milwaukee Road.*

The two new diners achieved the dignified look of a high-quality supper club, partially through use of mirrors in conjunction with the fluorescent lighting. The two new full-length tap cars (which were sometimes referred to as auxiliary diners) were carried between the dining car and the coaches, and had an aisle the full length of the car to accommodate standees waiting for meal service. A shoulder-high walnut-and-glass barrier separated the aisle from the tap rooms, which were themselves divided by a kitchen-galley in the center of the car. Attached to the inside of the barrier were tables for two, and the wall sides of the tap rooms were flanked by tables for three and booths for four. Glass-enclosed planters separated the booths from the tables. There were windows at the four booths, and the 12-foot walls alongside the tables were taken up by large

Despite the war, new coaches — along with diners, combines, and tap cars for the *Afternoon Hi* only — were permitted completion by the War Production Board. These were the only *Hiawatha* cars built new with skirts. Many felt that the cars of this series were the best-riding; certainly the liberal use of fluorescent lighting made them cheerful inside. In normal service on the *Hiawathas*, seats faced the camera and the smoking lounge was at the rear of the car. Gold stars served as night-lights between fluorescent tubes. — *All photos, Milwaukee Road.*

79

In 1943, just as they are today, boys were enthralled by trains. Two youngsters gave their utmost attention to the 105 taking train 5 — the *Morning Hiawatha* — out of Milwaukee; but one of them forgot his coaching and eyed daddy rather than the finned Beaver Tail. — *Both photos, C. P. Fox.*

80

hand-carved wood plaques depicting Indian lore, set off with square mirrors. The outside wall of the aisle had normal coach window spacing.

One of the new cars, coach 477, emerged with a red, white, and blue color scheme with "Buy War Bonds" in a flowing script beneath its windows. No. 477 was dispatched on a systemwide jaunt, after which it ran most frequently in one set of *Afternoon Hiawatha* equipment.

The passenger compartment in the two combines, 206 and 207, had the same design as the full coaches, except that a smoking area (consisting of leather-upholstered seats near the express room) replaced the smoking room.

All of the new equipment was put to maximum use. By August 1943, 100 and 101 each were averaging over 900 passengers per trip, and Nos. 5 and 6 averaged over 850 per trip. This was a 60 per cent increase in patronage over the previous year and is indicative of the contribution made by all passenger trains on all railroads during the war years. Although by that time the *Hiawathas* were overworked, they carried on in the best of *Hiawatha* tradition. Streamlined equipment was used unfailingly in *Hiawatha* service — no non-streamlined, non-air-conditioned, or non-reclining-seat equipment was ever used. Frequently the earlier models of streamlined coaches, and occasionally an earlier streamlined parlor, would be pressed into *Hiawatha* service, but quality was never sacrificed further. On the way to victory, the Milwaukee owned 207 streamlined passenger cars, and virtually every line-haul train operated with at least some streamlined cars in its consist.

Fifteen-car consists were common, and by the ninth birthday of 100 and 101 on May 29, 1944, the trains had rolled 3,275,000 passengers to their destinations without mishap. In 5 years 5 months as *Hiawathas*, trains 5 and 6 had served an additional 1,440,000 riders.

On December 6, 1942, the Office of Defense Transportation required that fast trains throughout the country be slowed to conserve equipment, and the *Hi's* were no exception: 15 minutes was added to all Twin Cities trains. At that time a stop at Camp McCoy, Wis., was added to the schedule of train 5; later the stop was transferred to train 101. After hostilities ceased in 1945 both westbound *Hi's* made Camp McCoy stops, and train 6's Sparta stop was shifted to McCoy, all to aid the post in serving as a discharge center. By 1946 this function had been reduced, and train 101 was the only *Hi* making the military stop. The stop was discontinued in November 1946.

Although the European phase of the war had ended, Japan still remained in the conflict. Consequently, the tenth anniversary of *Hiawatha* service was observed quietly with a luncheon in a dining car spotted adjacent to train 101 in Chicago Union Station. The luncheon was attended by H. A. Scandrett, by prominent Chicago businessmen, and by representatives of the press. The guest of honor was retired *Hiawatha* engineer Hugh McManus. Later conductor Ernie

Haddock gave the highball for 101, engineer Al Grandy opened the throttle of the 14, and 10 years of *Hiawatha* departures from Chicago were completed. Eastbound 100 was pulled by F-7 101 on the same date. In 10 years nearly 4 million passengers had traveled by *Afternoon Hi*, enabling it to gross $17,963,662. One well-informed source stated that the train had held first place in volume between Chicago and the Twin Cities since its inception.

(Far left) From the signal bridge at the east edge of the Milwaukee depot, the departure of train 6 was recorded on a track that is no more. (Left) A close-up of the ultimate in observation cars. — *Far left, W. A. Akin; left, Jim Scribbins.*

# FAMOUS 15

## The locomotive that sold the steam-powered Milwaukee Road on diesels

THE Minneapolis-Chicago speedway of the Milwaukee Road has been traversed by many types of motive power during the *Hiawatha's* existence.

The Class A Atlantics led the way and were in many respects the acme of high-speed passenger steam power. They were followed by the F-7 Hudsons which enabled train No. 6, the southbound *Morning Hiawatha*, to hold down what was perhaps the fastest regularly scheduled run ever made with steam power: Sparta to Portage, 78.3 miles, at 81 mph on a start-to-stop average.

Then in the fall of 1941 two 4000 h.p. A-A diesels were purchased and assigned to this exacting service. The road was well satisfied with its steamers, and Mechanical Engineer C. H. Bilty explained that the diesels were obtained simply because they could be quickly serviced at terminals and make a round trip daily between Chicago and the Twin Cities.

Throughout World War II Alco-GE-built No. 14 and Electro-Motive-built No. 15 gave their all, and the Atlantics and the Hudsons continued to do great things. There was no visible sign that the Milwaukee Road was displeased with steam. The picture changed when the conflict ended. In 1946 five EMD E7's bumped the 4-6-4's from

the *Hi's*; the next year Fairbanks-Morse power entered the pool. Present power for mainline trains is a fleet of Electro-Motive FP7's.

Thus in 10 years' time we have witnessed the transition of the Milwaukee Road from one of the leading exponents of the steam locomotive to a line on which the old faithful iron horse pulls only a handful of suburban runs. If the Milwaukee Road was well satisfied with steam until the middle '40's, why did it suddenly change horses in midstream? Why didn't it continue to rely on its outstanding steam power? The answer is found by examining the amazing demonstration of internal combustion traction given by No. 15, the road's first passenger diesel.

Many railroad hobbyists complain that diesels are impersonal machines, seeming less alive and therefore less to be admired than steam locomotives. No. 15, however, is individual enough as diesels go, since it is the only EMD E6 owned by the Milwaukee Road. More individual among diesel locomotives was her performance when she was in her prime. Consider for a moment the rugged service required of No. 15 and the way in which she met the challenge, and you will agree that it was the 15 which sold the steam-powered Milwaukee Road on diesels.

She left Chicago each evening at 9 with train No. 57, the famous

This article by Dick Nation and Jim Scribbins appeared in July 1953 TRAINS.

Seldom has the glory or the omnipotence of the steam age been more eloquently recorded than in this prewar scene photographed at the east end of the Milwaukee depot. The mighty Hudsons — one panting on First No. 6 and another serving as protection power (later to go on No. 46) — established records that would test the merit of any diesel. Famous 15 was soon to challenge the finest the steam age offered. — *C. P. Fox.*

Well within Chicago's city limits but still cruising at high speed on the Milwaukee Road's elevated right of way, the 15 approaches Grayland with the *Morning Hiawatha* in the summer of 1947. Chart on facing page reveals how well 15 met the timekeeping challenge. — *Wallace W. Abbey.*

| Miles | Stations | Dist. | Sched. Min. | May 29, 1947 Time | Speed | May 23, 1948 Time | Speed | November 2, 1948 Time | Speed |
|---|---|---|---|---|---|---|---|---|---|
| .... | MILWAUKEE | 0.0 | 0 | 1:52:56 p.m. | .... | 1:26:51 p.m. | .... | 1:37:00 p.m. | .... |
| 7.1 | Lake | 7.1 | 9 | 2:02:31 | 52.2 | 1:38:14 | 37.4 | 1:48:05 | 38.4 |
| 12.2 | Oakwood | 5.1 | .. | 2:06:18 | 81.0 | 1:41:52 | 84.3 | 1:51:52 | 80.9 |
| 15.6 | Caledonia | 3.4 | .. | ...... | .... | 1:44:02 | 94.2 | 1:54:08 | 90.0 |
| 16.9 | Tower A-68 | 1.3 | 17 | 2:09:21 | 92.5 | ...... | .... | 1:55:00 | 90.0 |
| 19.0 | Franksville | 2.1 | .. | ...... | .... | 1:46:11 | 94.9 | 1:56:24 | 90.0 |
| 23.2 | Sturtevant | 4.2 | 21 | 2:13:21 | 94.7 | 1:48:42 | 100.3 | 1:59:05 | 93.9 |
| 27.5 | Somers | 4.3 | .. | 2:16:00 | 97.2 | 1:51:17 | 100.0 | 2:01:40 | 100.0 |
| 32.4 | Truesdell | 4.9 | .. | 2:18:54 | 101.5 | 1:54:07 | 103.7 | 2:04:31 | 103.2 |
| 38.0 | Russell | 5.6 | .. | 2:22:19 | 98.4 | 1:57:30 | 99.2 | 2:07:53 | 99.7 |
| 42.1 | Wadsworth | 4.1 | 34 | 2:24:59 | 98.3 | 2:01:01 | 69.9 | 2:10:21 | 99.7 |
| 48.2 | Wilson | 6.1 | .. | ...... | .... | 2:06:01 | 73.2 | 2:13:56 | 101.7 |
| 52.7 | Rondout | 4.5 | 41 | 2:31:18 | 100.6 | 2:09:08 | 86.5 | 2:16:43 | 97.0 |
| 57.0 | W. Lake Forest | 4.3 | .. | 2:33:48 | 100.3 | 2:11:48 | 96.8 | 2:19:11 | 104.6 |
| 61.1 | Deerfield | 4.1 | .. | 2:36:04 | 107.6 | 2:14:07 | 106.2 | 2:21:31 | 105.6 |
| 64.7 | Tower A-20 | 3.6 | 40 | 2:38:20 | 95.2 | 2:16:17 | 99.7 | 2:23:41 | 99.7 |
| 73.4 | Edgebrook | 8.7 | .. | ...... | .... | 2:21:39 | 97.3 | 2:28:46 | 102.6 |
| 76.0 | Mayfair | 2.6 | .. | ...... | .... | 2:24:08 | 62.8 | 2:30:33 | 87.4 |
| 76.8 | Grayland | .8 | .. | ...... | .... | 2:24:59 | 56.4 | 2:31:13 | 72.0 |
| 79.6 | Tower A-5 | 2.8 | 62 | 2:48:13 | 90.5 | 2:27:16 | 73.6 | 2:33:16 | 85.7 |
| 82.1 | Western Avenue | 2.5 | .. | 2:50:56 | 55.1 | 2:29:56 | 56.3 | 2:36:12 | 51.1 |
| 85.0 | CHICAGO | 2.9 | 75 | 2:57:26 | 26.8 | 2:39:02 | 19.1 | 2:46:38 | 16.7 |

**RUNNING TIME** .................... 75 min.
**AVERAGE SPEED** .................... 68 mph

64 minutes 30 seconds
79.1 mph

72 minutes 11 seconds
70.7 mph

69 minutes 38 seconds
73.2 mph

### May 29, 1947

An exceptionally good assault was made on Lake Hill, and with a Grade-A start on the schedule, No. 15 pointed her nose toward Chicago and took off. Eighty-one mph was averaged to Oakwood, 92.5 mph to Tower A-68, and 94.7 mph to Sturtevant.

Over the slight hump beyond that junction the diesel averaged 97.2 mph to Somers, and finally broke the century mark by averaging 101.5 to Truesdell. Ranney curve cut the 15's speed, but the average was still above 98 mph to Wadsworth. Then, demonstrating that it had what it takes to go over the road, the engine maintained almost unbelievable speeds of over 100 mph for the following 19 miles: 100.6 to Rondout, 100.3 to West Lake Forest, and 107.6 to Deerfield — the highest speed recorded anywhere in our logs.

To Tower A-20, 95.2 mph was averaged, and the growler soared along at better than 90 well into the terminal limits of Chicago. Only after passing Tower A-5 was No. 15 permitted to catch its breath, and even then it was pushed along at the fastest permissible speeds in congested areas.

This run, more than any other, proved the 15's remarkable ability to stand up under a terrific beating, yet make up time. The diesel accomplished what might well be considered impossible — making up 10½ minutes on a very tight schedule. It was the fastest Milwaukee-Chicago run ever clocked by the authors.

### May 23, 1948

Slow running over the first 2 miles resulted in a low average speed to Lake, although No. 15 passed the tower at nearly 80 mph. The average speed was raised to 84.3 to Oakwood, 94.2 to Caledonia, and 94.9 to Franksville.

Then the mileposts flitted by even more spectacularly: 100.3 mph to Sturtevant, 100 to Somers, and 103.7 to Truesdell. No. 15 was hardly cramped by the curve at Ranney, but then it met the major obstacle of the run. A slow order passing a track gang at Wadsworth brought the speed down to barely 30 mph for about a quarter of a mile.

A clear road beckoned the 15 and the task of regaining lost time was begun. The qualities of the locomotive were again demonstrated when the needle on the speedometer rose to 73.2 mph to Wilson, 86.5 to Rondout, 96.8 to West Lake Forest, and on down the speedway at a cool 106.2.

Averages in the high 90's were maintained to the city limits at Edgebrook. The climb to track elevation ended the fast running, but a spurt near Tower A-5 brought the run to an on-time basis.

Arrival at Union Station was nearly a minute to the good — a fitting conclusion to a run powered by the unbeatable No. 15.

The May 29, 1947, run was scheduled to leave Milwaukee at 1:40 p.m. with a 2:55 p.m. arrival at Chicago. The May 23, 1948, and the November 2, 1948, runs were scheduled for 1:25 p.m. departures, with arrival at Chicago at 2:40 p.m.

### November 2, 1948

No. 15 was 12 minutes late out of Milwaukee and made an average run to Lake. The speeds, while respectable, were not as high as they were on the previous runs: 80.9 mph to Caledonia, 90 to Franksville, and 93.9 to Sturtevant.

Then the 15 gave another of its outstanding performances. It rolled the next 50.2 miles at speeds ranging from a low of 97 mph to a high of 105.6. The run followed the same pattern as preceding ones. Extremely high speeds between Sturtevant and Truesdell were followed by the inevitable slackening for the Ranney curve. The century mark was reached again between Wadsworth and Wilson. The diesel gained its second wind after passing Rondout and glided along at a smart 104.6 mph to West Lake Forest, then, still not satisfied with its efforts, pushed itself to 105.6 mph to Deerfield. The speed dropped a bit to Tower A-20, then as if it had yet to save its soul, the EMD averaged 102.6 to Edgebrook, the Chicago city limits.

The 15 had to restrain itself now, but it still ran at speeds which on many roads would be considered high in open country. With Tower A-5 behind, the engine assumed a more moderate pace, and speeds between Western Avenue and Chicago were a bit slower than usual.

The 85 miles from Milwaukee to Chicago had been covered in 69 minutes 38 seconds.

mail and express flyer, and arrived in Minneapolis at 6:15 a.m. This is a difficult assignment to say the least. Fifty-Seven's consist seldom amounts to less than 15 cars, more often is in the 20's, and sometimes is as heavy as 30 cars. Its schedule was and still is hot. Imagine making *Hiawatha* time with 20 to 25 heavily loaded mail and express cars! This was required of No. 15, for time-consuming intermediate stops belied the mail's slow over-all schedule.

No. 15 had a layover of little more than an hour and a half in Minneapolis, then left with train No. 6, the *Morning Hiawatha*, and sped to Chicago in 6 hours 50 minutes — an average speed of 62 mph, including stops. Embodied in this schedule for several years was one of the world's fastest runs: Sparta to Portage at an 81 mph start-to-stop average. Even more rugged than this was the last lap of the run: Milwaukee to Chicago, 85 miles in 75 minutes. This meant that time lost west of Milwaukee could be recovered only by some extraordinarily fast running on the home stretch. No. 15 held this assignment regularly until the summer of 1949. Then she was relegated to secondary trains; the newer E7's took over, to be bumped in turn by the present FP7's. It is worth noting that today's 4500 h.p. locomotives do not handle any heavier or faster trains than did the 15. If anything, the less powerful No. 15 outperformed them, because the newer units have a 95 mph gearing.

Picture then the character of a locomotive for which rolling uncounted miles in the 100 mph bracket was a daily assignment for some seven years with infrequent relief. Yet because she was a diesel — an impersonal, unromantic machine, slow to inspire affection — the 15 acquired little praise and no fame at all. To remedy this injustice and to arouse interest in the much-neglected art of train timing, we present the logs of three outstanding Milwaukee-Chicago runs of No. 15 while she was heading the *Morning Hiawatha*.

The physical characteristics and speed potentials of the Milwaukee-Chicago line should be mentioned. It is not the fastest track on the road, but it does have plenty of tangent and a density of extremely high-speed traffic that is exceeded on only a few lines between the large cities of the East. There is but one serious obstacle to high speeds eastbound — Lake Hill, a 5-mile grade partially within the city limits of Milwaukee. It reaches its summit at Lake, 7.1 miles south of Milwaukee. The balance of the line is virtually level with a few notable curves which do not impose any serious speed restrictions. In fact, there are no real speed restrictions between the terminal limits of Milwaukee and Chicago, though you wouldn't want to hit the curve at Ranney, now discontinued as a station, at much more than 90 mph. The speed restriction in the operating timetable for the Elgin, Joliet & Eastern crossing at Rondout, however, is worthy of mention: "Rondout . . . EJ&E RR crossing . . . *maximum* speed, passenger trains . . . 100 mph."

If one understands the full implication of that note, he is prepared for the logs on page 87.

The classic lines of the Electro-Motive E6 go on display before the camera of the Milwaukee Road's publicity forces. The location is not identified, but the author's guess is South Minneapolis during the turnaround for 57 and 6. Following the example of the F-7 4-6-4's, No. 15 was painted in an orange-and-gray livery. The Milwaukee Road's only E6 was one of those unexplained rarities in locomotive construction — an engine that, although it was built to the same patterns and standards as dozens of sister locomotives on U. S. railroads, somehow displayed exceptional speed and performance. — *Milwaukee Road*.

"The finishing touch to a perfect train," was the slogan used to describe Brooks Stevens' superb Skytop Lounges, which were introduced in 1948 on new Twin Cities *Hi* equipment. Only dome cars contained more glass area. — *Brooks Stevens.*

# SKYTOPS AND SUPER DOMES

## More diesels and enough new cars to make a 2½-mile Hi

JUNE 1946 brought additional 4000 h.p. two-unit EMD E7 passenger locomotives to the Chicago-Minneapolis service, bumping the last Hudsons from *Hi's* 5 and 100. As the 14 and 15 had been doing all along, the new locomotives made a daily round trip handling a standard train in one direction at night. At this same time, or shortly thereafter, the Alco, despite the fact that it had performed 99 per cent of the time, was quietly assigned to other trains.

On June 29, 1947, the prewar schedule of 6 hours 45 minutes was returned to train 101, and September 28 once again brought 6 hours 50 minutes to train 6, and 6 hours 45 minutes to train 100. Over a period of time, train No. 5 had acquired additional head-end cars and was not (and never has been) restored to its pre-December 6, 1942, schedule.

By now it was known that new Twin Cities *Hi's* were in the making. Their interiors and exteriors were styled by Brooks Stevens, a Milwaukee industrial designer. K. F. Nystrom continued to supervise the mechanical aspects. The Milwaukee's postwar coaches weighed in at an average of 111,260 pounds compared with the nearly 8600 additional pounds carried by cars constructed commercially to AAR specifications. Not only were Nystrom's products lighter (and he advocated even less weight) but their components were anywhere

from 3 per cent to 46 per cent stronger than AAR recommendations.

The year 1948 was billed as a *Hiawatha* year. One hundred fifty-three new cars, constituting the largest passenger-car order in the road's history and enough to make a 2½-mile-long *Hiawatha* if they were coupled end to end, were built to completely re-equip all *Hiawatha* trains and to add new *Hiawathas* to the roster. At least one published ad made reference to a *Pioneer Hiawatha* as the streamlined replacement for the *Pioneer Limited*, but when the new sleeping cars were delivered by Pullman-Standard, the *Limited* wisely was retained after all.

After a week-long exhibition tour before 43,635 persons — including a special showing for railfans who were members of the Railroad Society of Milwaukee — new Twin Cities *Hi's* entered service on the 13th birthday of trains 100 and 101, which coincidentally was the centennial date for the State of Wisconsin. In Chicago, at a luncheon in a diner adjacent to newly equipped 101, Illinois Governor Dwight H. Green and Milwaukee Road President C. H. Buford spoke in a 15-minute ceremony which was carried on radio station WMAQ. The Minneapolis sendoff of train 100 was aired on station KSTP and featured Patricia McLane, queen of the Minneapolis Aquatennial; Maxine Emerson and Edward Hampl, queen and king of the St.

There was speed aplenty — in this case a combined 140 mph — along the high iron when two *Hiawathas* met. The author was set up to shoot E7 No. 18 on train 101 at Powerton, Wis., on July 25, 1947, and had to run to gain a broadside angle after No. 6 popped out of Kelley's Cut from the opposite direction behind the E6. — *Jim Scribbins*.

Paul Winter Carnival; Edward Delaney, mayor-elect of St. Paul; Cliff Swanson, president of the Minneapolis city council; and Walter Finke, executive secretary of the Minneapolis Chamber of Commerce. All guests rode to St. Paul.

The new *Hiawatha* equipment had improved roller-bearing trucks and Westinghouse high-speed brakes with electric control. Dutch doors were used for the first time, and diaphragms were lined with a rubber tunnel to make passage between cars cleaner and less drafty. Exteriors were noticeably different. Gone was the fluting which had become a Milwaukee trademark. Sides were smooth and had only a trace of a skirt. Missing too were the wide diaphragms between cars. The new cars themselves were somewhat higher and a bit wider than earlier series.

The parlor-observation cars were considerably changed. The well-known Beaver Tail was replaced by the Skytop Lounge, which had a convex rounded rear end made up of 90 per cent glass. Glass panels, broken by framing, extended from the normal window level up the side of the car and into the roof. The profile of the Skytop was reminiscent of prewar Netherlands multiple-unit electric trains, and it was not unrelated to the turtle-back observations operated at the time on NYC's *Mercury*. In spite of all the glass and the planters which suggested a patio or garden, seats in this "rolling greenhouse" faced the interior. Oh, yes, it was possible to look across and around the heads of seated passengers; but the most important feature of an observation car, so fully exemplified in the immediately preceding Beaver Tails of 1939, was pointedly missing. The Skytop Lounges were, however, the most strikingly contoured termination of any train in the United States.

The solarium was separated from the body of the car by flower boxes fixed at approximately shoulder height between the side wall and vertical stainless-steel bars at aisle's edge. Beneath the planters in the body of the car were small end tables containing magazines. Within the main section were de luxe seats for 24 — big, comfortable, rotating, reclining chairs which were a pleasure to sink into. The forward end contained a drawing room with four seats in section style (which could be converted into a lower berth) and one individual chair.

The Milwaukee stayed with a wood finish, a specialty of Shops cabinetmakers, but the bleached walnut was of much lighter tone than in prewar cars. It was used extensively in parlors and coaches. Diners and tap-cafe cars were finished in darker shades.

The ceiling of the Skytop's solarium was tan. The thick structural member separating the roof from the windows at normal level was turquoise, as were the window frames between it and the rust-colored couch and chairs. Most of the ceiling in the main section of the car was yellow, but the portion above the luggage racks and the undersides of the racks were finished in turquoise. Above, below, and between the windows, as well as on the bulkheads at either end of the body to a height equal to the wood strip above the windows, was wood paneling. The familiar Indian oval appeared on the left bulkhead as one approached from the car's interior. The portion of the bulkhead near the ceiling was done in turquoise. Wall-to-wall carpeting completed the interior.

The aisle passing the drawing room was finished entirely in light wood. The end walls in the interior of the private room were of dark wood; the window wall was of light wood, as in the body of the car; and the fourth side was turquoise. All lighting in the body of the car was a continuous fluorescent strip recessed in the underside of the luggage rack. The drawing room had a fluorescent tube above the window, diffusing light toward ceiling and floor, and additional conventional ceiling fixtures. Two table lamps, as well as bullet lamps recessed in the main horizontal window frame, illuminated the Skytop.

The straight parlors were identical to the Skytops, except that seating was provided for 30, and the ladies' toilet (with an additional annex) was located at the rear (nonvestibule) end of the car.

Dining cars followed the usual 48-seat pattern of previous Twin Cities *Hi's*, with dark wood paneling in the passageway beside the kitchen (the cars always ran with kitchen end forward) and turquoise walls at either end of the dining room. The dining room was divided into three areas. The end thirds had lower ceilings of yellow and turquoise, a fluorescent fixture above the windows shedding light from top and bottom, the same wood treatment of the window area as in the parlors, and gray-green upholstery on the chairs. In the center section, woodwork was replaced with a light-colored background incorporating a leafy design extending into the ceiling area. Fluorescent tubes concealed in the top edge of this design unit reflected their light from the all-yellow raised center ceiling. Chairs in this portion were gray.

Directly ahead of the diners were cars split into cafe and tap rooms by a central kitchen-service area. Both portions had yellow ceilings and wood-paneled windows; a rose-colored band above the

Away from its usual *Morning Hi* assignment, diesel 15 arrives in Milwaukee with train 101. Pacific 184 will follow 101 with 29. — *Jim Scribbins*.

Displaying green "flags" for the *North Woods Section* following 5 hours behind, famous 15 nears Columbus, Wis., with No. 6 in 1947. — *Jim Scribbins.*

(Right) Splendid in its 1948 repainting, the lone E6 rumbles over the Menomonee River in Wauwatosa with First 6. — *Richard J. Cook.*

Running for Milwaukee, the spirited 4000 h.p. machine from EMD whips through the last curve into Wauwatosa with train 6, the re-equipped postwar *Morning Hiawatha.* — *Jim Scribbins.*

Although they were all "Erie-builts," Fairbanks-Morse diesels 21 and 22 had larger windshields and lacked the special chrome nose shields of the opposed-piston units purchased for the *Olympian Hiawatha*. (Above) No. 21 poses for a publicity photo on train 100 near Lamoillc, Minn., with the Mississippi River and the Wisconsin bluffs as backdrops. (Above right) A chrome-nosed FM puts in an appearance on No. 101 west of Wauwatosa, while the B-unit mate of a sister cab unit (right) crossing the Short Line Bridge in Minneapolis reveals an unusual "Route of the Hiawatha" legend on her flanks. — *Above, Milwaukee Road; above right, Jim Scribbins; right, Henry J. McCord.*

A new E7 has replaced the 15 on the point of the *Morning Hiawatha*, being led across 2nd and Clybourn streets in Milwaukee for the fast run to the Windy City. Soon the diesel will receive another livery and the *Hi* will be completely outfitted with new cars. — *W. A. Akin.*

Train 6, the *Morning Hiawatha*, runs past the modernized Wisconsin Dells depot at a leisurely 40 mph. The rear of the train is still on the Wisconsin River bridge. Fast running will resume momentarily. — *James G. La Vake*.

Cool breezes blowing off the Father of Waters help to keep a sultry June day under control as a pair of E7's in their most vivid paint scheme hustle *Afternoon Hiawatha* No. 100 past the Whitman Dam in Minnesota. Trains can be seen for some time as they follow the curving shore line along the bluffs through Hiawatha Valley. — *James G. La Vake*.

The *Afternoon Hiawatha* moves out from Winona, Minn., along the River subdivision on May 31, 1950. The Mississippi River is just beyond the trees. The Milwaukee Road does not remain in sight of the mighty waterway to the extent competitor Burlington does, but the Milwaukee's right of way still provides superb scenic vantage points at several locations. — *James G. La Vake.*

windows expanded to fill the entire wall area at the outermost edges of each room. Lighting fixtures were identical to those in the end thirds of the diner. The cafe section contained, with one exception, tables for two of rectangular and triangular design. The bar room's tables, primarily for four, were of semicircular, circular, and rectangular shapes. The rounded bar, flanked by large mirrors, nestled in a central corner formed by the service room and the outside wall. Above the back bar, set against a blue background, was a brown outline map of the United States with the routes of the *Hi's* lined in gold. The ceiling above curved to conform to the bar and contained an aluminum strip with a perforated design of an old-time locomotive with cars, illuminated from behind in yellow gold. The bulkheads of each room were of wood — the outer one in the cafe displayed the Indian oval; the outer one in the tap spiralled down around the end table to expose part of the exit door. New tap-cafe cars were used only on the *Afternoon Hi's*, since trains 5 and 6 were assigned the full-length cars constructed in 1942 to which a public-address system had been added.

Except for the seats, interiors of the coaches were nearly identical to those of the parlors, with the same continuous fluorescent lighting strip recessed in the luggage racks, and similar combinations of wood and pastels on walls and bulkheads. Men's smoking rooms were finished in wood paneling and had leather couches. Unlike in previous coaches, washbowl and toilet areas were secluded from smokers by opaque glass dividers and were fitted with two washbowls beneath large mirrors. Turquoise walls and a red leather couch for two completed the arrangement. Passageways alongside the men's rooms were done in wood, and flooring was gray-speckled linoleum. The ladies' smoking lounges were painted turquoise and cream. Both smoking rooms had framed prints on the walls: floral items for the women; wildlife scenes for the men. The passageway circling the ladies' area was wood-paneled on the window side, and the remaining surfaces were turquoise. Between the ladies' room and the vestibule were luggage shelves and, in some cars, a conductor's office space.

The body of the cars seated 52, the men's room 10, and the ladies' room 4. Seats were of the Sleepy Hollow type with adjustable footrests, and brown-and-yellow and green-and-gray upholstery was found in alternating cars. Some seats have been reupholstered in solid colors. In the same fixture as the fluorescent tubes were small blue night-lights which did not interfere with sleeping.

All told, EMD built more than 400 E7 cab units; Milwaukee Road owned 10 of them. Here 16B and 16A stir up roadbed dust through Watertown, Wis., with the eastbound *Morning Hiawatha* in June 1949. — *William D. Middleton.*

Another "new look" came to the motive power end of the *Hiawatha* in 1950, with the substitution of three four-axle FP7 units — totaling 4500 h.p. — for the pairs of six-axle EMD and FM units. Fore and aft views of No. 101 at Wauwatosa show how a simplified diesel color scheme — marked by an Indian oval below the headlight and side bands of maroon — blended with the window panels of the passenger equipment to form an unbroken line of color to the rear of the Skytop. — *Both photos,* TRAINS: *Wallace W. Abbey.*

Milwaukee Road tracks curve along the Menomonee and Underwood rivers immediately west of the Wauwatosa depot, offering a number of vantage points to photographers. Here No. 6 rolls behind Hoyt Park. — *Jim Scribbins.*

The colorful, unbroken consists of the postwar streamliners were among the prettiest sights in railroading, especially when a train such as No. 101 negotiating the curves near Wauwatosa was viewed from the air. — *Henry J. McCord.*

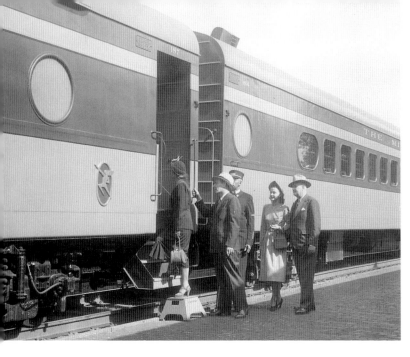

First-class patrons board Skytop parlor 187, *Coon Rapids*.
The car ahead is the "straight" parlor *Red River Valley*.

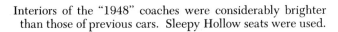

Interiors of the "1948" coaches were considerably brighter
than those of previous cars.  Sleepy Hollow seats were used.

Such specialties as Chicken Salad Hiawatha were served aboard the 48-seat dining
cars of the Twin Cities *Hiawathas*. — *Parlor, coach, and diner photos, Milwaukee Road.*

A truly distinguished tap room was designed for the *Afternoon Hiawathas.* A bar (left center) with mirrors and a map depicting the routes of the Speedliners complemented the imaginative seating, which terminated against a bulkhead (left) displaying a raised Indian oval. These cars also had a cafe room. — *Both photos, Brooks Stevens.*

Latest *Hiawatha* parlor cars feature extremely large and comfortable reclining, rotating seats (below left): 24 of them in the Skytop Lounge cars, 30 in the "straight" cars. Both car styles have a forward drawing room (below) that contains Touralux-type seats convertible to a lower berth. — *Both photos, Milwaukee Road.*

The usual consist for trains 101 and 100 was the Skytop Lounge, straight parlor, diner, tap-cafe, five coaches, and a brand-new express car. The consists of 5 and 6 were the same, but in these two a new RPO was substituted for the fifth coach; and train 5, because of its more local nature, carried additional express cars.

Motive power for the Twin Cities *Hi's* was two 2000 h.p. A units back to back — from either Electro-Motive or Fairbanks-Morse — and since the scrambling of units had not yet commenced, a "locomotive" always consisted of both its halves. The FM's were newer and introduced a much improved color scheme which carried to the head end the gray roof and maroon-and-orange sides of passenger cars. The maroon flank narrowed behind the cab door to become, in effect, a letterboard circling the orange nose. A maroon stripe also edged the pilot and trucks; fuel tanks and other underbody equipment were brown. During 1949 the EMD's were redone in this styling.

An FM unit, the 21A, was awarded the privilege of handling the exhibition train, and a likeness of the Alco (No. 14) shared with a Skytop Lounge the cover of the brochure describing the new equipment.

For the Railroad Fair in Chicago in the summer of 1948, the Milwaukee sent as its exhibit an abbreviated *Hiawatha* consisting of one unit of the 14 (in the new color combination), an express car, coach, tap-cafe, diner, straight parlor, and Skytop Lounge. On the fair's opening day, 10,000 spectators passed through the *Hi*, and on Milwaukee Road Day on July 27 that figure was exceeded.

The Twin Cities *Hi's* rolled along well through 1948 and 1949 and into the midcentury. During this time an aggressive advertising program in 204 newspapers and 6 national news and business publications won the Milwaukee recognition for stressing the restfulness and safety of *Hiawatha* travel compared with automobiles, especially in winter. At this time a booklet entitled "Let the Engineer Do the Driving" and a special brochure for children, "Meet a Modern Milwaukee Road Train," were distributed.

During the summer of 1950, new three-unit 4500 h.p. EMD FP7 locomotives were placed in service. They took frequent turns on the Twin Cities *Hi's*, and they brought another color combination to the CMStP&P roster. The maroon stripe was extended around the nose of the cab units and terminated rather uninspiringly at the edge of the access door below the Mars lights, but it did blend more successfully into passenger-car sides. The Indian oval was applied to the door beneath the headlight. The roof was black, and this black extended around the windshield and to the bottom edge of the side

Steam already was uncommon shortly before the latest re-equipping, when the author, hoping for the 14 and anticipating an EMD, was delightfully surprised by F-7 101 (above) powering train 101 west of Wauwatosa. Steam indeed was a rarity by June 1950, when the same engine appeared on the same train (right) at Oakdale, Wis. — *Above, Jim Scribbins; right, James G. La Vake.*

Nonreserved seats of the Skytop solarium could comfortably seat 12 people, but observation-car buffs complained that the view of the bluffs and Mississippi River had been better from the earlier Beaver Tails. — *Milwaukee Road.*

(Above) On a bitter cold afternoon in February 1955, No. 101's Skytop Lounge silently glides past the frozen pond of Wauwatosa's Hoyt Park. Glass-ended cars preserved the road's reputation for distinctive observations. — *Jim Scribbins*.

(Left) The view through the regular parlor seat windows contrasts with the sweeping panorama offered in the Skytop. The planters and large expanse of glass prompted the nickname "rolling greenhouses" for 186-189. — *Milwaukee Road*.

(Right) By the fall of 1950, most passenger-car roofs had been painted black to correspond with the new FP7 liveries. *Dell Rapids* pauses on No. 6 in Milwaukee. — TRAINS: *Wallace W. Abbey*.

A span of some 35 years of railroad progress is represented by the sight of a heavy USRA Mikado easing up to a water plug alongside a new Super Dome on a westbound *Hiawatha* stopped at New Lisbon. The first full-length domes in railroading went into service at the end of 1952 and their period briefly overlapped the steam era on the Milwaukee Road, which lasted until the end of 1955. — *James G. La Vake*.

(Left) Major air-conditioning components of the Super Domes were easily accessible for servicing. The enormous glass area required a cooling system of 16 tons capacity. Car 53 later was sold to the Canadian National. — *John F. Larison.*

(Below left) Approaching C&NW 's Proviso (Ill.)-Butler (Wis.) freight line on December 6, 1952, a special train previews four Super Domes to passenger sales representatives of eastern and southern roads. — Trains: *Wallace W. Abbey.*

(Below) *Afternoon Hiawatha* No. 100 highballs along the Mississippi River between Winona and La Crosse behind a trio of FP7's. This is the most picturesque stretch of "river running" along the route of the fleet Indian. — *Milwaukee Road.*

From a passenger viewpoint, the Super Domes were not the most successful of cars. The true advantage of a dome — forward visibility — was lost because the bulkheads were too high and the seats were too low. Also, the 12-wheel cars rode rough, at least by CMStP&P standards. Six of the 10 Pullman-Standard-built cars were sold to the Canadian National in 1964. — *Milwaukee Road.*

Along the Lower Dells of the Wisconsin River, a westbound *Hiawatha* passes one of the many rock formations that thousands of people come annually to see. Unfortunately for the road's rail passenger business, in the 1950's and 1960's many came by automobile. — *Milwaukee Road.*

ventilating grilles. More FP7's were acquired in succeeding months, but their noses lacked the Indian sign, and it was eventually removed from the units that did display it. Later the canted rectangular CMStP&P emblem was applied beneath the cab windows of most of the units. As the older EMD and FM units and the lone Alco went through the shops, this design gradually was applied to all of them. It was also carried over into all series of streamlined passenger cars, giving them black roofs and eliminating the maroon letterboard. Instead, maroon lettering was used on the orange upper stripe.

During this period, train 6 was given a conditional stop at Lake City, Minn., to connect with a bus bringing passengers from Rochester. This experiment was of such short duration that notice of it never appeared in any issue of the Milwaukee's public timefolder.

*Railway Age* revealed that as the *Afternoon Hi's* rolled into 1952 they were bringing in average revenues of $7.49 per mile, and their out-of-pocket expenses were $3.74 per mile. Both figures excluded diners and bar cars. The normal consists of 100 and 101 at the time were the express car, 5 to 7 coaches, tap car, diner, full parlor, and Skytop Lounge.

In March 1952, after at least one major carbuilder had hinted at such a design and speculation centered on two southwestern railroads as possible customers, the Milwaukee announced that it would obtain from Pullman-Standard full-length dome cars for *Hiawatha* use. The road conducted a contest among its employees to name the new cars. The first prize of $150 was won by B. H. Perlick, head of the tie bureau in Chicago, who submitted the term Super Dome. Lesser awards went to Milwaukeeans who suggested Master Dome, Ultra Dome, and Panorama Dome. Delivery of the Super Domes took place just before the holiday season, and they entered service at the 1953 New Year. They have been the only daytime *Hiawatha* equipment not built in the company shops.

The totally new design of the full-length domes presented a number of construction problems. The dome floor (8 feet 8 inches above the rails) had to be suitably combined with the bar's floor (less than 2 feet above the rails), and an entirely new approach to underframing had to be found, since the conventional center-sill type could not be used. A stairway to the dome and auxiliary power equipment for lights and for air conditioning at each end of the car were carefully located to give the best possible weight distribution for smooth, well-balanced riding qualities. Because of the huge glass-roofed area, which had 625 square feet of glass (35 per cent

more than other domes), an air-conditioning system of 16 tons capacity was employed. Special solar discs mounted on the roof measured the intensity of the sun's heat and regulated the air-conditioning output to cope with the rays. To support the 224,000-pound weight of cars 50-59, special General Steel Castings six-wheel trucks were designed. These trucks are probably the largest ever applied to passenger equipment. The dome windows of the $320,000 (apiece) cars remain the largest curved-glass units of their type.

The lower lounge, officially designated cafe-lounge, was a room with surf green walls and suntan ceiling. The room was ringed by small, square incandescent lamps. Outside windows featured Venetian blinds; these cars were the last CMStP&P passenger cars so equipped. Gold-toned mirrors, with an Indian design, were affixed to the posts between windows, and the upper portion of the divider between the room and the bypassing aisle contained frosted-glass paneling with a similar Indian design. Booths, upholstered with green or gold top-grain leather, were arranged in twos, fours, and fives to seat 28 at tables topped with Formica of a wavy-grained light wood design. Floor covering throughout the lower level consisted of a green rug with yellow Indian patterns. The divider followed the turn of the aisle to the front left outside corner of the room where there was a hand-wrought copper Hiawatha medallion by Italian sculptor Ianelli mounted on the far side of the aisle. Behind an imitation window frame on the inside rear wall was a color photo mural of the Cascades.

The dome was entered by way of stairs at the right rear and front left corners of the car. The first reaction upon going into the dome was a feeling of tremendous space, for here was a room nearly 80 feet long with two-thirds of its wall and top glass; the only solid portion of the ceiling was the air-conditioning duct, finished in a light blue. Seats of a modified Sleepy Hollow style, upholstered in rust with a wavy-M continuous design suggesting both Milwaukee and Indian, were at floor level, lending an additional impression of spaciousness.

Dome seating was for 68, mostly in doubles, but there were some single seats near each end. The sides of the seats were turquoise; window frames, walls, and bulkheads were all suntan. Marbleized rubber tile was dark blue beneath the seats, cream and light blue in the aisle. Three lights of the same type used in the cafe-lounge were above every other seat on alternate sides of the aisle, and all armrests contained individual ashtrays. Railings on the stairs and above the lower aisle adjacent to the single seats were square aluminum tubing.

Special black-and-white and color brochures were prepared for the advance showing of the Super Domes. The domes' appearance was also heralded by color advertisements and newspaper commentary and illustration. Good news coverage had also accompanied the first announcement of the cars' construction.

During the month between delivery and entrance into service, the Super Domes were exhibited along mainline *Hiawatha* routes and at such diverse locations as Green Bay, Wis., Kansas City, Mo., Sioux Falls, S. Dak., Sioux City, Ia., Des Moines, Ia., and Savanna, Ill. Although all of these communities except Kansas City had *Hiawatha* service, none of them were destined to be on the route of the Super Domes. Response to the showings was good; in Milwaukee several hundred persons inspected the car in the first hour of display.

On December 9 two round trips were made between Chicago and Rondout, Ill., with a passenger extra consisting of four Super Domes, a tap car, and six coaches to take 900 eastern and southern railroad passenger personnel from points as distant as Boston and Atlanta on a demonstration ride. On one of the trips the new cars were formally christened Super Domes by Jane Kiley, daughter of John P. Kiley, who was then Milwaukee Road President.

The publicity attendant upon the introduction of the first full-length dome cars in service anywhere could reasonably be assumed to have fulfilled one of the main objectives of their purchase: to build up railroad prestige in general and to get Milwaukee Road Super Domes talked about throughout the country.

However, experience proved that the Super Domes were not the most successful cars introduced to railroading. The view forward was restricted, and admittedly the cars were — by the Milwaukee's standards at least — rough riding. In 1964 and early 1965, the six Super Domes that had been rendered surplus by the termination of the *Olympian Hiawatha* were sold to the Canadian National Railways and placed in service across the Rockies.

These plaques were a proud symbol of one of the finest passenger trains in U. S. railroading history. They were later removed. — TRAINS: *Wallace W. Abbey.*

# YELLOW PAINT AND RED INK

## For President Crippen, "an unhappy task"

ON October 30, 1955, the Milwaukee Road assumed operation of the Union Pacific's *Challenger* and *City* streamliners between Chicago and Council Bluffs. Some changes of train numbers were necessary to avoid duplication of the operating designations of the UP trains which, unlike many interline passenger runs, use the same schedule number over all participating lines. (Since 1955, consolidations of the *City* trains have altered this somewhat.) Inasmuch as the *City of San Francisco* was trains 101 and 102, the original *Afternoon Hiawatha* was renumbered 3 and 2.

By the mid-1950's the declining patronage and rising expenses of railroad passenger operation were receiving nationwide attention in both the railroad and the consumer press. The Interstate Commerce Commission, using a formula that included both "solely related" and "apportioned" costs (*i.e.*, out-of-pocket costs and costs that must be shared with freight service), revealed that in 1955, for example, railroads had lost 476 million dollars on passenger service. Up to 1953, passenger revenues had at least covered direct expenses, according to ICC accounting rules. But by 1957 the out-of-pocket loss alone was 113.6 million dollars. In that year the Milwaukee suffered an ICC-formula passenger deficit of 24 million dollars. It was also in February of that year that the road moved to economize by combining the more or less duplicating services of the westbound *Afternoon Hi*, train 3, and the *Olympian Hi*, train 15; and of the eastbound *Olympian Hi*, train 16, and the *Morning Hi*, train 6. A new schedule was published effective February 18, and, as some other roads in similar circumstances had done, the Milwaukee in its public folder continued to present two schedule columns using both names and both train numbers with identical times, but in the operating timetables gave the numbers 15 and 16 to the combined train.

In terms of Twin Cities *Hiawatha* performance, the consolidated schedule added a Watertown stop and 15 minutes running time westbound, and 20 minutes and stops at Tomah, Wisconsin Dells, Watertown, and Oconomowoc eastbound. The Watertown and Oconomowoc halts were designed to compensate for the discontinuance of the last Milwaukee-Madison trains on that same date.

Two days prior to the contemplated reduction in service, the Wisconsin Public Service Commission objected, and announced its intention to hold a formal investigation of the matter. The Milwaukee nevertheless put the new schedule into effect, but operated First and Second 15's and 16's. The first sections were the Twin Cities trains, the second were the *Olympian Hi's*. Eastbound, First 16 made the Watertown and Oconomowoc stops, and Second 16 made the stops

Sixty-three hundred horsepower takes command of No. 2's 12 cars beneath the bluffs out of St. Paul Union depot. In this 1958 scene, the E9's carry their original numbers and the FP7 has not been repainted. — *William D. Middleton.*

Separate Twin Cities and *Olympian* sections of trains 15 and 16 often were operated during the summer of 1957. This is First 16, the Twin Cities section, barreling over joint Milwaukee-Burlington trackage near Newport, Minn., with its E9 cabs spliced by an Erie-built Fairbanks-Morse booster. — *Jim Scribbins.*

The cold, dull grip of January 1959 has hold of Hastings, Minn., as the Chicago-bound *Afternoon Hiawatha* led by an FP7 and two FM's makes its second crossing of the Mississippi River. Behind the train about a mile is St. Croix tower — where joint operation with the Burlington terminates — and ahead lies the River subdivision.
— *William D. Middleton.*

The flagman inspects No. 2 as it rolls through the curve between St. Croix tower and the Hastings bridge. This is one of three short segments of single track on the Chicago-Minneapolis line.
— *A. J. Hazelquist.*

119

When No. 3 whipped across the sandy, piney wastes of Camp McCoy, Wis., in 1964 the speed limit actually was 90 mph, but the Army's sign was still appropriate, since the start-to-stop average speed of 74.7 mph between New Lisbon and La Crosse made this one of the country's fastest runs. — *Both photos, Kent Kobersteen.*

at Tomah and the Dells. The departure of No. 15 from Chicago was at 2 p.m., midway between the previous times of the *Afternoon* and *Olympian Hi's*; and No. 16 left Minneapolis 15 minutes earlier than No. 6 had.

On April 15 all passengers were handled on the first section of each train; but the state commission insisted upon operation of a second section between Milwaukee and La Crosse until April 30.

This consisted of a single unit and one coach, and carried only its crew. It might be correct to state that effective at this time until the discontinuance of the *Olympian Hiawatha*, no westbound *Afternoon Hi* or eastbound *Morning Hi* existed.

The April 28 timetable restored the 1 p.m. departure from Chicago and added another 5 minutes to the over-all time to Minneapolis. The schedule was advanced because of the adoption of

The *Afternoon Hiawatha* stops at New Lisbon. There are 11 cars behind the lashup of an E9 and two FP7's. Over the years a substantial transfer of passengers took place here between mainline and Wisconsin Valley trains. Within minutes the scenic highlights of the driftless area on both sides of this central Wisconsin community will again be receding before the view of first-class passengers aboard the Skytop observation car. The car's red Mars warning light was activated automatically by an application of the brakes. The windshield wipers primarily were used for backup movements in the yards. — *Louis A. Marre*.

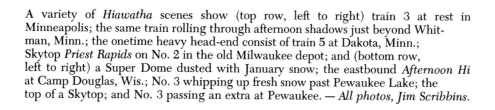

A variety of *Hiawatha* scenes show (top row, left to right) train 3 at rest in Minneapolis; the same train rolling through afternoon shadows just beyond Whitman, Minn.; the onetime heavy head-end consist of train 5 at Dakota, Minn.; Skytop *Priest Rapids* on No. 2 in the old Milwaukee depot; and (bottom row, left to right) a Super Dome dusted with January snow; the eastbound *Afternoon Hi* at Camp Douglas, Wis.; No. 3 whipping up fresh snow past Pewaukee Lake; the top of a Skytop; and No. 3 passing an extra at Pewaukee. — *All photos, Jim Scribbins.*

daylight saving time for the first time in Wisconsin. However, the departure remained at 1 p.m. from then on without any adjustment to compensate for variations in use of daylight and standard time.

On May 25, 1960, *Afternoon Hiawatha* service marked its silver anniversary. En route celebrations feted the train that was what no train before it had ever been. In Chicago Union Station, Indian Chiefs Daybreak and Still Day from Wisconsin Dells, Wis., greeted all passengers as they entered Hiawatha's teepee — the platform gate camouflaged as an Indian dwelling. In Milwaukee a teepee was erected in the central portion of the waiting room, and members of the Mah-Hedes (whites having an interest in Indian ways) performed ceremonial dances on the platform as the four *Hi's* passed through the station. A similar group, the Arapaho Tribe of Indian Guides (Boy Scouts), entertained passengers in Minneapolis.

Aboard the *Hi's*, all passengers were given a membership card denoting their acceptance into the Hiawatha tribe. Ladies received vials of perfume; men, small billfolds; and children, Indian headdresses. The *pièce de résistance* was the serving of the original menu foods at 1935 prices: 50 cents for lunch, and 65 cents for dinner. The Wisconsin Chapter of the National Railway Historical Society arranged for a group tour using train 5 to Wisconsin Dells and returning on train 2. At the Dells the Minerama, an O-gauge scale model of the Dells, including the Milwaukee in miniature, was opened specially for them. Fittingly, the task of hauling the oldest (by a half hour) *Hi*, No. 2 (ex-100), fell by coincidence to the road's oldest passenger diesel — the 15 — whose A and B units this trip were spliced by a newer FP7 booster. A number of railroad personnel who had ridden on the first trip of 100 or 101 were present for the anniversary: O. R. Anderson, general passenger agent; Russ Harrington, engineer of train lighting; Israel Townsend, waiter; W. R. McPherson, superintendent of transportation — passenger; and William Wallace, general passenger traffic manager.

During this period other changes were made from time to time in equipment and motive power for the *Hi's*. In common with many railways, the Milwaukee began to scramble its units, assembling various models and even units from different builders to work together as one locomotive. In some cases it was a matter of operating an additional booster to make a four-unit FP7; at other times, one or two FP7 boosters would be coupled between two E7 cabs. With FM's still operating, their B units frequently would be used to splice EMD cab units; and it was not unknown to find a locomotive consist-

124

(Above) Electro-Motive No. 2 has just coupled onto train 2 in Milwaukee on a snowy evening in late December 1969 and the FP45 prepares to make its maiden run. (Below) Train No. 5 accelerates west of Wauwatosa behind a pair of new FP45's. — *Above*, TRAINS: *Harold A. Edmonson; below, Jim Scribbins.*

ing of an E9 cab, an FP7 booster, an FM booster, and an FP7 or E7 cab. Until recently Twin City fast train power was standardized with a combination of one E9 and two FP7's totaling 5400 h.p. This was most frequently assembled with a cab-booster-cab lashup, but occasionally a cab-booster-booster combination would appear. All the FM's have been retired, so remaining units are entirely EMD. When EMD E9's carrying auxiliary generating equipment for push-pull service were received in spring 1961 they were broken in (multipling with standard steam generator units) on Twin Cities trains.

From November 1956 to May 1961, train 5 was operated between Chicago and Milwaukee without a diner (the restaurant car ran on earlier train 27, which had more of a demand for breakfast). Toast and coffee were offered in the lower level of the Super Dome. The latter was necessitated by the elimination of the cafe-parlor car from the *Chippewa*, whose equipment moved from Chicago to Milwaukee as 27. Because the diner was cut into the train at Milwaukee, No. 5 was always a few minutes late leaving there, but the delay was normally made up before arrival at Portage. Through diner operation from Chicago was restored when local Chicago-Milwaukee trains were upgraded with 1948-style tap-cafe cars. Early in 1949, train 100 received a second 30-seat parlor for a total of three parlors. The third car went west on *Olympian Hi* 15. A year later the situation changed with removal of the straight parlor from No. 5, leaving the train with only the Skytop Lounge. The *Olympian* parlor then returned as the straight parlor on No. 6, and 100 was reduced to the normal two cars for first-class passengers. With the consolidation of the *Olympian* and Twin Cities *Hi*'s, one parlor was removed in each direction of travel. The lineup was:

| Train 5 | Skytop Lounge only | Returned on | Train 2 |
| Train 15 | Two straight parlors | Returned on | Train 16, 1 car |
| | | | Train 2, 1 car |

This allowed for two parlor cars on the afternoon services and one on the morning service. In the fall of 1957, this was curtailed further to one parlor car in each direction on each train. Shortly before the discontinuance of the *Olympian Hiawatha*, all regularly assigned parlors became the STL type.

Some minor changes in scheduling took place after that time: The fall 1957 timetable transferred the Wisconsin Dells stop from train 16 to train 2 without change in the over-all running time of either.

In January 1958 a new bus route was instituted between Columbus and Madison, replacing the Watertown-Madison and Portage-Madison routes; and Columbus stops were inserted in the schedules of trains 15 and 2—fortunately without lengthening of the schedules.

The fall of 1958 saw the addition of 10 minutes running time to No. 15's schedule (half of this was allotted to additional station time in Milwaukee and St. Paul), 15 minutes to No. 16's (allotted entirely to road running), and 5 minutes to No. 2's. In what would seem to have been a good step to widen the gap between trains, changes in the fall of 1959 brought a 30-minute-earlier schedule throughout for train 5. This was partially nullified the following spring when the departure was moved to 15 minutes later and 5 minutes was added through inclusion of a Glenview stop, to end the last 75-minute run in either direction on the C&M. At the same time, train 16 commenced stopping at Glenview (its timing was shortened on the La Crosse division to compensate, and the over-all schedule was unchanged). The afternoon services had been stopping at Glenview for some time previously. One year later No. 5's schedule was restored to a 10:30 a.m. departure from Chicago and a 6:50 p.m. arrival (local times) in Minneapolis, again narrowing the interval between morning and afternoon services. In the spring of 1965 10 more minutes was added to 5, for a 7 p.m. arrival.

The April 1962 timetable finally recognized the smaller consists handled since the termination of *Olympian Hiawatha* service, and the schedules of *Afternoon Hi* 15 and *Morning Hi* 16 were tightened 10 and 15 minutes respectively. Adjustments in the spring of 1963 brought a 20-minute-earlier schedule for train 15 to compensate partially for daylight saving time. The train could not advance the full hour because doing so would break the connection from train 104 (*Challenger-City of Los Angeles-San Francisco*) from the West. Summer timings were particularly vexatious to the Milwaukee. Illinois, Wisconsin, and Minnesota could not agree on periods for use of daylight time, and there were four different change-of-time dates between spring and fall. In the fall of 1963, 5 minutes westbound and 15 minutes eastbound were added to *Afternoon* trains, plus additional stops at Wabasha, Minn., to make bus connections for Eau Claire, Wis. Existing bus connections between Winona and Rochester were amplified. (The Winona-Rochester bus service was discontinued in February 1969.) A privately operated bus already running between Duluth-Superior and Eau Claire was extended to La Crosse to connect with trains 5 and 2. These services, for which the Milwaukee sells interline tickets, enabled the *Hiawathas* to gain some passengers from areas lost to direct rail passenger service with the termination of the Twin Cities and Rochester *400's* by C&NW. The Wabasha-Eau Claire bus operation ceased in January 1965, but the stops and the added running time of the *Afternoon Hi* were not withdrawn.

Undoubtedly the most significant change in *Hiawatha* makeup in recent years was the complete changeover from the traditional orange and maroon to the yellow-with-gray-and-red-trim scheme used by Union Pacific. The original intent of the Milwaukee was to redo only those cars that were assigned to *City* train service. After approximately a year of experience, however, the new scheme was found to be more dirt resistant and easier to apply, and the change of livery was begun. By the summer of 1957, yellow cars were standard on the *Hi's*, although orange units (and combinations of orange and yellow units) frequently were on the head end. In 1958 all-yellow trains prevailed on the system except for Chicago commuter runs. Road freight locomotives remained in orange and maroon, and today the maroon bands are being eliminated. During the streamlined era at least three other large systems have adopted liveries emphasizing orange, so traditional association of that color with the Milwaukee was already compromised. The *Hiawathas'* new dress, even though it was originated by Union Pacific, may still be considered individual, since away from those two roads it is normally seen only in extensions of *City* streamliner service on Southern Pacific.

In the April 26, 1964, employee timetables the designations of the *Afternoon Hiawatha* (westbound) as train 3 and the *Morning Hiawatha* (eastbound) as train 6 were restored.

In January 1965 the last direct passenger service between Chicago and Superior, Wis. (via the Soo Line) ended, and a Chicago-Duluth storage mail car route was established using *Hiawathas* 5 and 6 east of St. Paul and Northern Pacific beyond. For this service, which· was diverted to the Q from the Milwaukee in the spring of 1966, NP contributed a streamlined car.

On August 4, 1965, the new Milwaukee Road passenger station was opened in Milwaukee, and the first train from the west to enter the station was *Hi* 6. One month later, the dining cars on 5 and 6 were changed from full-service type to Buffeteria style, following the successful use of one of these rolling cafeterias in special movements. Four tables nearest the kitchen were replaced by a food counter. Patrons place their food (chosen from a reasonably large selection)

on trays, pay the steward at the counter, and proceed to the tables. Two waiters are available to assist and to bring certain hot food items directly to the eight tables. Some of the tableware frills normally associated with dining cars have been dispensed with, but prices are lower and no one need go hungry.

With the discontinuance of passenger train service via the direct line between Savanna, Ill., and Milwaukee in the fall of 1965, an Omaha-Milwaukee storage car was routed via Chicago, thence by the first connecting train to Milwaukee, which happened to be No. 5. That particular car now is handled on another train, but the practice of coupling Milwaukee storage cars behind the Skytop Lounge continued. This was regrettable from an esthetic viewpoint, but inasmuch as the C&M is not a scenic subdivision, the consequences were not as unhappy as they might have been elsewhere.

For some time after the delivery of the road's bi-level suburban coaches, they were used as relief trains operated ahead of train 5 to New Lisbon and returned to Chicago ahead of train 2, and operated ahead of train 3 to Winona and returned as an equipment extra. This was not the practice, however, during the Christmas-New Year season of 1967-1968, when the road resorted to the earlier policy of operating regular *Hiawatha* trains of 20 or more cars during holidays.

In January 1967, parlor-car conductors were removed from No. 3 and No. 2 (these trains had been the conductors' last assignments). On September 1, 1967, all but two of the Railway Post Office cars operating between Chicago and St. Paul, including those on 5 and 6, were removed, and for a while 3 handled a Chicago-Minneapolis storage car. Some changes in schedules took place, and at the end of 1969 the *Hiawatha* timetable looked like this:

| No. 5 | Lv. Chicago 10:30 a.m. | Ar. Minneapolis 7:20 p.m. |
| No. 3 | Lv. Chicago 12:35 p.m. | Ar. Minneapolis 8:20 p.m. |
| No. 6 | Lv. Minneapolis 7:30 a.m. | Ar. Chicago 3:10 p.m. |
| No. 2 | Lv. Minneapolis 12:15 p.m. | Ar. Chicago 7:55 p.m. |

On April 1, 1969, straight parlors replaced the Skytop Lounges on trains 5 and 6 as the westbound train began handling head-end cars behind the parlor all the way to St. Paul. Somewhat earlier, midweek consists of the *Morning* and *Afternoon Hi's* were reduced to include but two or three coaches because of the decline in patronage. This in turn practically eliminated the need for three-unit locomotives. Four coaches became relatively normal during July and

August, and more were used only on holidays or for special movements.

During the 1960's the declining health of the rail passenger business left its mark on the *Hiawatha*'s onetime competition. The *Twin Cities 400* was discontinued in 1963, and by 1969 one *Twin Cities Zephyr* was simply a coach or two cut into the combined *Empire Builder-North Coast Limited* while the other ran with a much-abbreviated consist. The inevitable came in mid-August of 1969, when Milwaukee President Curtiss E. Crippen, rising to what he acknowledged as an "unhappy task," asked for ICC permission to discontinue the *Afternoon Hiawathas*. He cited an out-of-pocket loss in 1968 of $436,506, as well as increasing competition from the airlines and a new Interstate highway that parallels most of the Milwaukee's route and attracts motorists. Hearings were held at a number of on-line communities, and on January 21, 1970, the ICC ruled that the *Afternoon Hi* could be discontinued. On January 23, 1970, 34 years after the first run of the *Hiawatha*, the *Afternoon Hi*'s made their final runs between Chicago and the Twin Cities.

Winter descends upon the Milwaukee Road, dumping thick, wet, sticky snow on the roadbed and blanketing the *Afternoon Hiawatha* at Wauwatosa. Cars stall and airplanes are grounded, and people turn to the rails for transportation. On normal days, however, train patronage continues to decline, clouding the future of all streamliner fleets. — *Both photos, Jim Scribbins.*

127

Although a through Chicago-Star Lake (Wis.) timetable service did not originate until the summer of 1939, occasional sections of the *Afternoon Hiawatha* that went directly up the North Woods line were operated as early as 1935 to accommodate heavy loadings of vacationists and fishermen. In August 1938, such a train — with its consist looking quite like the original *Hi* of 1935 — curves west between Okauchee and Oconomowoc. The Atlantic will be replaced by a Ten-Wheeler at New Lisbon. — *Milwaukee Road.*

# NORTH WOODS HIAWATHA

## The Hi that was the fisherman's friend

THE portion of the Milwaukee Road that extends from New Lisbon to Woodruff, Wis. (and once went beyond) has been incorporated into the La Crosse division for some 30 years. In the past it was the Wisconsin Valley division. Railroadmen still refer to the long branch as the "Valley," and passengers transferring at New Lisbon are termed "Valleys."

Mention was made in Chapters 1 and 2 of the co-ordination of conventional train service north (west in railroad parlance) of New Lisbon with the original *Hiawatha* and the occasional operation during the summer of 1935 of a through section of the *Hiawatha* from Chicago to Minocqua. In June 1936 an expedited northbound schedule of 4 hours 35 minutes was inaugurated between New Lisbon and Minocqua, 168 miles. This was hardly breathtaking speed, and the southbound train required an additional 1 hour 10 minutes on weekdays. In both directions the remaining 19 miles to Star Lake required 55 more minutes. The maximum speed on the line was 55 mph; in many places it was less. The primary purpose of the train was to bring vacationists to the North Woods, and fishermen came in large numbers to the abundant lakes in the Tomahawk-Minocqua-Star Lake region. Stops were frequent and often were made not at established communities but at a resort entrance or

a depot serving a cluster of fishing camps. Ads mentioned the train as the "fisherman's friend."

An important amount of commercial travel took place to the small cities straddling the middle of the division — Wisconsin Rapids, Wausau, and Merrill — and to stops from which off-line points could be reached by bus or private automobile — Babcock (for Marshfield), Wisconsin Rapids and Junction City (for Stevens Point), Tomahawk (for Rhinelander), and Minocqua (for the resort areas west of there).

The equipment used for this service, which was labeled *Hiawatha — North Woods Section* and numbered 200 and 201, was completely air-conditioned: streamlined coaches, standard tap-lounge, and dining car. The equipment listing in the folder was not clear, leading one to suspect that a combination diner-parlor was used.

The motive power was suited to the physical characteristics of the line. A Ten-Wheeler that had been built at the turn of the century as a Baldwin Vauclain compound and had survived a change in class designation, three renumberings, and conversion to simple was put through the Milwaukee Shops [see page 230]. It emerged with a fifth number, 10, and a shroud which was nearly identical to that of the A's, with the same color combination, large aluminum wings, and even an air horn. The tender differed from the 4-4-2's

Displaying their usual ingenuity, the men of the Milwaukee Shops took two veteran 4-6-0's and camouflaged them to resemble the A's for the North Woods line service. Beneath the jaunty façade of sheathing and air horns, the 4-6-0's retained a turn-of-the-century scoop-fed firebox and cylinder-head stars. — *All photos, Milwaukee Road.*

tenders—it was squared off and was not flush with the cab roof. The cab was the open-gangway, curtain-protected type. No. 10 was hand-fired.

In the fall, trains 200 and 201 were cut back to Minocqua and divested of their names, and the folder clearly indicated the use of a diner-parlor. Running time remained the same until January 1937, when the carding for 201 was lengthened to its pre-*Hiawatha* schedule.

In April 1937, a Beaver Tail parlor and a restaurant-tap from the original *Hiawatha* trainset (now idle) were assigned to the trains, along with coaches identical to those of the second edition of the mainline speedster, and mail-and-express car 1205 (which had two side doors in the express section and became a permanent item of rolling stock on the *North Woods Hi*). The name of the train was restored, but with a slight modification: it was now *Hiawatha — North Woods Service*.

In June, service once more was extended north to Star Lake with the same faster schedule of the previous summer. In the fall, service was cut back to Minocqua, and in January 1938 train 201 again was slowed 30 minutes. This pattern was repeated annually until abandonment of the line beyond Woodruff in 1943.

In 1937, engine No. 11, of the same lineage as sister 10, joined the 10, permitting operation all the way behind streamlined power, since standard procedure was to change engines at Wausau. Occasional runs continued to be made behind "plain old" engines. The author once witnessed a Consolidation being dispatched from the house at Wausau to forward train 201.

Late in 1936, No. 10 underwent alterations. When the 4-6-0 had been streamlined the tops of its drivers were concealed like those of the Atlantics; now that part of its cowling was removed. However, the sheet metal was retained below the cab deck, and a narrow sheathing remained on the outside of the running boards. Maroon paint (F-7 style) edged the pilot, and the Indian-in-oval was applied to the tender sides, just as it had been added to the A's tanks. The 11 underwent the same changes later.

By the summer of 1939, business justified operation of through Star Lake service from Chicago, eliminating the change at New Lisbon. This required use of the second restaurant-tap car of 1935; since some of the Beaver Tails were now surplus, the additional parlor presented no problem. On the main line the trains operated 10 minutes in advance of 101 and 100, and were authorized daily by train order to run as Second 5 to New Lisbon, Second 6 New Lisbon to Milwaukee, and Second 46 Milwaukee to Chicago. Out of Chicago on the C&M three 75-minute trains to Milwaukee left in rapid succession: Second 5 at 12:50 p.m., 101 at 1 p.m., and *Chippewa* 21 at 1:05 p.m. — all with Beaver Tails.

Since the train from Minocqua departed from New Lisbon before the arrival of Second 5, some locomotive hocus-pocus took place there. The Hudson arriving from Minneapolis on local 58 (both F-7 streamliners and F-6 Baltics were used) was cut off and placed on the head end of Second 6, along with 58's engine and train crews. The engine and crews arriving on Second 5 were hastily turned to take over the storage cars, RPO, express cars, and coach of the momentarily deserted 58.

With the arrival of fall, through Chicago operation was suspended. The summer of 1940 saw through operation on Fridays, Saturdays, and Sundays only — this time combined with the *Chippewa* from Chicago to Milwaukee and treated as a section elsewhere. Because of the combining on the C&M, a straight parlor had to be substituted for the Beaver Tail on days of through operation. Running time on the Valley was improved by a half hour in each direction compared with the best previous summer schedules.

December 1940 brought substitution of a standard diner-parlor car for the Beaver Tail and restaurant-tap cars, since these cars were transferred to the *Midwest Hiawatha*. In 1941 summer operation was north on Fridays and Saturdays only; south on Fridays, Saturdays, and Sundays with full parlor and diner.

In August 1943, North Woods business was 25 per cent higher than in August 1942, despite the Office of Defense Transportation restrictions on extra sections. The transfer at New Lisbon was especially busy. But even such seasonal increases could not prevent abandonment of the Woodruff-Star Lake tip of the Valley, which was not supported by freight business. The following summer, traffic was even more promising, and Chicago-Woodruff through operation took place daily from May 26 through September 6. This set the practice for succeeding summers and for winter holidays. Apparently no policy was set on whether Minocqua or Woodruff was the end of the line for *Hiawatha* service. At times in the off season 201 would terminate at Minocqua and 200 would begin its journey from Woodruff.

During the course of the war the trains became too large for the Ten-Wheelers to handle, and "big" power in the form of F-5 Pacifics was imported. This class originally had been used in the

The rustic sign at New Lisbon faced passengers transferring from mainline *Hi's* to the Valley trains. — *All photos*, TRAINS: *Linn H. Westcott.*

"Picture a lazy summer afternoon in the driftless area of western Wisconsin: temperature high, humidity high, big bulbous clouds barely moving in an almost breezeless pale blue sky." That's what John F. Boose wrote in the July 1941 issue of TRAINS Magazine as he described the atmosphere at New Lisbon, a quiet town of 1000 people in America's heartland. Quiet, that is, until 3:45 p.m., when train 200 from Star Lake backed into a stub-end track adjoining the depot after coming down the east leg of the wye (right) on the Valley line.

Passengers have unloaded, and Ten-Wheeler No. 10 has been uncoupled and serviced and now is backing onto its train once again as baggagemen load cargo. Unseen behind No. 10, train 58 has arrived from the Twin Cities and is backing into a siding.

New Lisbon has come to life! Already the eastbound *Afternoon Hiawatha* has arrived, and departed at 4:01 p.m. Now an F-7 cruises into town with the westbound *Hi* as No. 10 waits with train 201.

Train 101's Hudson hastily takes coal to prepare for a 4:11 p.m. departure, as transferring passengers board train 201. Meanwhile, No. 58 comes onto the main alongside the station platform with 10 mail-and-express and baggage cars, plus a single coach.

At 4:15 the *North Woods Hi* — a 4-6-0, M&E 1205, two 4400-series coaches, standard diner, and parlor car — departs over the west leg of the wye, while 58 pauses before continuing its slow trip to Chicago.

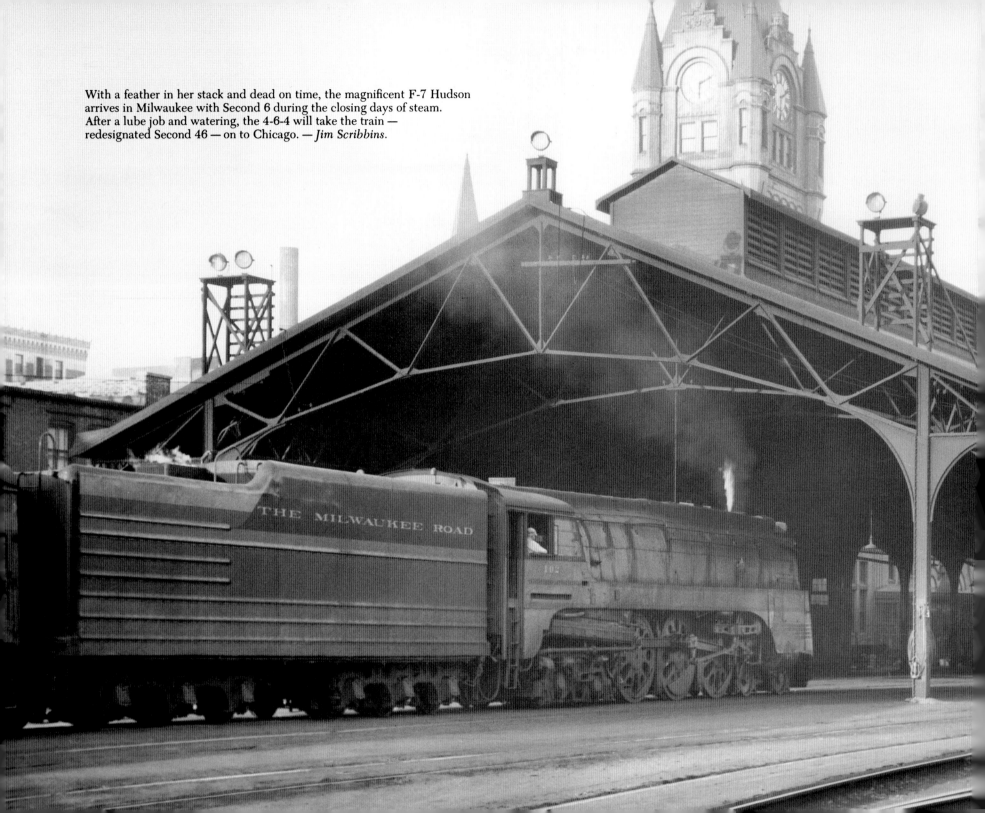

With a feather in her stack and dead on time, the magnificent F-7 Hudson arrives in Milwaukee with Second 6 during the closing days of steam. After a lube job and watering, the 4-6-4 will take the train — redesignated Second 46 — on to Chicago. — *Jim Scribbins.*

Following delivery of postwar E7's and dieselization of the *Midwest Hiawatha*, the Sioux Falls line shrouded Pacifics were sent to the Valley line. The upper photo shows the southbound *North Woods Hiawatha* behind No. 812 crossing the Eau Claire River at Schofield, Wis., at 1:10 p.m. on March 15, 1947; the lower photo depicts No. 801 pulling the same train along the banks of the Wisconsin River between Brokaw and Wausau on March 23. Consists could vary slightly from week to week: the restaurant car in the earlier scene has been replaced in the later picture by one of the original tap-diners. On-time performance was always important on the southbound runs because No. 200 had to connect with the *Afternoon Hiawathas* at New Lisbon. — *Both photos, David Kuechle.*

(Above) Passengers off the *North Woods Hiawatha* watch the trio of FP7's that will rush them east on train 2. On the Valley side of the New Lisbon depot, the Alco burbles its own peculiar chant. — *Jim Scribbins.*

(Far left) The snows of a dissipating winter are in evidence as the 812 highballs through Schofield with train 200 in late March 1947. A little over 2 hours away is New Lisbon . . . in the near future is an RS-2. — *David Kuechle.*

(Above left) In the spring of 1947, total dieselization arrived on the Valley line. All road work was performed by Alco RS-2's on freight and by RSC-2's on passenger trains. Here the southbound *North Woods Hiawatha* parallels backwaters of the Wisconsin River near Brokaw. — *David Kuechle.*

(Left) By 1957 No. 202 was just another coach-only train without a name. The view of two of the train's three coaches leaving Wausau records the transition from orange-and-maroon colors to yellow. — *William D. Middleton.*

137

Rockies and in the Cascades. After electrification in these areas, the F-5's had moved east to the Mobridge (S. Dak.)-Harlowton (Mont.) district; and following the introduction of 4-6-4's there, the 4-6-2's went, among other places, to the Manilla (Ia.)-Sioux Falls (S. Dak.) line and into Chicago suburban service. The 820 worked trains 200 and 201 during the summer of 1946, and in early 1947 streamliners 801 and 812 were on duty maintaining cruising speeds of 54 mph with seven-car consists.

In the summer of 1947, four 1500 h.p. Alco RSC-2 road-switchers helped the Valley to become one of the first two por-

A decade after the *North Woods Hiawathas* ceased to exist, 202 and 203 still were running between Wausau and New Lisbon (above), connecting with the *Afternoon Hi's*. One of the last RSC-2's to be found in passenger service transfers occasional through cars to train No. 2 (below) before trundling alongside the Yellow River north of Necedah (right). — *All photos, Louis A. Marre.*

tions of the CMStP&P to be totally dieselized. It was common to ride a through section behind an Atlantic or a Hudson on the main line, and then to gurgle along through the piney woods behind the newest product of Schenectady's diesel line. The six-wheel-truck units were classed by the road as 15-ARS and numbered in the 900's. They were painted in the same attractive design as the road's yard switchers, and their appearance was considerably more pleasant than that of the mainline passenger units. Gray hood and cab roof were separated from orange sides by a maroon stripe, and frame and trucks were painted black. A bell protruded jauntily

above the headlight on the front end. The long hood was forward in running position, suggesting a steam locomotive profile. During summer seasons the 900's often were doubleheaded to handle 12 cars of the *North Woods Hiawatha*. In those postwar years standard diners frequently operated with straight parlors of the 1937 series and coaches of all three earlier editions of the *Hi*. The Alcos remained in service until spring of 1968.

Through the end of the 1949 season, summer bus connections were provided for *Hiawatha* patrons destined to stations between Woodruff and Star Lake, but this service was discontinued after that time. January 1949 brought restoration of Beaver Tail parlor service, except on days of through operation, and also the use of one of the 1937 tap cars which had been reconstructed to 1942 design for trains 102 and 103. On January 21, 1951, the *Hiawatha — North Woods Service* was terminated at Wausau. Its Beaver Tail was gone for all time, replaced by "parlor car, dining and buffet service." But the train was extended again to Woodruff in May, and through Chicago operation took place in the summer on a limited basis: Fridays, Saturdays, and Sundays, and the entire week of the Fourth of July holiday. Eastbound on the main line, the Woodruff-Chicago train followed big *Hi* 100 (unlike in all preceding years) so that the two FP7 units which usually brought Second 5 from Chicago could return to Union Station with Second 6. For the first time that summer's timefolder referred to the train as the *North Woods Hiawatha* instead of *Hiawatha — North Woods Service*. In the fall of 1951 one of the top-grade *Grove* parlor-diners constructed in 1948 at the Shops was assigned to Nos. 200-201. During the through operation of the following summer, the 1938 buffet-parlor *Hanson* and a 1938 diner worked the opposite set of equipment. In the summers of 1952-1955 the convenience of no-change-of-trains-at-New Lisbon was available on weekends only.

In 1955, procedure was altered to operate the *North Woods Hi* 5 minutes behind regular train 101, with a New Lisbon arrival of 4:15 p.m. Second 6, however, departed Lisbon at 3:55 p.m., and diesels and crews were shuffled among Second 5, 58, and Second 6 as they had been with steam operation.

On October 30, 1955, the trains were renumbered 202 and 203 to correspond with the change in numbers of the mainline *Hi's*. On April 29, 1956, they were permanently cut back to a New Lisbon-Wausau round trip with coaches only, and the name *North Woods Hiawatha* was quietly eliminated.

On a tranquil summer day early in August 1941, Atlantic No. 4 lays a steady stream of thin black smoke over the community of Mannheim, Ill. The *Midwest Hiawatha* would not observe its first birthday until December 7 — a date on which Americans would be preoccupied with other events. — *Alfred W. Johnson.*

# MIDWEST HIAWATHA

## "The audacity to challenge entrenchments"

WHATEVER ELSE might be said about the Milwaukee Road's line between Chicago and Omaha, it possesses an uncanny ability to avoid centers of population. It misses Rockford, Ill., and Dubuque and Des Moines, Ia., and scores a near-miss on Cedar Rapids, Ia., by running through adjacent Marion. All of this, at least in recent times, did not make the road a leading contender for passenger travel between Lake Michigan and the Missouri Valley.

Whatever complacency the other roads between those gateways might have felt in regard to the Milwaukee, though, was shattered on December 7, 1940, with the first trip of the *Midwest Hiawatha*. Here was a railroad that depended upon city or highway buses and upon doodlebugs as means of entry into the cities situated squarely on its competitors' main lines, yet it possessed the audacity to challenge these entrenchments. Although several streamliners already operated between Chicago and Omaha, the Rock Island's *Rocky Mountain Rocket* was the only one that provided a convenient schedule between those points, and that was westbound only. The upstart Milwaukee established a decent daytime schedule in both directions. (However, it was quickly countered when the Q cut time on its standard-equipped *Exposition Flyer* westbound and began daytime *Zephyr* service eastbound.)

From the start the *Midwest Hi* was a double-destination train. The Sioux Falls (S. Dak.) section of the service (trains 132 and 133) continued on from Manilla, Ia. As with the original *Hiawatha*, the earliest departure of the *Midwest Hi* (Nos. 102 and 103) was eastbound. Class A Atlantic No. 4 headed the first trip of train 102 after its christening by 8-year-old Sandra Bock, granddaughter of General Agent W. E. Bock. Earlier in the day, ceremonies had been held for the Sioux Falls portion of the service before 132 left Sioux Falls and Sioux City on its first run. In South Dakota, 12-year-old Ellen Poss, daughter of the Chamber of Commerce president, participated in the celebration; and in Iowa, Jerry Marks, of the mayor's staff, did the honors. All three girls were dressed as Indians. Bands played at both Sioux Falls and Sioux City. Sioux City radio station WNAX interviewed railroaders and passengers, and Omaha stations KOIL and KFAB featured the *Hiawatha* in a program that included talks by the mayors of Omaha and Council Bluffs. The mayors, accompanied by a number of other dignitaries, rode to Madrid, Ia., on No. 102 and returned on 103. At Marion, the high-school band and a crowd of 3000 people turned out to watch the passage of the *Midwests*. At Savanna, Ill., L. F. Donald, newly appointed assistant general manager of Lines East, made a speech. At other

The *Midwest Hiawathas* employed not only the motive power from the original *Hiawathas* but many of the 1937 cars, plus the 1935 tap-diners. The six cars of the train pictured crossing Iowa — a mail-and-express car, a tap-diner, two coaches, a drawing-room parlor, and a Beaver Tail — were the normal consist until World War II traffic required the addition of two more coaches. — *R. D. Kimmel.*

Chicago-bound, the *Midwest Hiawatha* slows for its stop at Madrid, Ia., where it will receive passengers off a connecting train from Des Moines, 28 miles to the southeast. — *Verne Philips.*

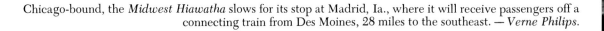

As the bright afternoon sun of May 11, 1941, reflects off Atlantic No. 4's streamlined sheathing, the engineer of the eastbound *Midwest Hiawatha* studies the train orders the conductor has just handed him during the 4:51 p.m. station and crew-change stop at Marion, Ia. — *A. H. Dunton.*

Late on a July 1947 day, No. 103 glides to a stop at Perry, Ia., 362 miles from Chicago. After the Atlantic's final crew change en route to Omaha, Nebr., the train will go to Manilla, where the Sioux Falls section will be switched out. — *Henry J. McCord.*

stops and in open country en route, the *Hiawathas* were greeted by local citizenry.

The capable Class A's handled 102 and 103, and quickly set the pace on some of the fastest steam timings in the country. The Sioux Falls portion of the service received motive-power treatment akin to that of the *North Woods Hi.* Two F-5 Pacifics, Nos. 801 and 812, were taken to the Milwaukee Shops in March 1941 and were covered with jackets resembling those of the F-7 Hudsons, but without vestibule cabs. The 4-6-2's retained their squatty four-wheel-truck tenders of modest capacity. The locomotives looked pushed together when compared with a 4-6-4, but they were neat in design, attractive in all respects, and entirely capable of hauling the not-too-heavy train on subdivisions with a 70 mph maximum speed limit.

Looking as fresh as the day it left Alco five years earlier, 4-4-2 No. 3 whips up the dust through Bensenville, Ill., at 1:07 p.m. on April 12, 1942. The *Midwest Hiawatha*, just 1½ years old, is operating on an 8-hour schedule that demands nearly a 61 mph average speed, including stops, over the 488-mile route between Chicago and Omaha. The maximum permitted speed was 90 mph. — *Henry J. McCord.*

The air is cold on this 9th of February 1941, and Atlantic No. 4 emits a continuous plume of steam and white smoke as the passage of a seven-car *Midwest Hiawatha* obscures the Chicago commuter station of Mont Clare, and (on the facing page) swirls up the snow across Harlem Avenue into the suburb of Elmwood Park. This Beaver Tail car was part of the 1936 *Hiawatha* equipment. Photographer Alfred W. Johnson was one of the few pioneer camera artists who consistently took rear-end "going" shots as well as the more traditional "coming" pictures.

Two 1912 Pacifics, Nos. 801 and 812, were specially streamlined to pull the Sioux Falls (S. Dak.) section of the *Midwest Hiawatha* after the train was split at Manilla. Although the Omaha section retained the Atlantics, as well as the train numbers 102 and 103, the Sioux Falls section was fully equal in equipment — and in fact, carried the Beaver Tail car, shown leaving Sioux Falls in the photo at lower left on the facing page. (Below) At Canton, S. Dak., the *Midwest Hi* takes on passengers while the westbound *Sioux* is split into sections for Rapid City and Sioux Falls. (Right) An F-2 "blows her nose" through the cylinder cocks as she leaves Sioux Falls. — *Both photos above left, Milwaukee Road; all others, Henry J. McCord.*

The *Midwest Hiawatha* averaged 61 mph over-all between Chicago and Omaha in territory that permitted a maximum of 90 mph. The line was double track except for the westernmost 61 miles between Manilla and Council Bluffs, which were under CTC. Manilla enjoyed an importance far beyond its size (just as New Lisbon, Wis., did) as a junction point for the district to Sioux City and Sioux Falls.

Nos. 102 and 103 stopped at Davis Junction, Ill. (bus connection to Rockford); Savanna (engine crew change); Green Island, Ia. (Dubuque rail connection); Marion (train crew change); Madrid (rail connection to Des Moines); Perry, Ia. (engine crew change), Manilla, and Council Bluffs. Elgin, Ill., was a conditional stop to receive or to discharge passengers destined for Savanna and beyond; and Delmar and Tama, Ia., were soon added as stops for revenue passengers only. Beyond Manilla, the Sioux Falls section stopped at Charter Oak (No. 133 only), Mapleton, Sioux City, Akron, and Hawarden, Ia., and at Canton, S. Dak.

At Canton, train 132 connected with train 22 from Rapid City, S. Dak. (the schedule of the latter had been considerably readjusted) to provide an 8-hour-faster, one-night-out service from the Black Hills to the Windy City. An editorial in the Rapid City *Daily Journal* declared that this ended the isolation of that city, and 41 Rapid City businessmen purchased a full-page ad congratulating the Milwaukee for the indirect expansion of *Hiawatha* service to their area. Not to be outdone, a group of 34 businessmen in Marion followed suit. Both ads opined that the *Midwest Hiawatha* was a train in which railroad and patrons could take pride, and one that would be unsurpassed for some time to come.

The original tap-diners of the first speedliners (5251 and 5252) were used on the new service, along with drawing rooms, Beaver Tails, and coaches from the 1937 set of equipment. The tap-diner and the drawing-room parlor (also the 1937-style mail-and-express car) went to Omaha, the Beaver Tail to Sioux Falls. Originally the train carried only two coaches (one to each terminal). Between Manilla and Sioux Falls, tap-express cars 151 and 152 (from the *Hi's* of 1937) were officially designated "cafe-lounges." With World War II came an expanded consist, and normally four coaches were handled, resulting in an eight-car train. Evidence indicates that semistreamlined coach 4000 was permanently assigned to the Des Moines connection.

At the time the Twin Cities trains were given partially new equipment in 1942, express-taps 151 and 152 were returned to Milwaukee Shops, where they were stripped to their underframes and rebuilt as tap-diners. Their exteriors were identical to those of the entirely new cars, and they accommodated 19 persons in the tap room and 32 in the dining room. Since they had no blind end (as their predecessors did), they could be coupled between the Omaha parlor and the coaches rather than adjacent to the mail-and-express car. With this change — and until August 1946, when food-lounge service was specifically designated as Tip Top Tap-Diner — the timefolder did not indicate the type of dining car used on the Manilla-Sioux Falls section. One of the original tap-diners of 1935 might have been assigned to 132 and 133 in 1944, since by that time their bar rooms had been modified to permit entrance from either end of the car. However, the Milwaukee is unable to confirm this.

During the Second World War the Milwaukee learned that a young Navy radioman, John Gessaman, of Louisa (west of Marion) carried with him a photo of the *Midwest Hiawatha*, and that he frequently asked about his favorite train in letters home. Iowa Division Superintendent O. H. Beerman issued a bulletin instructing enginemen to whistle when they were passing the Gessaman home as a salute to the sailor who was so fond of the Milwaukee and its train. When John returned to the U.S., he was given a ride in No. 3 on the head end of a *Midwest*.

Between their inauguration and June 1944, Nos. 102 and 103 carried 800,000 passengers, and in the succeeding year they shared in the tremendous traffic increases of the *Hiawathas* by carrying 400,000 riders.

Although additional diesel passenger units were acquired in 1946, the *Midwest* remained intermittently under the guidance of the Atlantics for at least another year. Diesels (two-unit E-7's) are known to have operated (with a 10-car consist) as early as July 5, 1946. This writer had the pleasure of riding behind Atlantic No. 4 on train 102 at summer's end the following year; and a railfan who frequently observed the *Midwest* at the time reported that A's on the head end were common. When diesels were run, the procedure was to split the units at Manilla, one-half of the locomotive handling each section west of there. In about 1946 the *Midwest* began handling a full express car for Sioux Falls in addition to the mail-and-express car always carried to Omaha.

During the summer of 1948 new coaches, drawing-room-parlors, and diner-lounge cars entered service. Refurbished Beaver Tails

The *Midwest Hi*'s single E7 unit awaits a 12:40 p.m. departure from Omaha on August 29, 1948. At Manilla, Ia., the diesel unit and cars of the Sioux Falls section will be added for the long run to the Windy City. — *L. O. Merrill.*

*Earling* and *Merrill* (off the most recent *Afternoon Hi*) ran to Sioux Falls, and upgraded tap-diners operated north of Manilla. By this time the train was fully dieselized.

Tap-diners 170 and 171 were the only cars actually designed for exclusive *Midwest* service. Their exteriors were identical to that of a regular diner, and interiors had a kitchen at the forward end, a 32-seat dining area, and — separated by a glass divider — a 16-seat refreshment area. Beverage seating accommodated three fewer persons than in cars 151 and 152.

In September of the following year, drawing-room Beaver Tails *Mitchell* and *Miller* replaced the other two 1938 observations; and five months later buffet-parlors were substituted for the drawing-room-parlor and tap-diner to Omaha. For this assignment, drawing-room-parlors *Hanson* and *Manchester* (1938) were rebuilt with a kitchen in the drawing-room space and tables in place of parlor chairs adjacent to the kitchen. Effective in July 1951, the Omaha portion became coach-only; cars 170 and 171 ran only between Chicago and Sioux City; and north of there, only coaches and the Beaver Tails operated. In January 1953 a full diner (1948 type) replaced the tap-diners, but the latter were restored two years later.

By September 1955, the news was out that effective with the fall schedule adjustments, Union Pacific streamliners would be handled by the Milwaukee east of Omaha-Council Bluffs, adding five passenger trains in each direction on the route of the *Midwest Hi*. *Railway Age* hinted that "possibly" the *Midwest Hi* would be combined with the *Challenger*. One week before the changeover of streamliner routing this was confirmed by the Milwaukee in a bulletin which read in part: "The *Midwest Hiawatha*, trains 103-133 and 132-102 . . . will, effective October 30, be consolidated with

Diesels first appeared on Nos. 102 and 103 in 1946. At the time this photo was taken west of Bensenville, Ill., on June 25, 1947, the gray-and-orange E7's were frequently in charge, although the A's were not bumped entirely until 1948. — *B. Milner.*

the *Challenger* as trains 107-207 and 208-108, and thereafter will be known as the *Challenger-Midwest Hiawatha.*"

The departure of the eastbound *Challenger* from Los Angeles was changed from midday to late evening to allow the train to operate on the Milwaukee portion of its route in daytime. The westbound *Challenger* had always been a morning run from Chicago (since its return to service as a streamliner); but the schedules in both directions varied considerably from accustomed *Midwest* timings.

The *Midwest Hiawatha* actually consisted of two coaches destined for Sioux Falls which were attached to the *Challenger* proper. Ahead of the CMStP&P mail-and-express car on the first westbound run, which was also the first departure of a Streamliner from Chicago on Milwaukee tracks, were E7 units 18A and 18B spliced by two FP7 boosters. The train, including Sioux Falls cars, was yellow; but the locomotive, displaying "107" in the number boxes, was still orange and maroon. Inasmuch as a glass-topped coach was part of the *Challenger*'s equipment, the *Hiawatha* service to Omaha became a dome train. A tap-cafe car operated between Manilla and Sioux Falls. Through cars to Omaha and Los Angeles required reservations, so the Sioux Falls cars were also operated on a reserved basis. The schedule was accelerated—largely through elimination of smaller intermediate stops—until, despite the 79 mph limit, it nearly equaled that of the original 90 mph trains of 1940. Enthusiasm for the new service was apparent. A group of railfans drove from Milwaukee to Davis Junction to observe the first passage of westbound 107, and approximately 300 persons witnessed the maiden run at Perry.

Some bus connections were retained for the new service. Highway service was available between Dubuque and Savanna to deliver

Released from *Olympian Hiawatha* duty across the mountains by electrics, Fairbanks-Morse diesels 12-A and 12-B bring No. 102 around a curve toward the depot at Marion, Ia., at 5:08 on an afternoon in 1951. — *Charles E. Arnold.*

With a mixture of skirted and fluted equipment in its consist, the *Midwest Hiawatha* heads west past smoke-covered Bensenville yards in January 1947. — *Henry J. McCord.*

to train 107 and receive from 108. Buses from Des Moines made direct connections at Perry, with both trains providing convenient access to all points served in either direction. The 4:30 a.m. departure from Sioux Falls, however, must have been something of a handicap.

The scheduling of the *Midwest* is compactly illustrated in this chart:

| Effective: | Original | **Train 103-133** 12/6/42 | 8/29/43 | 9/28/52 | **Train 107-207** 10/30/55 |
|---|---|---|---|---|---|
| Chicago | 12:45 p.m. | 12:45 p.m. | 12:50 p.m.[1] | 11:50 a.m. | 9:00 a.m. |
| Omaha | 8:45 p.m. | 9:00 p.m. | 9:20 p.m.[1] | 8:35 p.m. | 5:10 p.m. |
| Sioux Falls | 11:55 p.m. | 12:05 a.m. | 12:25 a.m.[1] | 11:45 p.m. | 8:30 p.m. |
| Running time: (hrs. min.) | | | | | |
| To Omaha | 8  0 | 8  15 | 8  30 | 8  45 | 8  10 |
| To Sioux Falls | 11  10 | 11  20 | 11  35 | 11  55 | 11  30 |
| Stops: | | | | | |
| To Omaha | 11 | 12 | 12 | 12 | 5 |
| To Sioux Falls from Manilla | 6 | 6 | 6 | 7[2] | 6 |

| | Original | **Train 132-102** 12/6/42 | 8/29/43 | 9/28/52 | **Train 208-108** 10/30/55 |
|---|---|---|---|---|---|
| Sioux Falls | 9:20 a.m. | 9:25 a.m. | 9:25 a.m.[1] | 8:25 a.m. | 4:30 a.m. |
| Omaha | 12:35 p.m. | 12:40 p.m. | 12:40 p.m.[1] | 11:55 a.m. | 8:10 a.m. |
| Chicago | 8:35 p.m. | 8:55 p.m. | 9:10 p.m.[1] | 8:40 p.m. | 4:30 p.m. |
| Running time: (hrs. min.) | | | | | |
| From Omaha | 8  0 | 8  15 | 8  30 | 8  45 | 8  20 |
| From Sioux Falls | 11  15 | 11  30 | 11  45 | 12  15 | 12  0 |
| Stops: | | | | | |
| From Omaha | 11 | 12 | 12 | 12 | 5 |
| Sioux Falls- Manilla | 5 | 5 | 5 | 6[2] | 6 |

[1] Effective July 1, 1951, schedule advanced 1 hour between all points westbound and 45 minutes between all points eastbound with no change in elapsed running time. Stops include positive and conditional.

[2] East Wye Switch, S. Dak., added February 1948.

Mount Carroll, Ill., was added as a conditional stop in May 1942, and East Wye Switch (near Elk Point, S. Dak.) was added in February 1948. Green Island was changed to a conditional stop in September 1949, when the Dubuque train connection was removed and a bus was substituted between Delmar and Dubuque. Five years later, Green Island again became a positive stop when the Dubuque bus connection was moved there. A bus was substituted for the Des Moines rail connection in September 1951 with the same time schedule. During the early 1950's Nos. 102 and 103 made a conditional stop at Coon Rapids, Ia., but the stop was not in effect long enough to appear in any issue of the timefolder. When the *Challenger* was combined with the *Midwest Hiawatha* in the fall of 1955, stops were reduced to Elgin, Savanna, Marion, Perry, and Manilla. The westbound-only stop at Charter Oak on the Sioux Falls portion was eliminated.

On December 6, 1942, a speed slowdown went into effect by order of a Government war ruling; and in 1952 another speed reduction took place to comply with an ICC restriction to 79 mph in territory not protected with cab signals (the limit was 59 mph north of Manilla where no block signals were in use). The reduction in time for trains 107 and 108 was primarily through the elimination of intermediate stops.

In the spring of 1956, the *Challenger* and the *City of Los Angeles* were combined, resulting in a nighttime schedule on CMStP&P rails, and the road's April 20 service bulletin concluded: "With the change in the *Challenger* schedule, Milwaukee Road day trains between Chicago and Omaha, Sioux City, and Sioux Falls will be discontinued."

On Saturday, April 28, 1956, the *Midwest Hiawatha* departed for the last time.

The beginning of the end came for the *Midwest Hiawatha* in the fall of 1955, when Union Pacific's through streamliners switched from the Chicago & North Western to the Milwaukee Road between Omaha and Chicago. The *Midwest Hi*'s cars and name were combined with UP's *Challenger*, shown climbing out of the Mississippi River Valley on November 19, 1955, behind an A-B-B-A diesel combination after a servicing stop at Savanna, Ill. Effective April 29, 1956, the *Challenger* was combined with the *City of Los Angeles* on an evening departure out of Chicago, and daytime service between Chicago and Omaha, Sioux City, and Sioux Falls was discontinued. — *William D. Middleton.*

The classic Beaver Tail car will forever be synonymous with *Hiawatha.* — *B. Milner.*

# OLYMPIAN HIAWATHA

## To fill a void, "a perfect train"

WHEN the victory of the Allies in World War II became evident, the visions of people and industries could turn again to peaceful ambitions. Trains in the United States not only were full, they were crowded — a circumstance that in most railway general offices brought optimism regarding the future of passenger traffic. Lines that were not operating streamlined trains announced intentions of doing so, and those whose rails already were brightened by lightweight, cheerfully hued varnish declared that their modern services would be expanded as soon as cessation of hostilities permitted.

A void in streamliner service was obvious in the Pacific Northwest. Seattle was the terminal of three transcontinentals, but none of these offered service comparable to trains that served Los Angeles, San Francisco, or Seattle's rival metropolis, Portland. TRAINS Magazine for December 1944 printed a reader suggestion that three northern routes offer a co-ordinated every-third-day coach streamliner service from the east (similar to the Chicago-Florida streamliners running then); and coincidentally, the same issue carried a news item to the effect that Great Northern would operate a daily streamlined *Empire Builder* as soon as new equipment could be delivered. In June 1945 the Milwaukee Road issued a general statement that "passenger service will be further modernized and augmented to serve you even better than in the past." After reorganization of the road on December 1, 1945, persistent rumors pointed to streamlining of the *Olympian*. Northern Pacific meanwhile announced an order for new cars and diesel passenger locomotives without indicating what their operation would be. In spring 1946 the rumors regarding the *Olympian* streamlining were confirmed, and at least once the contemplated running time was estimated at "slightly over 40 hours."

The April 6, 1946, issue of *Railway Age* reported that CMStP&P had ordered "6 mail, 6 baggage-dormitory, 24 coach, 6 dining, and 6 recreation-lounge cars from the company shops and, from Pullman, 18 sleepers and 6 compartment-drawing room Beaver Tail cars for use on six 12-car Seattle trains." An announcement by Passenger Traffic Manager F. N. Hicks at the same time indicated that the consist of the new trains would be diesel locomotive, RPO, baggage-dormitory, 4 coaches, diner, recreation-lounge, 3 sleepers, and compartment-drawing room Beaver Tail. Later the same month a release stated that five 6000 h.p. diesels (builder not specified) had been ordered to power the new Seattle trains.

Within a short time, the Milwaukee distributed a brochure with accurate sketches of the locomotive (readily identifiable as a Fair-

Through the Belt Mountains, 100 miles or so north of Yellowstone Park, is a gash — much like the Wisconsin Dells — known locally as Sixteen Mile Canyon and usually described in tourist brochures as Montana Canyon. Early in its career, the 5 (first of the FM's) leads the *Olympian Hiawatha* beneath the rocky walls deep in the gorge. — *Milwaukee Road.*

157

On the La Crosse division, an F-6a with lifted smoke deflector speeds *Olympian Hiawatha* equipment on a June 9, 1947, westbound test run. — *Milwaukee Road.*

(Far left) Industrial designer Brooks Stevens (center, with associates Reed and Floria) was the stylist for the most recent *Hiawathas*. Glass-topped lounge in the sketch at his right never made the train. — *Milwaukee Road.*

Probably the high point of all the liveries used by CMStP&P was displayed by the chrome-faced FM diesels of the Seattle speedliners. — *James G. La Vake.*

banks-Morse product), the color scheme for the cars, and the radically different observation car. It also depicted interiors which had wall decorations of mural-type drawings and photos. A running time of approximately 45 hours between terminals was predicted. Although references were made to Hiawatha emblems and Hiawatha-type coaches, the train itself was mentioned only as the Speedliner. Important in view of later developments was a statement that sleeping cars would consist *entirely* of bedrooms and roomettes. Apparently no firm decision had been reached on a train name, and possibly the road was considering joining other transcontinental lines in eliminating intermediate-type sleepers. The timefolder for August 21 of that year carried on its back cover a sketch of the Skytop Lounge observations and referred to the trains as *Olympian Hiawathas*.

The rival *Empire Builder* became a streamliner in February 1947. Although CMStP&P constructed most of its equipment in its own shops, it did experience difficulty obtaining components from suppliers. Because the road felt that construction of 12 room and room-solarium sleeping cars at Milwaukee would not be economically feasible, it contracted with Pullman-Standard to build them. At P-S, the Milwaukee order had to wait its turn behind earlier orders. The road's insistence upon retaining its own radical solarium design instead of adopting the new production-line "tear-drop" variety did not speed matters.

In 1945 extensive upgrading of the right of way west of Minneapolis had begun in anticipation of speedliner service. Bridges were strengthened, heavier rail was laid, curves were eased, and a line change of 16 miles was carried out on the west end of the Hastings & Dakota division between Aberdeen and Mobridge, S. Dak. In addition, the line between Aberdeen and Harlowton, Mont., the westernmost subdivision of the H&D, and the entire Trans-Missouri division were converted from manual block to automatic block signaling. Between Aberdeen and Hettinger, N. Dak., and between Rhame and Marmarth, N. Dak., the new block system was tied in with what the Milwaukee terms controlled automatic block, which is a CTC-type operation except that train crews line the switches of passing tracks themselves in accordance with signal indications transmitted from the dispatcher's office.

The line east of Aberdeen had been signaled in the Chicago, Milwaukee & St. Paul project that commenced in 1912. This involved 2382 track-miles and was claimed to be the largest signaling project (measured in track-miles) on record. Between 1915 and 1917 color-light (three-lens type) signaling was installed in both electric zones, and the Chicago, Milwaukee & St. Paul asserted that it was the first railway to adopt color-light block signals for an extended project.

When the idea of extending *Hiawatha* service to Tacoma was first considered, the maximum speed for CMStP&P passenger trains west of Minneapolis was 70 mph; in many locations the limit was 60 to 65 mph, and in some of the more rugged mountain sections it was even lower. The improvements preceding the inauguration of *Hiawatha* service resulted in a general maximum speed limit of 80 mph (this subsequently was changed to 79 mph under ICC signal rules) except on some subdivisions of the Coast division, where the maximum was 70 mph. Naturally, severe restrictions were imposed where they were needed in the Belt, Rocky, Bitter Root, and Cascade mountains; but even beneath the Continental Divide itself, in the long valley between Butte and Deer Lodge, the *Hi* could — and did — move along at 80.

In November 1946 newspaper articles made the first reference to use of new tourist-type sleeping cars, and the 6000 h.p. Fairbanks-Morse passenger locomotives began to arrive from General Electric's Erie (Pa.) works (where they were constructed for Fairbanks-Morse, since FM's Beloit [Wis.] locomotive facility had not yet been finished). The first two units of No. 5 were painted in the usual orange and gray in order not to give away the decorative scheme of the forthcoming train. Other units, delivered in the new year, appeared in *Olympian Hiawatha* garb but omitted the chrome name strips on the cab units. At first these units operated between Chicago and the Twin Cities, but in the spring they were transferred to handle the *Olympian* from Minneapolis through to Tacoma.

An announcement was made in April that the *Olympian Hiawatha* would enter service on June 29, 1947, on a 45-hour timing between Chicago and Seattle, with an additional 1 hour 15 minutes running time to or from Tacoma. The spring edition of the passenger folder carried the schedule and equipment listing for the forthcoming trains without train numbers. Appropriately, the June 1947 *Popular Mechanics* displayed a color drawing of the *Olympian Hi* (featuring the Skytop Lounge) in a nighttime mountain scene. On June 23 one set of equipment being sent to Tacoma to commence the eastbound run was operated in revenue service carrying rowing crews of several Eastern and Midwestern universities to participate in the Lake Washington regatta at Seattle.

159

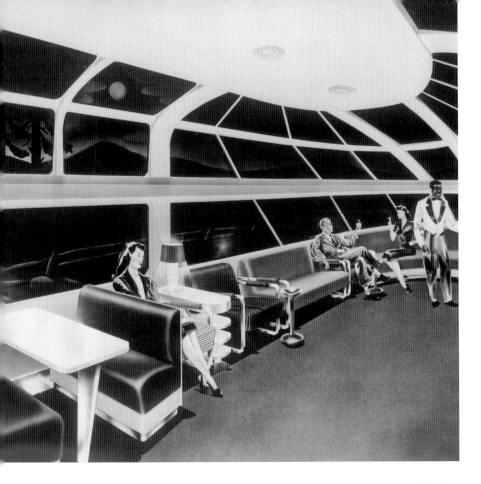

The finishing touch to a perfect train was the Skytop Lounge and the extensive glass of the solarium. It was a pity seating was not arranged to face the scenery. In this view at Pullman-Standard, one of the *Creek* cars stands beside an NYC room car. The P-S Sky-tops were broader of beam than the parlors built at Milwaukee. — *Milwaukee Road*.

Brooks Stevens' designs were closely followed by Pullman-Standard, as careful comparison of the sketches with the finished cars shows. *Solar View* did not fare well as a car name, however; and the train name did not appear adjacent to the vestibule. — *Milwaukee Road*.

Milwaukee Road individuality persisted in the ample glass of the Skytop Lounge, but the lack of wood paneling was evidence of P-S ideas. To extend glass farther forward would have created difficulties. — *Milwaukee Road*.

The Skytop Lounge of No. 15 paused near the Public Service Building in Milwaukee — site of the city's interurban terminal. — *Edward Fisher*.

During most of its career, the *Hi* faced the necessity of backing down the tail of the wye into the stub depot at Butte, Mont. — *Linn H. Westcott*.

161

On Sunday, June 29, 1947, the *Olympian Hiawatha* (trains 15 and 16) entered service. The existing *Olympian* schedule was transferred to the name and numbers of the road's "second" Tacoma train of the 1911-1930 period: the *Columbian*, Nos. 17 and 18. For the first time in 17 years, two daily passenger trains again were running on the Milwaukee between Lake Michigan and Puget Sound. A. A. Grandy manipulated the throttle of EMD E7 No. 18 on that first departure from Chicago. The Railroad Society of Milwaukee, which was operating an excursion on the Chicago North Shore & Milwaukee electric railway, scheduled its trip so that the group could be at Rondout, Ill., for the initial passage of *Hiawatha* 15. Those present estimated that the 12-car speedliner was moving at close to the authorized 100 mph maximum when it banged over the Elgin, Joliet & Eastern diamond and beneath the North Shore bridge.

What did the Milwaukee Road receive for each of its new *Olympian Hi's* in exchange for 1.5 million dollars per train?

Up front (west of Minneapolis) was a three-unit 6000 h.p. Erie-built FM machine sporting the zenith of CMStP&P passenger-power decoration. The roof and the top of the nose were gray. Below the ventilators was a maroon stripe corresponding to the window striping of passenger cars. The bottom third of each unit was orange. Trucks and underbody appliances were brown. On cab units (the arrangement of a locomotive was A-B-A) the center stripe terminated on an angle beneath the forward end of the ventilator. From that point forward, sides and nose were orange, with a large stainless-steel panel surrounding the headlight and extending back beneath the classification lamps. Corrugation on the panel was similar to the stainless-steel fluting applied to the exteriors of some Pullman-Standard passenger cars. Beneath this "centerpiece" were chrome letters on a maroon background spelling THE MILWAUKEE ROAD. This maroon stripe, which was edged in stainless steel, extended back to join the center flank of the same color, setting off the name of the train in stainless steel. The pilot was orange with a thick maroon stripe beneath the coupler. The FM's were the first Milwaukee road-passenger units to have exposed knuckles. More important, the units shattered years of tradition by running through the electrified zones of both the Rocky Mountain and Coast divisions.

Between Chicago and Minneapolis, routine orange-and-gray EMD E7 units, which had been in service for over a year, pulled 15 or 16 in one direction and an overnight train on the opposite

run. Behind the locomotive were freshly styled (by Milwaukee designer Brooks Stevens) cars of larger dimensions than former *Hiawatha* cars. They were slightly wider and higher, and had rounded rather than squared-off roof contours. Only a hint of a skirt remained, and the wide diaphragms were missing. Interiors of the diaphragms, however, had a noticeably improved rubber lining that provided a "tunnel" between cars and offered passengers a smoother and cleaner passage.

Gone from the exterior was the familiar maroon window area that extended throughout the train. Stevens preferred to set off each car as a unit. Maroon was used to emphasize the window area of the body of each car. As on the locomotive, the top portion of this center spread was narrower than the bottom portion, resulting in a tapering outward toward the ends of the car. A few inches above was a thin maroon line which followed the angle of the window board and extended past smoking, toilet, and vestibule areas below the window level. The usual maroon letterboard and gray roof were used, together with brown trucks and appliances. Vestibule doors had circular windows and — for the first time on the Milwaukee — were split horizontally. This permitted trainmen to open only the top half when it was necessary to catch "19" orders or to inspect the train. Windows of smoking rooms and of aisles bypassing them were partially rounded to set them off from the square windows in most of the car. Windows closest to the blind end were round to correspond with vestibule windows. Beside exterior doors was the stainless-steel Indian medallion which had always been the *Hiawatha* trademark.

Interiors of the cars were nearly identical to those of the cars built one year later (described in detail in Chapter 7), except that a darker wood was used. The principal design distinction in coach interiors was a wood window strip paneling that duplicated the idea expressed in the maroon exterior window areas. The two windows closest to each end had no woodwork — only the regular wall surface. At least some coaches so built still retain these interiors.

Diners were decoratively divided into thirds, but unlike the diners for the *Morning* and *Afternoon Hi's*, these seated only two persons at each of the four triangular center tables. The total seating capacity was 40. Tables for four projected from the walls, slanting from either end toward the center of the serving area. All tables were cantilever-suspended, eliminating legs. Bulkheads of the dining room were decorated with large photo murals of Western scenery.

At a time when all but the Canadian railways were abandoning the intermediate, or tourist, accommodation and price structure (and north of the border the cars were standard heavyweights), the Milwaukee showed its faith in that class by retaining it and providing it with entirely new cars. Unknowingly, the move was prophetic, as the Budd Company and the Canadian railways would prove in years to come.

The color scheme of the Touralux cars was similar to that of the coaches. Each car contained 14 sections with an upper and a lower berth somewhat larger than in conventional cars. Berths were designed so that they could be partially premade to reduce the time required to change them from seats to beds in the evening and back to seats in the morning.

The walls, aisle sides, and headboards in the Touralux cars were of wood finish to the tops of the windows. Above that, they were turquoise, as were the undersides of the upper berths and the ceiling. Fluorescent lights were recessed above the aisle, and additional incandescent lamps were recessed on each side of the window and in the confines of the upper berth. The contour of the seats was more formfitting than that found in any standard sleepers. Each section was upholstered in maroon velour and was fitted with a small drop-leaf table of the parlor-car type. One car in each train containing 8 Touralux sections and 24 coach seats was reserved for the exclusive use of ladies and children. This service was of sufficient importance to rate full-page magazine color ads. Touralux toilet areas were similar to those in the coaches. The décor of the ladies' lounge rooms was executed by Betty Meyer and Audrey Peterson of the Brooks Stevens staff.

The berths in the *Mount*-series cars were superior to those being offered first-class passengers on the new edition of Nos. 15 and 16. Despite 2½ years of advance planning, testing, and construction, the speedliner to the Pacific Northwest had been rushed into service to meet its competition without a full complement of streamlined cars. Pullman passengers rode in a 6-section, 6-bedroom car and a 3-compartment, 2-drawing-room car, both of which served on the standard predecessor. There was one consolation: first-class passengers could avail themselves of what must have been the fastest open-platform observation car ever operated. In fact, not even all of the Shops-built cars were ready when the starting gun was fired, and a few trips were made with earlier *Hiawatha* coaches, diners, and tap-lounge cars scattered in some consists.

The regular lineup of the *Olympian Hiawatha* when it entered service was RPO-express car, baggage-dormitory, three reserved-seat coaches, the tap-grill, the coach-Touralux for women and children, two Touralux cars, the diner, and two standard sleepers — 12 cars.

The westbound schedule called for departure from Chicago at 1:30 p.m. (a half hour behind the *Afternoon Hi*) and arrival in Seattle the second morning at 8:30, in Tacoma at 9:45. No. 16 departed Tacoma at 1:30 p.m. and Seattle at 2:45 p.m., and arrived in Chicago at 1:45 the second afternoon. Between Chicago and Minneapolis the new trains were given the usual *Hiawatha* timing of 6 hours 45 minutes. West of there, the pace was more leisurely, although a start-to-stop average of approximately 60 mph was maintained to the edge of the Rockies at Harlowton. West of Minneapolis, stops generally were made only at terminals, resulting in the longest distances between intermediate station stops for any Milwaukee Road train, not excluding the *City* streamliners of today. The longest distances were: Miles City to Harlowton, Mont., 216 miles; Mobridge, S. Dak., to Marmarth, N. Dak., 189 miles; and Othello to Renton, Wash., 177 miles. On the initial schedule, stops in either direction were made at Milwaukee, Portage, and La Crosse, Wis.; St. Paul, Minneapolis, and Montevideo, Minn.; Aberdeen and Mobridge, S. Dak.; Marmarth, N. Dak.; Miles City, Harlowton, Three Forks, Butte, Deer Lodge, and Missoula, Mont.; Avery, Ida.; and Spokane, Othello, and Renton, Wash. The fall timetable added conditional stops at Hettinger, N. Dak.; Roundup, Mont.; and Ellensburg, Wash.

Although scenery en route was not the primary determining factor of the schedule, the "driftless area" of Wisconsin, the upper Mississippi Valley, the main range of the Rockies, and the Cascades were traversed in daytime hours.

After eight months of operation, the women's and children's coach-Touralux car was removed from the consist. The *Olympian Hi* continued through most of 1948 with its heavyweight standard Pullmans. Finally, on November 29, the first non-company-built *Hiawatha* car appeared between the diner and the sleeper-observation: a sparkling 10-roomette, 6-bedroom *Lake*-series car fresh from Pullman-Standard. (Actually, the first such car, delivered two weeks earlier, had been assigned temporarily to the *Pioneer Limited* until 1 and 4's own streamlined sleepers, of somewhat different design, began arriving along with the *Olympian* cars.)

The first Skytop Lounge bedroom-observation cars (of the *Creek* series) arrived early in December; and during the holiday season

Train 15 hurtles through Sturtevant, Wis., at the maximum behind its FP7 trio in August 1953. Soon the 4-8-4's will put on a good show for the fans. — *Jim Scribbins.*

Only the flagman samples a September morn from the rear of a *Crystal*-series car. — *James G. La Vake.*

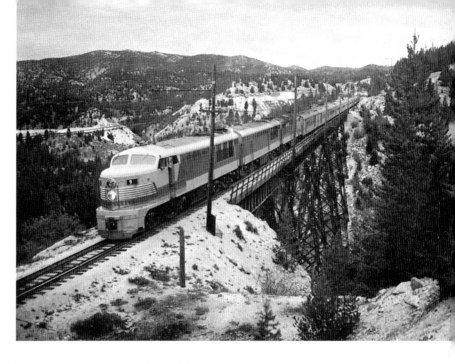

Miles City, Mont., 1119 miles from Chicago's Union Station and 1108 miles from Tacoma, Wash., was always a busy servicing stop. — *Don E. Wolter.*

Near the top of the Continental Divide, the still-new *Olympian Hi* holds steady for a publicity photograph. — *Milwaukee Road.*

(Far left) In the early 1950's, E-21 posed deep in Sixteen Mile Canyon. This shot became a well-known publicity scene. — *Milwaukee Road.*

(Middle left) Carrying an extra 10-6 sleeper, No. 15 breaks from the narrow confines of Montana Canyon. — *Milwaukee Road.*

(Left) A classic illustration of how close the *North Coast Limited* could be at times. That's NP's main between EP-4-powered No. 15 and Bruce Black's camera at Bearmouth, Mont.

Approximately 20 hours late because of Cascade snowslides, and running as a passenger extra behind 21-A, train 16 comes off the Columbia River bridge into Beverly, Wash., on February 11, 1949. — *Wade Stevenson*.

(Right) No. 16 drops down a 2 per cent grade around huge loops into Vendome, Mont. Regenerative braking enables its EP-4 to repay power it used ascending. — *Dick Steinheimer*.

(Far right) Towering escarpments dwarf even a mighty "Joe" and its train, as E-20 takes the eastbound *Olympian Hiawatha* along the Jefferson River in Montana. — *W. E. Malloy Jr.*

Barely south of Seattle's city limits, No. 16, behind an attractive pair of Erie-built FM's, has over 2000 miles of travel to look forward to before coming to a final halt at Chicago.
— *Stuart B. Hertz.*

The late winter sun doesn't help much to ease the foreboding of snowstorms in the black clouds as the westbound *Olympian Hiawatha* makes a chilly pause in Butte. Ahead are the Bitter Roots, the Inland Empire, and the Cascades — all good "snow country." — *Donald Sims.*

Photos of steam-powered *Olympian Hi 's* are difficult to find because 15 and 16 both crossed the Idaho division at night. So, a photo of S-3 4-8-4 No. 267 taking the eastbound *Columbian*, train 18, out of Spokane, Wash., will have to help fill the void. — *Philip R. Hastings.*

Until he saw these two photos, the author was unaware that passenger GP9's had been employed on the Idaho division. Apparently their use there at least partially coincided with the running of the FP7's. Here, 2427 and 2429, which later pulled the *Chippewa Hiawatha*, have brought No. 15 into Othello, Wash., approximately 4 hours late and are about to deadhead on to Tacoma behind bi-polars E-4 and E-2.
— *Both photos, Wade Stevenson.*

consists were mixed. The fifth and sixth Skytops arrived in mid-January, and at long last the *Olympian Hiawatha* was completely streamlined. The January 23, 1949, folder proudly announced a roomette-bedroom and a bedroom-Skytop Lounge for each consist —"the finishing touch to a perfect train." Coincident with this, a new parlor car was added to No. 15 for the benefit of late-afternoon Chicago-Twin Cities first-class passengers.

Cars 12 through 18 lived up to the Milwaukee reputation for outstanding solariums. They were broader at the rear than were the company-built parlor Skytops, and the glass area of the roof extended farther forward along each side. Originally designer Stevens had suggested extending the glass panels at the junction of the roof and the side of the car from the Skytop Lounge throughout the entire train. Presumably some provision would have been made for curtaining them in the sleeping cars. This would have eliminated the usual luggage racks over coach seats (baggage would have been placed beneath the car floor, bus-fashion) and would have presented something of a substitute for a train of dome cars. Also advanced by Stevens was the idea of using smooth unpolished slabs of aluminum or stainless steel for car sides. These would have been easily detachable to permit ready removal of any section damaged by, say, a grade-crossing automobile encounter. The resultant train would have been silver and orange; no maroon would have been used. The designer's color slides, shown before a well-remembered gathering of the Railroad Society of Milwaukee, depicted a train that would have been as radical and futuristic in appearance as were some of the new automobiles of the time. The impression received at this meeting was that Pullman-Standard vetoed most of these concepts, but the road stood firm on its demand for the Skytop Lounge.

By the time the *Creek-* and *Lake-*series cars were received, the road had decided (as was evidenced by other new *Hiawathas* effective in 1948) to dispense with the idea of blocks of maroon on individual cars; so the room cars came from P-S with a solid maroon window panel their full length. In the case of the Skytop Lounges, the window stripe and the letterboard terminated angularly at the forward end of the solarium. Except for the uppermost structural window framing, which was gray, the solarium was orange. Beneath the solarium windows was a fluted band of Pullman stainless steel. Under this wraparound was chrome script designating the train as the *Olympian Hiawatha*.

Inside the glass enclosure was a tail couch seating 6; on the right side were single, double, and single chairs; and on the left were four single chairs. Next were magazine racks of end-table design, topped with reading lamps. Beside the front window on the right were a single chair and a card-table booth seating four. The left side was taken up with a small sofa seating two; the balance of the space was an entryway from the corridor passing the bedrooms. Except for the table lamps, interior lighting of the Skytop was solely small bullet incandescent lamps recessed into the largest horizontal structural member of the window frame. As on the Twin Cities *Hiawathas*, such lighting presented a problem. One widely traveled habitual user of first-class rail service expressed it thus: "The illumination is not sufficient for easy reading, yet it is bright enough to prevent looking out to the darkened landscapes of night." Large color pictures of outdoor scenes relieved the monotony of the forward bulkhead.

The corridor along the left side of the cars gave access to eight double bedrooms. These were lettered A through H from the vestibule end. A, D, E, and H were of the sofa type with beds crosswise to the car. The others had a small sofa and a movable armchair, and their beds were parallel to the train, as in a roomette. This arrangement permitted adjoining rooms A-B, C-D, and so on, to be sold as suites with the walls between them folded to make one large room. B, D, F, and H were "forward riding." Bedroom E was equipped with a special movable window which could be opened easily to permit loading of stretcher patients directly into the room.

The vestibules of the 10-6 cars were at the rear, and these were the only *Hiawatha* cars so designed (Milwaukee's streamlined sleepers used on the *Pioneer Limited* and other trains also had rear vestibules). In order, from vestibule to forward end, were roomettes 10 to 1 (odd numbers on the right side) and bedrooms F to A. The large rooms were arranged in the same sequence as those in the Skytop, and one room also had a special window for stretcher loading.

Unlike in the cars of some other streamliners delivered at approximately the same time, Milwaukee's bedrooms all contained toilet annexes. As an interesting sidelight, in the vicinity of Cedar Falls the Milwaukee passes through the Seattle watershed. For obvious reasons, toilets could not be used in that area, so a special device was installed on the doors of the toilet annexes to permit their being locked from the aisle by the porter. On each trip an announcement was made on the p.a. system: "Attention porters — time to lock up. We are now entering the Seattle watershed."

(Far left) Heading down to Tacoma from Seattle on the last leg of its run, the *Hi* ducks beneath a covered highway bridge not far from Black River Junction. Tracks in the foreground belong to NP and GN, in the background to UP. (Left) Othello-bound E-2 leaves Seattle's Union Station and passes the original *Train of Tomorrow* dome diner in Union Pacific pool-train equipment. Date: 1951. — *Far left, J. F. Larison; left, Fred H. Matthews Jr.*

Seven years later, the motors have changed but the procedure is still the same: No. 15 runs backward out of Seattle. E-22 A and B were original locomotives on the first CM&StP electrification. — *Both photos, Fred H. Matthews Jr.*

Nowhere in the room cars were the road's typical fluorescent lighting and liberal use of wood finish evident. The interiors were strictly Pullman — of metal, and finished primarily in tones of light tan and brown. Each roomette and bedroom had its own individually controlled speaker for the *Hi's* public address system. Except on the Skytop solarium, the exterior contours were Pullman, and somewhat different from those of the company-built cars. Vestibule steps and the blind ends of the 10-6 cars had hints of the usual P-S curved skirts; and roof lines were rounder than on the Milwaukee Shops cars. Windows of the two end bedrooms in each car, and aisle windows opposite them, were of Milwaukee design. Exterior doors contained round windows (*à la Hiawatha*), but they were not in line with the other windows of the train. Ten *Lake* cars were acquired: 6 for normal *Olympian* service, and 4 for extra use. The name Pullman did not appear anywhere on the cars; they were lettered THE MILWAUKEE ROAD and carried numbers as well as names. Even the bedding used was marked with the letters CMStP&P, although the cars were operated by Pullman Company employees.

As a result of this arrangement, a Pullman conductor and a Milwaukee Road sleeping-car conductor (for the Touralux cars) were present on each train. In more recent years, the Milwaukee Road sleeping-car conductors and porters found their employment transferred to the Pullman Company; and from that time, one sleeping-car conductor sufficed for all cars. Former CMStP&P sleeping-car employees were given first choice at Pullman-operated cars on the Milwaukee; and at least two Pullman conductors who had run on the *Olympian Hiawatha*, bid runs on the *Empire Builder*. The Milwaukee still has its own porters on *Hiawatha* parlor cars which remain railroad-operated.

With brief exceptions, six sets of *Olympian Hi* equipment were always used. Although it would have been feasible to make a quick turnaround at Tacoma to return east on the same day as arrival, the *Hi* chose to lay over from one morning to the following afternoon. This ensured an on-time departure to the East even in bad weather. The winters of 1950 and 1951 were severe, and there often were times when the road's prudence paid off. No. 16 would depart from Seattle Union on the advertised, while over at King Street the competition (which had only five sets of equipment) was under the handicap of turning a train hours late from behind the Cascades before it could leave 2 or 3 hours late.

Even before the room sleepers were delivered, the Milwaukee

Shops constructed a second batch of coaches for 15 and 16. These 20 cars were identical in decoration to the cars built for the Twin Cities *Hi's*. The big difference between this group and all other *Hiawatha* cars was the omission of the "backward riding" seats against the bulkheads at the forward end of the car, thus decreasing the seating capacity to 48. All passengers faced the direction of travel. Even though the competition always had leg rests, these cars came without them.

"To provide better connections from the east" No. 15 was rescheduled to operate 2 hours later between all points in February 1948. This also allowed for a better spread in the Chicago-Minneapolis services, but it sent the *Hi* through Spokane (the largest intermediate station between Minneapolis and Seattle) at the awkward hour of 1:45 a.m. — and there was no setout sleeper. Efforts continued to obtain sleeping-car business between the eastern and western metropolises of Washington. Conductors were given instructions to release by wire from Deer Lodge to the depot ticket office in Spokane any unsold sleeping-car accommodations in the hope that these could be sold from that office to Seattle or Tacoma. This timetable changed all previous conditional stops to positive, and added a positive stop at Cle Elum, Wash. — the last terminal on the road. Commencing in January 1949 a parlor car was added on No. 15 for the Chicago-Minneapolis trade. The car returned on train 6 or 100, until consolidation of the *Olympian* and the Twin Cities *Hi's* resulted in elimination of this additional first-class carriage. For several years during this time, a fourth coach was added between Chicago and the Twin Cities on 15 for local business on Fridays, Sundays, and peak days before holidays. Like all *Olympian* coaches, it was operated on a reserved basis. There were also times when only two coaches instead of three were operated through to Tacoma. For a time, in 1950, reservations were made only for long-haul coach passengers: from Chicago, Milwaukee, and the Twin Cities to Butte and beyond; and from Tacoma, Seattle, and Spokane to Aberdeen and east thereof. A conditional stop at Lemmon, S. Dak., was included in April 1949 and a positive stop at Winona, Minn., the following September.

The discontinuance of the women's-and-children's car and the mail-and-express car made it possible to handle the train with only two 2000 h.p. units for the entire trip. The three-unit FM's were reduced to two units, and the "leftovers" were combined with one new unit into three additional two-unit engines. These operated through from Chicago to Tacoma. A coal miners' strike late in 1949 brought an effort to conserve coal; the FM's turned back at Harlowton, handled the *Columbian* as well as the *Hi*, and ended steam passenger operation across the prairies. The EP-3 Westinghouse Quill-type motors took over on the Rocky Mountain division, and the EP-2 General Electric bi-polar motors climbed through the Cascades. At last the *Hi* was electrified! Moreover, on the Idaho division the Streamliners, as they were called there, were pulled by standard nonstreamlined Hudsons 131 and 132, which had been converted to oil and had been sent west during the war. With the exception of eastbound B&O trains that ran through the Baltimore tunnels, this instance is the only one known to the author in which a passenger train regularly used three forms of motive power to complete its run. The coal strike ended, but not the use of motors and steam power. In fact, three Class S-3 4-8-4's — 262, 263, and 269 (the road's newest steam power) — were converted to oil shortly and sent to the Idaho division. They were later joined by 267. Approximately three years later, after the final batch of FP7 diesels were delivered, Nos. 104 and 105 were used to bridge the gap between the electric zones. The two Hudsons had been scrapped, and the Northerns were assigned to freight service.

In 1950 newer FM units, which did not have the stainless-steel front panel, occasionally were used on the long run to "Harlo." In the summer of 1950 electrification received additional emphasis with the purchase of the Class 4 motors which had been built by GE for shipment to the Soviet Union. Cold War tensions had prevented their delivery. The "Little Joes" are similar in appearance to EMD cab units except that the Class 4's are double ended. Two (E-20 and E-21) had boilers installed in one cab, making them "single ended." During the next six years they were assigned to handle 15 and 16 between Harlowton and Avery, replacing the Quills. Except for the addition of a gold-lettered THE MILWAUKEE ROAD on the center of each side, they were painted in the same manner as the road's FP7 units delivered at the same time. From the fall of 1951 until "Union Pacific Day" in 1955, an EP-4 graced one of the covers of the system passenger folder.

E-22 and E-23 (which had been part of the first order of motors for the beginning of Rocky Mountain division electrification in 1916) were upgraded in February and August 1953 respectively into more modern passenger machines. They were given roller-bearing engine trucks that had been removed from Class F-7 Hudsons, and the outer end of the lead unit of each two-unit motor was streamlined with contours not unlike some present-day European electric locomotives. Painted with black roof, thin orange stripe, and maroon sides, they were used first on Rocky Mountain division passenger hauls. They were designed to equal a 4500 h.p. diesel in performance, and they cost 20 cents per locomotive-mile less to operate. In May 1955 E-23 received a third unit, but by 1957 it had been reduced to two units. In 1956 all the Joes were in freight service. E-22 and E-23 were transferred to the Coast division, where they handled 15 and 16, the remaining passenger trains. The bi-polars were transferred to the Rocky Mountain division, and it became customary for the motors to be changed at Deer Lodge. There also were many times when a diesel arriving at Harlowton from the east was forced to continue into the electric zone because the scheduled motor was not able to relieve it. Some, if not all, of the passenger motors received the yellow and gray colors adopted wholesale in 1956.

In January 1950 train 16 was involved in two misadventures. On the 16th the first of its two units broke away from the train as a result of a highway grade-crossing entanglement with a truck at Duplainville, Wis. The truck scraped the side of the unit, taking off battery box covers and the rear sill steps, and apparently striking the uncoupling lever, causing it to raise the pin lifter and detach the lead unit. Wreckage of the truck also knocked off a pipe connection to the main reservoir, deactivating all air-operated devices, including engine controls, horn, and bell, and preventing reversal of the traction motors. Because the 17 miles into Milwaukee is all downgrade (some of it relatively steep) the runaway proceeded unchecked through the suburbs, into the city and terminal, through the depot, and stopped only when it reached the ascent from street level to elevation directly beyond the Menomonee drawbridge east of the Milwaukee passenger station.

On January 29 Coast division 16 stopped on the 1.7 per cent ascending grade on the west slope of the Saddle Mountains near Renslow, Wash., while the engine crew dismounted to extinguish a fire in a traction motor. While the bi-polar stood for over an hour, the air leaked off; the engine nudged its train, and the whole works began rolling backward downgrade, even though hand brakes were set on the cars. The startled fireman and engineer did not have a chance to climb aboard. The 200 passengers were treated to a ride at speeds up to 35 mph for 6 miles until the wayward *Hi* halted on a level section 1 mile west of Kittitas.

175

Fortunately, neither of these events resulted in any injuries to passengers. At the period of the two mishaps, time was readjusted on 16 to bring it into Minneapolis earlier, and to allow 35 additional minutes on the last lap into Chicago.

In a different way, No. 15, through the penmanship of then Assistant Superintendent J. W. Wolf of Montevideo, Minn., won some extensive press coverage. Wolf was in the cab of the *Hi* on the night of November 8, 1947, and the FM's were making the authorized maximum through Olivia, Minn. Ahead he saw a young girl running across the track directly in front of the speedliner. The child won the race by about 4 feet, and the rush of air from the train's passing blew her coat over her head. Wolf put his thoughts about the incident on paper; they were published by the Olivia *Times*, and thereafter received even more extensive circulation.

The *Olympian Hi* grossed $1,148,605 in its first two months of operation in 1947. During the entire year of 1948 the earnings of 15 and 16 varied from a 7 cents-per-mile *loss* to earnings of $2.17 per mile. By comparison, the *Afternoon Hi's* earned $2.89 to $4.64 per mile, the *Morning Hi's* $2.07 to $5.37 per mile, and the *Midwest Hi's* 18 cents to $1.65 per mile.

The Seattle speedliners moved along, promoted on special designs of menus and in special brochures depicting travel to California via the Pacific Northwest. The distinctive fronts of the FM units were emblazoned on luggage stickers, and ticket envelopes showed an FM-powered *Olympian* meeting its Skytop-equipped counterpart in a Cascade-like surrounding. Later, the "meet" was replaced with a Super Dome in a setting undoubtedly inspired by the Alpine wonders of Lake Keechelus.

The timetable for spring 1951 added a conditional stop at Bowman, N. Dak.; and for January 1953, a stop at Baker, Mont. Neither of these improvements could offset the re-equipping of the competing *Empire Builder*, and the change of running time of the *North Coast Limited* from three-nights-out to two-nights-out. In between, in spring 1952, No. 16 was given a conditional stop at Tomah, Wis., to receive Milwaukee and Chicago passengers.

Of more importance was the inauguration on the *Olympian Hi's* of Super Dome service — the first full-length dome service on any railroad — during the Christmas holidays of 1952. The inaugural date was to have been January 1, 1953, but the cars began moving out of Chicago in 15's consist approximately 10 days earlier, giving Puget Sound travelers an added Christmas present.

At the same time, leg-rest coach seats were finally introduced. The first conversions were made in some of the *Falls* coach-tourist cars. The transformation was gradual; at first only one coach on each train was fitted, but as various members of the 480-551 series coaches went through the Shops, they came out as 40-seat leg-rest types. Eventually 18 cars were reseated for *Olympian* service, and leg-rest seating was provided in still more cars when the Milwaukee became a partner in the Overland Route.

In June the westbound *Empire Builder* was rescheduled at 44½ hours Chicago to Seattle, and the Milwaukee countered with a like timing in both directions. No. 15's departure from Chicago was advanced to 3 p.m. (30 minutes earlier) and its arrival at Seattle to 9:30 a.m. (1 hour earlier); in the process the gap was narrowed between No. 15 and train 101 between Chicago and the Twin Cities. No. 16 departed Seattle at 3:15 p.m. (instead of 2:45 p.m.) and retained the usual 1:45 p.m. arrival in the Windy City.

Unlike the trains of Great Northern and Northern Pacific, CMStP&P's streamliner never was staffed permanently with a passenger representative or a hostess. At peak travel times the road did assign passenger salesmen from on-line and off-line offices to such duty, thus keeping them freshly knowledgeable about the appointments of their top train. For some time during the mid-1950's, these men handled advance reservations for the evening meal.

With the fall 1953 timetable revisions, 16 commenced being flagged conditionally at Wisconsin Dells, and for the first time only one Touralux car was normally operated. From that time on, the number of Touralux cars per train fluctuated, as did the coach assignments.

On April 20, 1954, the new Tacoma station was opened. The first train to arrive there was the *Columbian* (No. 17) and the first to depart was *Hiawatha* 16. During open house two days later, 1500 persons toured the brick-and-glass edifice that was topped with a 32-foot decorative pylon. During the dedication, Larry H. Dugan, vice-president and western counsel for the road, pointed out that the modern station would place the Milwaukee in a better position

The telephoto lens has distorted the crossover and squashed the four FP7's rapping the stack through Sturtevant on the head end of a long No. 15. The operator will need a sharp, quick eye to inspect the train. — *R. M. Clark.*

(Right) Deep in the heart of Montana's Belt Mountains, a Florida East Coast lookout-lounge carries the markers of the eastbound *Hi*. Pennsylvania tear-drop observations also filled in when the Skytops were in the shops. — *Jim Scribbins.*

(Middle right) In August 1959, No. 16 drops downgrade toward St. Croix Tower, Minn. Slide-detector fences protect the eastbound track which is operated by the Milwaukee. The Burlington operates the westward track to St. Paul, giving the two single-track lines the equivalent of a double-track railroad. — *William D. Middleton.*

(Far right) It's springtime 1949, and the melting snow is retreating from the Milwaukee's right of way at Hyak, Wash., at the top of the Cascades. Skytop riders are looking back at the east portal of Snoqualmie tunnel. — *Chester G. Horton Jr.*

to continue to provide the type of service that had made the road an important factor in the growth of the Puget Sound country. The location of the new depot adjacent to the Tacoma shops and engine terminal saved considerable switching movement.

Two years later the smaller but equally modern new Butte depot, located directly on the main line, was opened. Thus the previous backup move necessary to enter or to leave the old station was avoided.

On January 21, 1955, trains 17 and 18, the *Columbian*, secondary companions to the *Olympian Hiawatha*, were discontinued between Avery and Tacoma. Thereafter, 15 and 16 stopped at St. Maries, Ida., and at Warden, Wash.; and the various types of reduced-rate tickets, such as those for the clergy and disabled war veterans, that had been prohibited on the westernmost *Hiawatha*, were accepted. Employees' passes were accepted for travel in coaches between stations west of Minneapolis, and later for through travel from stations east of Minneapolis to stations west. Employees also were permitted to ride in sleeping cars upon payment to the conductor of 30 per

cent of the tourist or first-class rail fare (plus berth or room charge) when there were unsold accommodations available on the train west of Minneapolis.

The spring timetable evidenced further curtailment of 17 and 18 to Marmarth, N. Dak.; Baker, Mont., became a positive stop; and Ringling and Superior, Mont., were added as regular stops for the *Hi's.* Arrangements for co-ordinated rail and bus service (via Greyhound) were made to other stations, but this was of little consequence. Two and one-half months later, 17 and 18 were cut back to Aberdeen, with no changes in the schedules of 15 and 16.

Although the Milwaukee joined in the operation of Union Pacific *City* trains through the Council Bluffs gateway on October 30, 1955, raising the importance of the Omaha line considerably, the schedule of the *Olympian Hiawatha* always remained in first place in the timefolder. On that same date Bowman became a positive stop for 15, and the Warden (Wash.) stop was eliminated.

After the Milwaukee decided to use Union Pacific colors on all of its passenger equipment (except suburban cars), new brochures

depicting the *Hi* in yellow, red, and gray appeared. One of these even contained a photo (worked over by an artist) of a Little Joe in new colors. Actually, E-20 and E-21 were in freight service by that time and remained orange and maroon.

February 18, 1957, marked the consolidation of the *Olympian* and Twin Cities *Hiawathas* east of Minneapolis [see page 116]. Twenty minutes was added to the schedule, resulting in a Chicago-Seattle time of 44 hours 50 minutes; and eastbound 30 minutes was added to make an over-all time of 45 hours. For No. 15, 40 minutes had been added between Chicago and the departure from Minneapolis; the time west of there actually represented a 20-minute reduction. The eastbound time was allotted entirely to a longer stop at Minneapolis.

On April 16 the operation of consolidated trains between Chicago and Minneapolis finally took the shape intended: No. 15 carried storage-express Chicago-Minneapolis; RPO-express St. Paul-Tacoma; baggage-dormitory and two coaches Chicago-Tacoma; diner, Super Dome, three coaches, and two parlors Chicago-Minneapolis; and Super Dome, diner, Touralux, standard sleeper, and Skytop Lounge sleeper Chicago-Tacoma. This resulted in 16 cars Chicago-St. Paul, 17 cars St. Paul-Minneapolis, and 9 cars beyond. No. 16's equipment was the same except that it included only one parlor, and a full RPO east of St. Paul rather than a storage-express.

At times a separate Twin Cities section was made up in Minneapolis to depart on time when Tacoma 16 was late; and often during the tour season for Yellowstone National Park and the Pacific Northwest, a separate Coast section would be operated in both directions.

Gradually the use of two diners and two dome cars in one train ceased. It was normal for the consolidated trains to use engines from the Chicago-Minneapolis pool for that distance; a locomotive ran in one direction on 15 or 16 and returned overnight on train 4 or 57. West of Minneapolis a combination of one E9 and one FP7 generally was used (and this practice persisted to the end), first to Harlowton, then ultimately to Tacoma. Even these units worked their way in and out of Chicago. The engine arriving in Minneapolis on 16 was forwarded to the Windy City on local train 58 the same

The late-morning sun is hot as the yellow cannonball ejects from the east portal of Tunnel No. 1 at Tunnel City in July 1958. The E9 of train No. 16 carries the number of a recently scrapped 4-8-4. Ahead lies fast running across Wisconsin's driftless area. — *Jim Scribbins.*

In early morning the *Olympian Hiawatha* crosses the bridge over the stream between Lake of Isles and Lake Calhoun as No. 16 arrives in Minneapolis from the West Coast. — *William D. Middleton.*

morning. Westbound the units ran on local 55 to Minneapolis and continued west on 15 the same evening.

At the time of the consolidation of the schedule east of Minneapolis, the remnants of the *Columbian* were reduced to a turnaround run between Minneapolis and Ortonville, Minn. The spring time changes eliminated 17 and 18 altogether. The schedule of 15 was advanced 1 hour (with no change in over-all running time) to coincide with daylight saving time in Illinois and Wisconsin. For the first time in years this brought the streamliner through Spokane before midnight. On July 1 a stop was inserted for the hamlet of Summit, S. Dak. (primarily to serve Watertown, approximately 30 miles off line to the south). Nine months later it was stricken when remaining local trains 5 and 6 terminated their service between Minneapolis and Aberdeen, and conditional stops were added to 15 and 16 at Ortonville, Minn., and at Milbank and Webster, S. Dak. The *Olympian Hi* was now *the* passenger train west of Minneapolis. (For the first three months after the *Olympian*'s streamlining, a third passenger train had operated across parts of the Rocky Mountain and Idaho divisions. This was Nos. 7 and 8, an overnight local between Butte and Spokane, which was a remnant of the predepression *Columbian*.) The fall schedules added 25 minutes to the running time between Chicago and Seattle in both directions.

A spot of sunshine was the brief reign of train 16 as the world's fastest point-to-point run. With the fall 1957 timetables, the previous record holders, CB&Q's *Twin Zephyrs*, lost their title through a slight lengthening of their Prairie du Chien-La Crosse (Wis.) peak run of 84.4 mph. The Milwaukee, by transferring the Wisconsin Dells stop to train 2, cut the Tomah-Portage (Wis.) time for No. 16 to 45 minutes for the 61.9 miles, resulting in an average of 82.5

Looking quite Continental and cleverly hiding its age, E-22 leads No. 15 through Maple Valley. The long early-morning descent from the Cascades is completed, and the speedliner will enter Pacific Coast Railroad track to reach the Seattle area. — *Robert E. Oestreich.*

181

This trio of photos by Robert E. Oestreich hints at the glories of Snoqualmie Pass in Washington by which the Milwaukee wins its battle up the Cascades from Puget Sound. The high, curving trestle above is only one of several.

An E9 and two FP7's emerge from 2-mile-long Snoqualmie tunnel, longest on the Milwaukee Road.  Snow lingers late here at the top of the Cascades, and passengers will see many more scenic views as the *Olympian Hiawatha* follows Lake Keechelus.

5400 h.p. does battle with the ascent of Snoqualmie Pass. Few locations in U. S. railroading compare scenically with this subdivision of the Milwaukee Road. The train in these May 1961 photographs is No. 16, soon to make its final run on May 22.

Empty seats explain why the *Olympian Hiawatha* was one of the first victims in what could be called the decade of discontinued name passenger trains. — *All photos, Robert E. Oestreich.*

The scarred face of an Electro-Motive cab unit peers into the Skytop Lounge for the last time on the afternoon of May 22, 1961. As always, the *Hi* will be drawn backwards from Tacoma to Seattle, where engines will switch ends.

(Left) Diesels have moved around the train and prepare to couple to head-end cars in Seattle's Union Station as newsmen rush to photograph the last departure.

(Below left) Short-haul passengers leave train at Renton while others prepare to board the final run to Chicago. Soon the Skytop will recede into the horizon — forever.

(Below) The last *Olympian Hiawatha* and the last Milwaukee Road passenger train into Seattle from Chicago arrives at Union Station early in the morning of May 24, 1961.

185

mph start to stop. This was over much of the same route traversed by the never-to-be-forgotten steam run of 81 mph with *Morning Hi 6* during 1940 and 1941. The next fall, even though 16's run remained CMStP&P's best, addition of 1 minute caused the world speed crown to pass to Illinois Central.

Despite this CMStP&P speed exploit, the service offered by four domes per train on the Seattle streamliners of the other railways was taking its toll. The airlines too were skimming off much expense-account first-class travel. Contemporary advertising and promotional pieces distributed to connecting lines emphasized the economy of rail coach (whose fare was 40 to 45 per cent *less* than air-coach fares) and further pointed out that Touralux berths (found on no other U. S. train) were not as expensive as plane seats.

On November 1, 1958, the Milwaukee took the unprecedented step of eliminating intermediate, or tourist, class rail fares, and coach tickets were accepted for travel in the Touralux cars upon payment of the space charge for an upper or a lower berth. This resulted in a fare that was $51.20 lower than the price for a lower berth in a standard car on paralleling lines, and $27 less than air-coach service. At first the "coach in tourist" arrangement was intended to be only a wintertime travel promotion aid, but it was extended for a second six-month period, then made permanent.

On March 9, 1959, the Skytop bedroom cars were quietly removed from the consist as an economy move. On some trips there was such a lack of sleeping-car patronage that the dormitory car was dispensed with and the dining-car crews were housed in unsold berth or room accommodations in the revenue service cars.

In the summer, however, business was better, and the Skytop Lounge was reinstated in June. Commercially published (nonrailroad) picture postcards of Seattle Union Station depicted an *Olympian Hi* not only with the dormitory but with *four* coaches. This expansion of business was only temporary, even though the September 27, 1959, timetable took up 30 minutes west of Spokane to bring 15 into Seattle at 7:45 a.m. (There was no change in 16's time.)

On November 15 the Milwaukee entered into a travel promotion scheme which has been equaled only on Canadian National and Baltimore & Ohio. The practice of honoring coach tickets in Touralux cars was made permanent, and a 15 per cent reduction in the rates for berths in those cars was instituted. For example, a Touralux lower between Tacoma and Chicago which had been $19.10 now was $16.25. Roomette and bedroom accommodations in the first-class cars were sold in connection with coach tickets west of the Twin Cities. Passengers to or from points east of St. Paul paid a modest additional charge equivalent to first-class rail fare on the La Crosse and Milwaukee divisions. Meal prices could be reduced for *Olympian* riders if they paid for their meals at the time they purchased their tickets. In this way, the maximum of 11 possible meals on a round trip between Puget Sound and Lake Michigan were tabbed at $16.05. Purchased on the train at regular menu prices they totaled $23.75.

This arrangement was labeled by the road as its "Travel-Dine-Sleep Package." There were no cutbacks in any item of service or food in the *Olympian Hiawatha*'s diner. Everything about the speedliner retained its quality. Family-plan fares remained in effect to give even greater savings. As one publicity stunt, all passenger department personnel wore large lapel buttons asking, "Did I Tell You?" When a prospective passenger asked the meaning of the legend, the ticket or information clerk expounded on the advantages of the new system.

In theory, one total price, including rail fare, meals, and sleeper (if used), was to be quoted in giving information to potential customers. Other offices might have had different experiences, but the staff of the Milwaukee ticket office indicated that not everything was as simple as it might have been. Sleeping-car business represented a small percentage of the total sales for the train, and coach passengers who considered it worth an additional $29.15 to occupy a roomette between Minneapolis and the Coast (or $19.10 for a Touralux lower all the way from Milwaukee) were few and far between. There simply did not appear to be much opportunity for upgrading the seats of coach passengers to sleeping-car accommodations. Frequently these coach passengers would ask why their fare on the *Hiawatha* would be $7.35 additional one way, or $16.05 additional round trip, compared with the seat fares using a combination of two other railways and a change of trains in St. Paul. When informed that the extra amount represented the cost of meals (at a reduced rate), they often asked, "How much is it if I don't eat?" Considerable talking was required to convince them that meals on the "lower priced" trains would cost much more than the $16.05 added to a CMStP&P round trip. Frequently after the arrival of 16, people would appear at the ticket counter with unused meal coupons to be refunded. (Meal tickets were not sold to passengers whose travel was entirely within Illinois, Wisconsin, and Minnesota.)

When the end of the six-month experimental period neared, announcement was made that it would be extended with the modification that first-class tickets would be required in the roomette-bedroom cars during the summer. In the fall, T-D-S was extended once more, but the honoring of coach tickets on the first-class cars was not restored. In fact, with the September 25 timetable the Skytop bedroom cars originated in Minneapolis; Skytop parlor cars substituted out of Chicago.

Some minor schedule changes took place during this time: the spring 1960 timetable listed Milbank and Webster as positive stops, and in the fall folder time had been added to 15 on the Idaho division to bring it into Spokane and Seattle 10 minutes later; but this time was recouped on the last lap to retain the 9 a.m. arrival at Tacoma.

On December 6, 1960, CMStP&P filed with the Interstate Commerce Commission notice of its intention to discontinue the *Olympian Hiawatha* between Minneapolis and Tacoma. The economics of such a move could not be denied. For the year ending with October 1959 the operation west of Minneapolis brought in $2.51 per mile, but expenses were $4.23 per mile. In the following 10 months it was evident that the Travel-Dine-Sleep plan, despite the fact that it provided sleeping accommodation at less than air-coach fare, had not achieved its goal of increased patronage on the *Olympian Hi*. The receipts per mile were $2.40; expenses per mile were $4.36. The out-of-pocket loss was over 2 million dollars in each of these accounting periods. Out-of-pocket expenses are those directly attributable to the operation of the train, such as crews' wages, maintenance of locomotives and cars, dining-car losses, and so forth — those items that could be eliminated entirely if the train in question did not run. Another method of computing operating costs of a train is the one used by the Interstate Commerce Commission. This is known as the full cost basis. This includes not only all of the direct costs of a train, but also a percentage of additional costs for its route, such as maintenance of track and signal systems. Using this full cost basis, the red ink resulting from the operation of 15 and 16 beyond the Twin Cities was even more distressing: a loss of over 3 million dollars for each

of the accounting periods mentioned in the request to discontinue the service.

Not even fares below the lowest airline charges could lure passengers from the tin birds or from automobiles. One can only guess at what circumstances might be if the full costs of highway construction were paid by highway users, or how many persons would fly if the price tag on plane tickets represented the cost of providing the flight with its necessary ground services. A great deal of *Olympian Hi* business seemed to be California passengers traveling in one direction of a round trip via the Pacific Northwest, but it became increasingly difficult to encourage this traffic (in one direction) via Seattle each time the diverse-route charge increased, as it did with each fare adjustment from fall 1958 onward.

Then, too, with the exception of Aberdeen, all cities of consequence along the route of the *Hi* west of its double-track territory also were served by good-quality streamliners of paralleling roads. In fact, in many places in Montana and Washington, Milwaukee Road and Northern Pacific are so close together they appear to be one double-track railroad. Unlike the competition, the *Hi* was not bolstered by a Portland terminal; and there simply weren't as many people going to Seattle as to San Francisco or Los Angeles.

The Milwaukee requested authority to terminate the *Olympian Hiawatha* service on January 8, 1961. The Interstate Commerce Commission ordered operation of the trains until May 8 to allow time for a thorough investigation. Even off-line newspapers such as the Portland *Oregonian* editorialized on the situation. The *Hiawatha* service was kept up to its regular standards, even to the serving of complimentary coffee to all passengers once each day. For the usual spring change of timetable, a condensed folder was issued, since the ICC edict was still several days away.

The Commission came up with a compromise: the *Olympian Hiawatha*, as such, could be discontinued, but a passenger service (with diner and sleeper) would have to be scheduled between Minneapolis and Butte, Mont. So on Monday, May 22, 1961, the last *Olympian Hiawathas* departed from their Chicago and Tacoma terminals.

# CHIPPEWA-HIAWATHA

## Where aging Pacifics dimmed their headlights for deer

THE Milwaukee's secondary main line from Milwaukee north into the upper peninsula of Michigan, like the Chicago-Omaha route, managed to bypass more communities of importance than it reached. In fact, with the exception of Green Bay, Wis., and Iron Mountain, Mich., none of the communities along the route surpassed the definition of a small town. Along the first subdivision, populations did not exceed 4000; on the second subdivision, the figures for all intermediate towns were under the 1000 mark. But the railroad, as it did with the *Midwest Hiawatha* in the Chicago-Omaha service, plunged into the market with a more or less streamlined train on Friday, May 28, 1937.

The train, named *Chippewa* in recognition of the Indian tribe which once inhabited much of northeastern Wisconsin and upper Michigan, slashed 2 hours off the best previous running time on its route. At the moment of No. 21's first departure from Chicago for its northern destination, Iron Mountain, Mich., homing pigeons were released from Chicago Union Station. (They arrived at Green Bay 1 hour 26 minutes after the train.)

Behind the capable 84-inch drivers of an A, No. 21 followed the *Afternoon Hiawatha* by 15 minutes to Milwaukee, whence it was forwarded over mostly 70 mph line by aging F-3 Pacifics that had been specially painted gray, orange, and maroon and carried the CHIPPEWA name on their tenders.

The running time north of Milwaukee was 4 hours 50 minutes in each direction. Stops (regular or conditional) were made at Plymouth, Elkhart Lake, Hilbert, Green Bay, Coleman, Crivitz, Wausaukee, and Pembine, Wis. In Green Bay the Oakland Avenue station, adjacent to the roundhouse on the west side of the Fox River, was used by 21 and 14. Within a few months Chilton, Wis., was added as a conditional stop in both directions, and Deerfield, Ill., where No. 21 was subject to the "green and white" from the start, was made a conditional stop for 14. During its entire career, the eastbound *Chip* departed Milwaukee at approximately 8 p.m., affording a convenient connection with late-evening departures from Chicago. The departure of 21 from Chicago always provided a close connection from the *Chicago Arrow*, the fast Wabash-Pennsylvania train from Detroit — and thus a fine method of transportation from the Wolverine State's metropolis to its hinterland.

In October, Nos. 21 and 14 were extended from Iron Mountain to Channing, Mich., 24 miles. They were given an Iron River (Mich.) connection, which was somewhat erratic westbound since it was operated as a mixed train. For a while during the formative period,

(Left) *Chippewa* train 21 arches through the intersection of 5th and Clybourn in Milwaukee in its original form: gaily painted F-3 Pacific, standard M&E, two 4400 coaches, and standard diner and parlor. The veteran 4-6-2 spread its cinders across the first subdivision of the Superior division at 65 or 70 mph, then assumed a more relaxed pace for the remainder of its run.

(Below) A year or two later — in 1938 — CMStP&P had completed its last steam renumbering and had added the Beaver Tail as 21 eased alongside a classic lineup of waiting automobiles at Coleman, Wis. Note the Ford bus and the stately Packard. — *Left,* TRAINS *collection; below, Keweenaw Central Railway collection.*

In the mid-1940's, good old 151 blasts out of Milwaukee depot beneath a generous umbrella of soot and steam. Visible above the roof of the 1938 coach and standard diner is the outline of another F-3 waiting to follow with Madison-bound train 29.
— *Allan D. Krieg.*

On February 5, 1949, the crisp bark of No. 152's exhaust is audible all the way up the hill from Grand Avenue tower. The temperature is below zero, and the *Chip* is in all its glory with a fine shrouded steam locomotive and the latest-type cars. — *Jim Scribbins*.

21 was given the impossible task of changing engines, transferring baggage, and adding its mail and express within an allotted 2-minute time at Milwaukee. For some time 21 ran 1 minute behind *Hiawatha* 101 from Chicago to Milwaukee.

In March 1938 the *Chippewa* was extended through 92 miles of near-wilderness to its farmost terminal, Ontonagon, Mich., on Lake Superior's shore. At least in the early 1940's, the policy was for enginemen to run with the headlight on dim so as not to blind (and immobilize) deer which frequently stood between the rails. During the *Chip*'s career, the schedule of 21 called for a departure from Chicago between 12:30 p.m. and 1:15 p.m.; an arrival at Channing at approximately 8 to 8:30 p.m., and at Ontonagon between 10:50 and 11:15 p.m. No. 14 left Ontonagon between 10:45 a.m. and 11:20 a.m., and unvaryingly arrived Chicago at 9:35 to 9:40 p.m.

The third equipping of the Twin Cities *Hiawatha* in the fall of 1938 resulted in the transfer of original Beaver Tail parlor cars *Nokomis* and *Wenonah* from *North Woods Service* to Nos. 21 and 14. Although sketches in the timefolder and in ads depicted the cars with CHIPPEWA emblazoned beneath their rear windows, this was not the case; the gold HIAWATHA was firmly embedded on the tail and remained so throughout the life of the cars.

The *Chip* had started life with streamlined coaches (those of both 1934 and 1937 design were used), standard diner, standard parlor, and a streamlined express car. The head-end car subsequently became a standard RPO-express and then a streamlined RPO-express. The RPO's operated only on the Superior division. Between Chicago and Milwaukee full express cars were always used, necessitating transfer of head-end traffic at Milwaukee. April 1939 saw the diner and Beaver Tail removed from the Channing-Ontonagon portion of the run. By summer, though, they were back, and a privately operated bus connection was running from Green Bay to Sturgeon Bay (in Wisconsin's Door County peninsula, an area often likened to seacoast New England) along with a railroad-operated bus between Coleman and Marinette, Wis. That October 21 began originating in Milwaukee and receiving its passengers from Chicago via *Afternoon Hi* 101. No. 14 continued through to Chicago, an operation that prevailed as long as the train itself lasted. For the northbound run, equipment came to Milwaukee as train 27 from Chicago, and this was the permanent arrangement whenever 21 did not travel over the C&M.

The following summer, through operation from Chicago was scheduled on Fridays, Saturdays, and Sundays (actually the train was a combined *Chip* and *North Woods Hi* between Chicago and Milwaukee). At the same time the diner and Beaver Tail were permanently terminated at Channing. In fact, from that time on, the trains beyond Channing usually consisted of the mail and express and one coach. In the bitter peninsula winter there were times when even two lightweight cars were too much for a Pacific, and a Mikado would substitute through the woods. One memorable night an L-2 2-8-2 took 12 hours to buck its way through snowdrifts on the Third Subdivision.

In October 1940 the usual fall adjustments were made, together with extension of the Marinette bus to adjacent Menominee, Mich., and substitution of another railroad bus route for the Iron River train connection beyond Channing. At times during the following years, the bus connection was made from Sagola, Mich., instead. Fourteen's consist was altered to the extent that its diner was cut out at Milwaukee (for use to the Windy City next morning), and the additional Milwaukee-Chicago parlor, which had been inaugurated in July, was changed to a buffet-parlor.

Duluth, South Shore & Atlantic announced that it would hold its overnight train 7 (Marquette, Mich.-Duluth, Minn.), scheduled to depart Sidnaw, Mich., at 9:08 p.m., until 10 p.m. in order to protect the connection from 21, which was due at 9:34 p.m. This connection was later refined by the South Shore through rescheduling of its train to arrive at Sidnaw at the same time as 21, and the Milwaukee put a hold of 15 minutes on its train when necessary to wait for passengers from the smaller road. This writer's first observation of a South Shore passenger train was from 21 at Sidnaw. The wine-colored Duluth-bound varnish left first and was followed through the timber by the *Chip* on a somewhat parallel route for a while. This arrangement lasted until the end of CMStP&P passenger service through Sidnaw.

The usual summer operation took place in 1941, and with it the *Chippewa* acquired restyled steam power. F-3-a Pacifics 151 and 152 were run through the Milwaukee Shops and given the same shrouding as the 801 and the 812 on the Sioux Falls section of the *Midwest Hiawatha*. Because of the permanency of their assignments, they were fitted beneath their running boards with small CHIPPEWA signs identical in shape to those of the A's.

By January 1942 the U. S. was in the Second World War, and passenger travel was increasing rapidly. No. 21 was operated through

Soon to become a *Hiawatha* (only the standard diner remains), *Chippewa* 21 accelerates past a clear board into manual block territory at North Milwaukee tower on Saturday, April 3, 1948. — *Jim Scribbins.*

from Chicago permanently, and the dining car on 14 went through to Chicago. An additional parlor car and at least one coach were always added to the southbound *Chip* during its Milwaukee stop. The standard consist of both trains south of Channing was mail-and-express cars, five coaches (of the 1934, 1937, or 1939 type, and often mixed), standard diner, and Beaver Tail. Even though it was estimated that recently introduced *400* streamliner service to Green Bay and Ishpeming on Chicago & North Western had taken business from the *Chip*, the normal consist held consistently at eight cars. We railfans often wondered what type of single-unit diesel could be assigned to an eight-car train, since on the North Western the rule of seven cars behind a single unit seemed to be unbreakable. We finally settled on a contemplated 3000 h.p. Baldwin.

Nos. 151 and 152 chugged along doing a capable wartime job. When relief was needed, it usually came in the form of the 150, the road's other F-3-a. No. 150 was also the normal second engine in the case of doubleheading — which was resorted to whenever the consist exceeded eight cars. Engines were always changed at Milwaukee; the 151 and the 152 never ran in or out of Chicago. Later, when diesels became more plentiful after the war ended, Class F-6 Hudsons often operated through to Green Bay, turned, and brought No. 14 back; or if No. 21 was late, the F-6's would return from the Bay on night train 2, the *Copper Country Limited*. The big power was permitted only on the First Subdivision. The Pacifics running out of Milwaukee would take water in either direction at Hilbert

(Left) Leaning into a curve near the edge of the Kettle Moraine area between Plymouth and Elkhart Lake, No. 172 (identical to the regularly assigned 151 and 152 except for the shrouding) sprints along with the *Chippewa-Hiawatha*. Train 21 consists of cars showing both the 1947 broken window stripe and the 1948 continuous stripe. — *John Sachse*.

(Far left) In a day when road crews still could switch their trains in terminals, the Superior division crew waited to back the M&E and coaches onto their train in Milwaukee. — TRAINS: *Wallace W. Abbey*.

(Below) A decade later, the train again is called *Chippewa*, not *Hiawatha*; and a typical consist that will remain on the train to the end — M&E, vending-machine coach, and coach — zips along between Saukville and Fredonia, Wis. — *Jim Scribbins*.

and Crivitz, Wis., and at Channing, and coal at Crivitz. In bad weather water was also taken at Elkhart Lake, and coal (if needed) at Hilbert and Channing.

Trains were long, of course, during holiday weekends and when ski meets took place at Iron Mountain, and extra parlors were sometimes used. At such times extra sections were operated south from Green Bay. They actually would be run as Second 10, and would depart a few minutes ahead of the regular train.

On June 1, 1944, the 74-mile Copper Range Railroad placed in service a connection from McKeever (where 21 and 14 made a special stop for it) to Houghton, Mich., affording a daytime service to the Copper Country. Although the CR's little train was named *Chippewa* and was designated by the same numbers, it was not streamlined. It consisted of an old wood combine and an equally antique coach pulled by a 2-8-0. One report says that all brass was polished and all wood was restored to its original condition when the venture was started. The train lasted a bit longer than the war; on November 24, 1946, it was discontinued.

Some four months earlier the Milwaukee had reopened its Washington Street station in Green Bay's business district. For 21 this meant heading into Washington Street, backing a half mile from the stub depot to the mainline junction switch, and then crossing the Fox River to Oakland Avenue. No. 14 performed the reverse, backing into Washington Street from the east edge of the bridge. During the summer of 1948 new mail-and-express cars, coaches, and diners emerged from Milwaukee Shops and were gradually placed in the consists of 21 and 14, together with the latest-model Beaver Tails *Mitchell* and *Miller*, recently bumped from the Twin Cities *Hi's*. The fall folder made the train's acceptance into the tribe official: *Chippewa-Hiawatha*. Unlike other members of the tribe, this one always had its name hyphenated.

On the cold night of February 2, 1950, No. 14 was involved in the only accident in which a passenger on a *Hiawatha* was killed. Running at 63 mph in a 65 mph zone, the six-car Pacific-powered limited went over a broken rail at Saukville, Wis. The engine and

the mail and express remained upright, but the three coaches, the diner, and the parlor overturned.

Three days later a gas-electric motorcar was placed in service as Nos. 14 and 21 between Channing and Ontonagon. It carried the same numbers and used the *Hiawatha* designation throughout, and the schedule page of the timefolder conveyed the impression that 14 and 21 were through trains. Only the equipment notes identified the doodlebug. On that same date a private operator attempted a Houghton connection by bus from Mass, Mich., parallel to the Copper Range Railroad. This lasted less than five months northbound, but 15 months in the opposite direction. The motor fared better, running until January 1952.

On December 9, 1950, No. 21 made its last trip between Chicago and Milwaukee on a year-round basis, although through operation took place on a daily basis from Chicago in June, July, August, and September of the following four summers, and on weekends only from Independence Day to Labor Day of 1955. After that date there was no through operation whatsoever. On the last day 21's consist was a 1500 h.p. FP7, 1938 coaches, diner, and Beaver Tail (all of its passenger cars were prewar, indicating that the *Chippewa-Hiawatha* was already beginning to falter). Earlier that fall, the prewar procedure of cutting out 14's diner at Milwaukee to use on a morning train to Chicago had been revived.

Dieselization crept upon the *Chip* gradually. As more and more internal combustion machines entered service, diesels often would handle the train between Chicago and Milwaukee. Dieselization north of Milwaukee commenced late in the fall of 1950, most often in the form of Fairbanks-Morse single units belching exhaust in the best Beloit manner. Stray runs took place behind Pacifics until the summer of 1951, but for all practical purposes, dieselization had come by December 1950.

One effect of dieselization was noticeable: with 4-6-2's 151 and 152, No. 14 was nearly always 5 or 10 minutes late into Milwaukee. With a single unit, and the same size train, it could be counted on to be 5 minutes ahead of time.

Early in 1951, trains 19 and 10 — locals between Chicago and Green Bay — were discontinued. Most of their stops were assigned to 21 and 14 on a conditional basis. This, together with the lowering of the maximum authorized speed to 59 mph (it was later reduced somewhat more) to comply with ICC signal regulations, resulted in a slight lengthening of the *Chippewa*'s time north of Milwaukee.

199

In September 1951 a cafe-parlor car (of the *Grove* series of 1948 design) was assigned to the train in place of the full diner and the Beaver Tail, restoring food service through to Chicago on 14. (In a switch two years earlier, the *Mitchell* and the *Miller* had gone to the *Midwest Hi*, and the *Chip* had received the *Earling* and the *Merrill*.) During that summer the additional Milwaukee-Chicago parlor was reduced to a Sunday-only operation. After delivery of the Super Domes made conventional tap cars of the *Hi's* surplus, such a displaced car frequently would deadhead on train 9 on Saturday nights and return on 14 on Sunday afternoons to supplement the cafe section of the *Grove* car.

Nos. 21 and 14 were cut back to Channing permanently on December 28, 1953.

Effective October 1956 parlor seats and full meals were no longer obtainable on the *Chip* north of Milwaukee. The cafe-parlors were replaced by cars officially designated as "lunch coaches." These were ex-parlors *Hanson* and *Manchester* (which had been revised for *Midwest* service) renumbered as coaches 563 and 564. Their kitchens had been converted to smoking rooms; vending machines (dispensing sandwiches, pastry, coffee, candy, and soda) had been installed where the tables had been; and coach seats had replaced their parlor chairs. The Milwaukee-Chicago parlor once again was placed on a daily schedule.

On February 18, 1957, the only major change to the schedule of 21 took place when it was operated one hour later than usual. This occurred because the mainline connection from Chicago was rescheduled when trains 15 and 3 were consolidated. That same date No. 14, as a separate train, was removed from the C&M timetable, and Minneapolis local train 58 was run from Milwaukee on the *Chip*'s time. The *Chip* on the main line became just one coach (sometimes two) cut into 58 at Milwaukee.

The plunging popularity of the trains was reflected in the April 1957 timefolder. In it the *Chippewa* name once again appeared without *Hiawatha*. In October the Coleman-Menominee bus also disappeared. In spring 1958 the Washington Street depot in Green Bay was closed, and the schedule of 14 was adjusted (for the first of two summers) to conform to daylight saving time. Twenty-One's schedule had been adjusted to daylight time the previous summer but had never returned to standard time. Departure from Milwaukee remained at approximately 2:30 p.m. to the end.

In 1958 three Electro-Motive GP9's, Nos. 2427, 2429, and 2431 (new numbers 201, 203, and 205), were painted yellow with gray-and-red trim to match the road's most recent color scheme and were permanently assigned to passenger service on both the *Chippewa* and *Copper Country Limited* between Milwaukee and Channing/Champion. They were the only road-switchers to receive this treatment and have since been restored to the usual orange and black.

On August 21, 1959, the Milwaukee petitioned, under provisions of the Transportation Act of 1958, to put an end to the *Chippewa*; and not even a three-unit, 19-car No. 14 on Labor Day could avoid the inevitable. The Iron River bus came to a halt on September 26. No. 21 made its last run on February 1, 1960, and when No. 14 arrived in Milwaukee the next evening, an era had ended on the one-time Superior division.

On December 9, 1950, No. 21 has arrived in Milwaukee from Chicago for the last time on a year-round basis. — *Don Smith.*

The end came for the *Afternoon Hiawatha* on January 23, 1970, as southbound No. 2 passed St. Croix Tower (above and below) at midday and northbound No. 3 tied up in Minneapolis (facing page). — *Above and below, Norman Priebe; facing page, John Gruber.*

# EPILOGUE

THE ICC decision approving termination of the *Afternoon Hiawatha* was issued on January 21, 1970. Nos. 2 and 3 made their last trips on Friday, January 23, with a minimum of publicity and only a small amount of railfan activity.

The final consist of No. 2 comprised 102C-2 (an FP7 and an FP45), an express car, five coaches, Super Dome 58, diner 121, and Skytop *Coon Rapids*; of No. 3, 35A-35B (an E9 cab and booster), an express car, five coaches, Super Dome 57, diner 123, and Skytop *Dell Rapids*. Thereafter, four of the FP45's were assigned to freight service, train 6 began stopping at New Lisbon (to connect with the rescheduled Valley train) and at Wisconsin Dells, and the Skytop Lounge cars went to Milwaukee for storage.

The *Morning Hiawathas* continue in service, but *the Hiawatha* — the train that instituted the legend behind 4-4-2's, rolled to even greater achievement behind 4-6-4's, and partook of both prosperity and financial loss behind the variants of dieselization — is now but an item of record . . . and of cherished memory.

# WAY OF THE HIAWATHAS

THE ROUTE of the *Hiawathas* offers scenic and railfan interest. Chicago to Milwaukee is the first subdivision of the Milwaukee Division; Milwaukee to Hastings is the first, second, and third subdivisions of the La Crosse Division; Hastings (St. Croix Tower) to St. Paul is under the jurisdiction of the CMStP&P-CB&Q joint timetable; and St. Paul to Minneapolis is the fourth subdivision of the "LaX." Train and engine crews change at Milwaukee, engine crews at La Crosse. C&M crews are Milwaukee-based. La Crosse Division crews are both Milwaukee-based ("La Crosse men") and Minneapolis-based ("River men"), and some engine crews work from Portage to La Crosse to Milwaukee and terminate at Portage.

The observant passenger departing Chicago will note the use of Pennsylvania Railroad-type position-light signals on trackage under the Union Station Company's jurisdiction to Western Avenue. After the C&NW is crossed there, the coach yard and engine terminal are passed to the east.° Tower A-5 marks the end of the Chicago Terminal, and here the line to Omaha diverges to the west. C&NW crossings occur at Grayland (freight) and at Mayfair (passenger), after

which the line drops to street level. The freight connection from Bensenville (via C&NW) joins from the west opposite Tower A-20, and at Rondout are encountered the crossing of the Elgin, Joliet & Eastern, the junction of the Janesville-Madison line west, and the beginning of CTC operation which continues to Milwaukee. Trains normally keep right, although both mains are equipped with block signals for either direction. Sturtevant is the junction point with the Milwaukee-Kansas City route to the west and with the Racine branch to the east.

Entering Milwaukee, carferry docks are to the east at the Kinnickinnic Bridge, where double freight mains diverge to parallel the passenger mains. C&NW passenger trains enter Milwaukee Road trackage from the east at Washington Street, and immediately after crossing the Menomonee River trains burrow beneath the Post Office and slip into the Milwaukee Road station.

The Milwaukee Shops and engine terminal are approximately 5 minutes beyond the depot between the junctions of the freight tracks at Cutoff Tower and the route of the former *Chippewa* (now used by C&NW passenger trains) at Grand Avenue. At Elm Grove, junction of the Air Line from the east — an alternate, infrequently used freight entrance to Milwaukee — the westbound track loops

---

*As used in this description, east is on the right side of a train traveling from Chicago to Minneapolis, on the left side of a train en route from the Twin Cities to the Windy City.

Belching in the best of Beloit opposed-piston tradition, Erie-built 11-B digs its flanges into the Canal Street curve accelerating the *Chippewa-Hiawatha* from Chicago's Union Station. A gateman guards the crossing as the train prepares to duck beneath the throat tracks of North Western Terminal. Then it will climb to above street level for a fast exit from the Windy City. By now the conductor is collecting tickets in the head coach, and hopefully, at least a few passengers are anticipating *Hiawatha* club steaks in the *Grove* parlor-diner. — TRAINS: *Wallace W. Abbey*.

205

In midafternoon of an early September 1952 day, train 15, the *Olympian Hiawatha*, thurumphs across the C&NW Wisconsin Division crossing at Mayfair in Chicago and heads into 90 mph territory. — TRAINS: *W. A. Akin.*

Train 6 passes Tower A-20 behind a brace of E9's in the summer of 1969. The train order signal adjacent to the tower governs mainline trains; the signal at the left governs freights from Bensenville. — *Jim Scribbins.*

In July 1969, 22 years after the photo at the lower left was taken, the CNS&M overpass is gone as train 3 crosses mains under CTC control. — *Jim Scribbins.*

A Railroad Society of Milwaukee CNS&M trip was timed so that excursionists could be at Rondout for the June 29, 1947, inaugural run of the *Olympian Hiawatha.* The train, photographed from the North Shore's bridge, slams across the EJ&E. — *Richard D. Acton.*

207

Floating ice attests to a relatively mild winter day near the end of December 1967 as No. 6, the *Morning Hiawatha*, rumbles across the Kinnickinnic River draw-bridge. Immediately ahead is the assault on Lake Hill. — *Phil Stemo.*

The engineer of outbound train 2 (above) tests the Mars light while he awaits the highball at the open east end of the new Milwaukee depot. Milwaukee's new Post Office was later constructed above this portion of the platforms. On Wednesday, August 4, 1965, No. 6 (above right) became the first eastbound train to arrive at the new Milwaukee Road station. Spanning the tracks is the 6th Street viaduct, which originally was constructed by the North Shore Line. As these photos illustrate, eastbound trains normally use the No. 3 track. Later Chicago & North Western trains began to use the station too. — *Both photos, Jim Scribbins.*

to gain a more favorable gradient, then returns to its mate at Brookfield, the junction of the original Milwaukee & Mississippi line west toward Janesville. Shortly thereafter the Soo Line is crossed at Duplainville. *Hiawathas* pass through Milwaukee's nearby lakelands. Pewaukee Lake is most visible, since it is adjacent to the railroad; other waters are more distant. The line diverging west to Madison and a crossing of C&NW's original Badger State route are found at

Milwaukee's new Post Office completely covers the east platforms of the Milwaukee Road station, as evidenced by these views of trains 3 (left) and 6 (above). The west end remains open for scenes such as the meeting of No. 6 and C&NW *Flambeau 400*, No. 153 (below). Light-colored cars are the Permacel train. — *All photos, Jim Scribbins.*

No. 3 hurries past recently constructed Cutoff Tower in 1967. About to follow is Soo Line 233. — *Jim Scribbins.*

In the Christmas card setting of Wauwatosa on December 25, 1965, the *Morning Hi* crosses the Menomonee River bridge. — *Jim Scribbins.*

Milwaukee's 35th Street viaduct still affords a vantage point similar to that in this 1947 view of train 6 with new FM's, but the footbridge is gone. — *Charles McCreary.*

An extra section of the westbound *Hi* passes beneath the C&NW freight belt in Wauwatosa. — *Armin Krueger; collection of Robert Eschenberg.*

Watertown. East of Rio come the first glimpses of the Baraboo Range. A branch from Madison and the "Old Line" (from Milwaukee via Horicon) join the main line at the canal entering Portage.

From this terminal, semaphores rather than the searchlight signals used since Western Avenue in Chicago govern to the Twin Cities. Much of the lower dells of the Wisconsin River can be seen approaching Wisconsin Dells, and a splendid view of the upper dells is afforded from the bridge leaving the station. This is the

speedway through sand and pines which for years has been the Milwaukee's racetrack. New Lisbon brings the junction with the line to Wausau and Woodruff. Then the bluffs of the driftless area become increasingly prominent; the most noticeable formation is encountered entering Camp Douglas, where the former Omaha Railway (now C&NW) is crossed. Tomah Shops (opposite the depot) supply maintenance of way material, and cars that might be seen there ultimately will become camp and work cars.

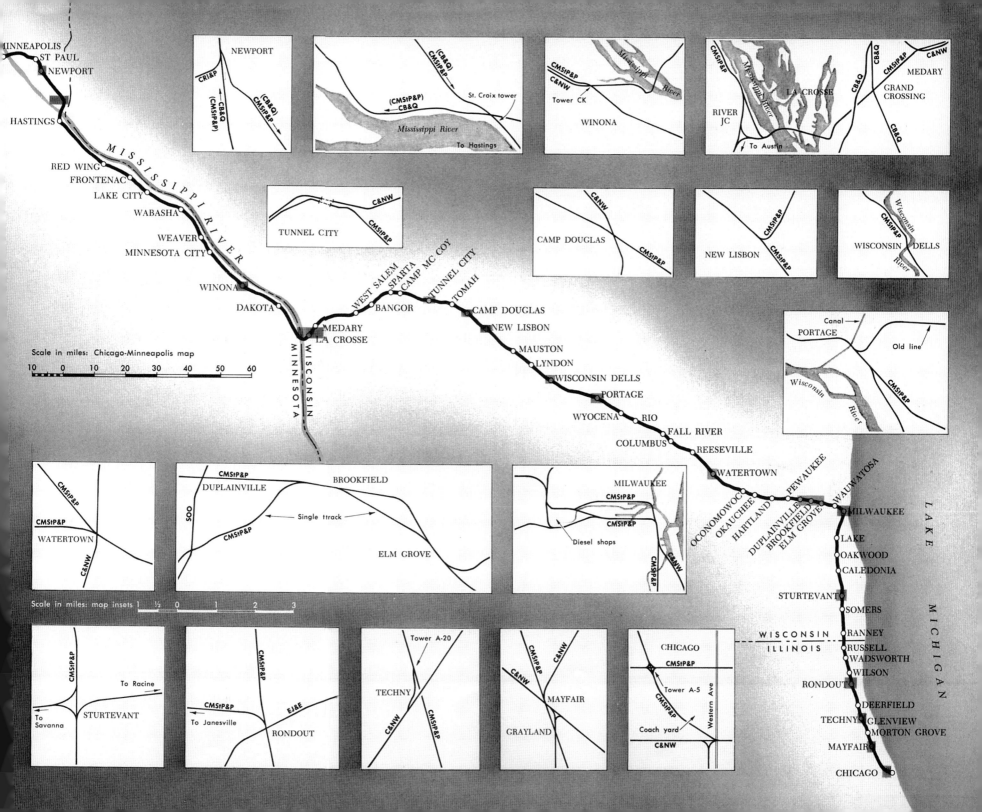

Eight cars of a summer 1969 No. 2 whip past the tower at Duplainville, Wis. The tower, at one of the busier locations in the greater Milwaukee area, controls the crossing of the Milwaukee and the Soo main lines. Just behind the camera is the highway that figured in the runaway locomotive episode on page 175. — *Jim Scribbins.*

The temperature at Pewaukee Lake, Wis., on January 30, 1954, is minus 10 degrees. The photographer accepts the hospitality of some ice fishermen who invite him to share their fire. Then the westbound *Afternoon Hi* appears, and the camera freezes an instant of time. — *Jim Scribbins.*

214

The Milwaukee introduced 1969 by break-
ing in its new FP45's on Twin Cities trains,
then putting them on the *City* streamliners.
A normal *Hiawatha* E9 stands idle on
local 12/23's layover as 7200 h.p. hustles
No. 6 into Watertown. — *Clinton Jones Jr.*

The *Afternoon Hi's* did not stop at Columbus until Madison bus connections were
instituted in place of Milwaukee-Madison
and Madison-Portage local passenger trains.
The Greyhound, operated on a charter
basis for the road, is exchanging passengers with train No. 3. — *Jim Scribbins.*

FP7-trio 94 leads *Afternoon Hiawatha* 101 over the Fox-Wisconsin canal drawbridge at Portage Junction. The turnout to the Madison branch from the eastbound main is visible at the far end of the bridge. The switch to the "Old Line" to Milwaukee via Horicon is beneath the train. Although the tower remains, it has been boarded up for some time. — *Jim Scribbins.*

Wisconsin Dells is one of the few places on any railroad where passengers can detrain adjacent to a major tourist attraction — a circumstance of geography the Milwaukee Road uses to advantage. Train 2 still carried two parlors when this 1957 photo was taken. — *Jim Scribbins.*

On a summer afternoon in 1952, First 5 brakes to a stop at the Juneau County seat. Signals are displayed for a *North Woods Section* that follows. Mauston now has a much smaller frame depot and plays host to one westbound train per day. — *James G. La Vake.*

Skytop Lounge and Super Dome riders look back at the east portal after train 2 has emerged from Tunnel 1 at Tunnel City.

A riot of color: An orange-maroon-black FP7 leads yellow E9's and an orange-olive Great Northern storage car as No. 5 pops out of the west portal.

With Great Northern and Pennsylvania head-end cars, and a tap-lounge (photo at right) spliced into the consist for the benefit of Skytop passengers, No. 5 crosses the Black River at the west edge of La Crosse. A new crew has assumed operation of the train at this division point.

The bluffs in the vicinity of Camp Douglas, Wis., are a scenic delight. This is No. 2 accelerating away from the Chicago & North Western crossing.

After following the Father of Waters from Weaver, Minn., the *Afternoon Hiawatha* passes the Whitman locks and dam. — *All photos, Jim Scribbins.*

First 16, the *Morning Hiawatha*, passes St. Croix Tower onto the single-track approaching the Mississippi River bridge into Hastings. — *William D. Middleton.*

The *Afternoon Hiawatha* skirts St. Paul's Pig's Eye Yard at speed on the left-handed eastbound main track while Tacoma-Chicago time freight 264 waits to follow on this sunny January 19, 1959. — *William D. Middleton.*

FM's idle in Minneapolis while a Rock Island unit clears the trainshed and the stub-station's Baldwin performs switching. — *Henry J. McCord.*

Departing *Afternoon Hi* shares a platform in the Minneapolis depot with a CRI&P Kansas City train. — *Jim Scribbins.*

Skytop parlor contrasts with smoke jack and intricate steelwork of the Minneapolis depot. — *Jim Scribbins.*

221

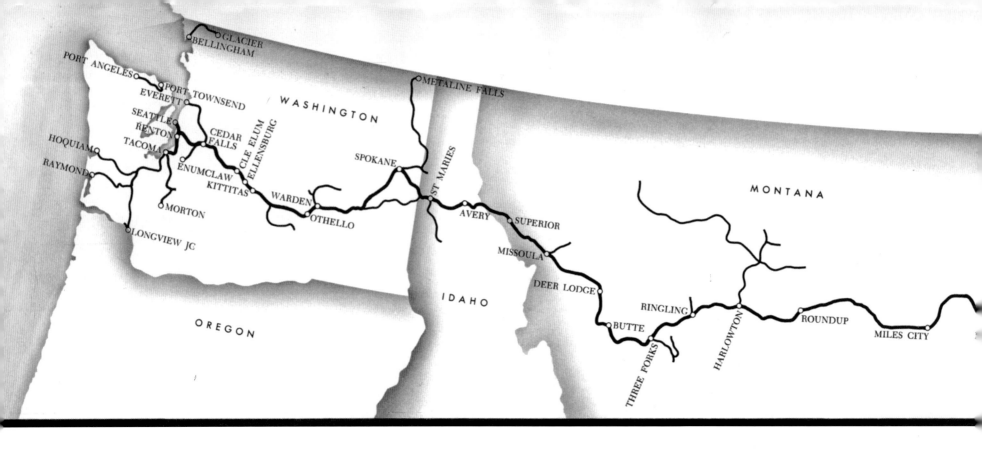

At Tunnel City a short stretch of single track, governed by CTC, penetrates Tunnel No. 1. The original bore, which is now abandoned, is on the left westbound. The paralleling railway is C&NW, and after emerging from its own tunnel it stays near until La Crosse. From West Salem the path descends toward the Mississippi. The tower at Medary controls the crossing with C&NW, and the Grand Crossing Tower controls that with the Q.

Immediately out of La Crosse the Black and Mississippi rivers are bridged with a single track (CTC controlled), and lines diverge to Dubuque and Austin before the iron once more becomes the double track which sends the fleet *Hiawathas* beneath towering bluffs along the Father of Waters. At Tower CK in Winona, the Black Hills line of the North Western is crossed for the last time. Near Weaver the river disappears from sight, although the bluff-tops on the Wisconsin side often remain in view; but between Wabasha and Lake City the Mississippi returns in widened form as Lake Pepin, then is completely lost from sight. After negotiating a long valley marked with rock outcroppings, trains reach Red Wing with another view of the Mississippi.

At Hastings the third section of CTC single iron crosses the big river once more to St. Croix Tower, where left-handed operation with the Burlington begins. Westbound trains use the Q, which is at water level and beside the river in places. Eastbound trains use the Milwaukee track, away from the river and much higher; but the height allows a fine panorama of the Mississippi when trains are dropping down to St. Croix Tower. At Newport, Rock Island trains enter from the west, and the joint line proceeds beside the CB&Q and CMStP&P yards, then moves beneath the bluffs and around the long curve into St. Paul. West of the Union Station two CTC-controlled ascending main tracks bring the *Hiawathas* past the Minnesota Transfer Railway roundhouse and yard, which are on the east side of the tracks. The *Hi's* cross the Mississippi for the final time via the Short Line Bridge, continue through South Minneapolis coach yard, and enter the Minneapolis depot.

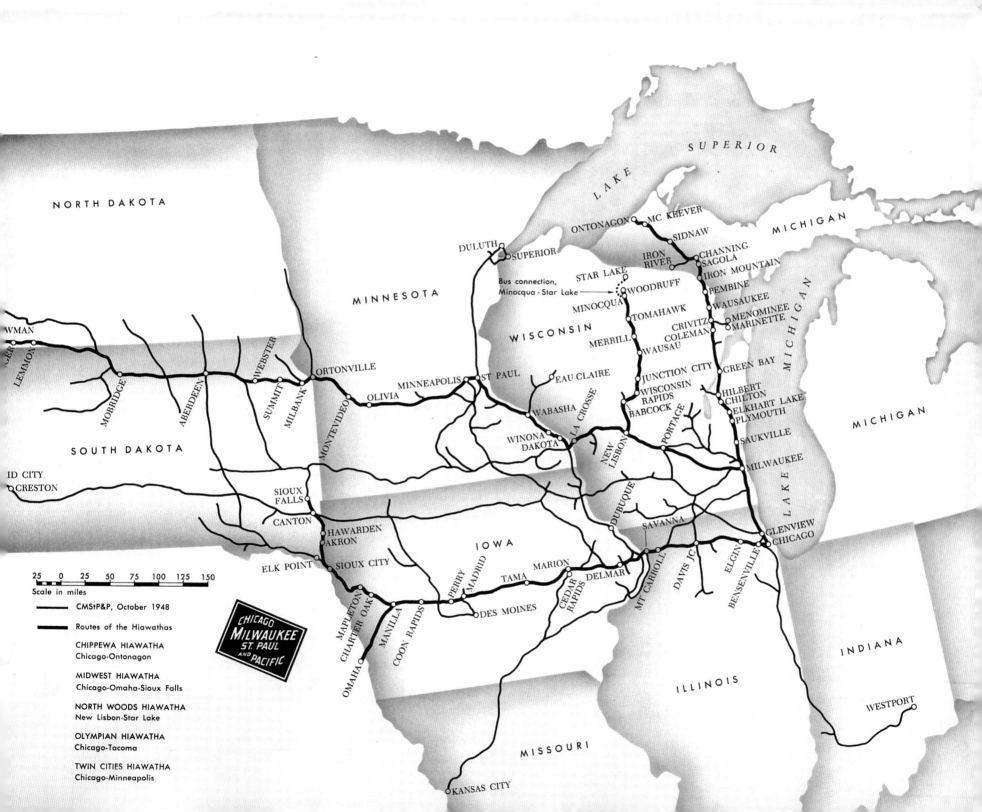

LAKE SUPERIOR

NORTH DAKOTA

MINNESOTA

WISCONSIN

MICHIGAN

MICHIGAN

SOUTH DAKOTA

IOWA

ILLINOIS

INDIANA

MISSOURI

LAKE MICHIGAN

WMAN
GER
LEMMO
ID CITY
CRESTON

MOBRIDGE
ABERDEEN
SUMMIT
MILBANK
WEBSTER
ORTONVILLE
OLIVIA
MINNEAPOLIS
ST PAUL
EAU CLAIRE

MONTEVIDEO
WABASHA
LA CROSSE

SIOUX FALLS
CANTON
HAWARDEN
AKRON
ELK POINT
SIOUX CITY

WINONA
DAKOTA

NEW LISBON

PORTAGE

DULUTH
SUPERIOR

ONTONAGON
MC KEEVER
SIDNAW
CHANNING
SAGOLA
IRON RIVER
IRON MOUNTAIN
PEMBINE
WAUSAUKEE
MENOMINEE
MARINETTE

STAR LAKE
Bus connection,
Minocqua - Star Lake
WOODRUFF
MINOCQUA
TOMAHAWK
CRIVITZ
COLEMAN
MERRILL
WAUSAU
JUNCTION CITY
GREEN BAY
WISCONSIN
RAPIDS
BABCOCK
HILBERT
CHILTON
ELKHART LAKE
PLYMOUTH
SAUKVILLE

MILWAUKEE

DUBUQUE
SAVANNA
GLENVIEW
CHICAGO

MAPLETON
CHARTER OAK
MANILLA
COON RAPIDS
PERRY
MADRID
DES MOINES
TAMA
MARION
CEDAR RAPIDS
DELMAR
MT CARROLL
DAVIS JC
ELGIN
BENSENVILLE

OMAHA

WESTPORT

KANSAS CITY

25  0  25  50  75  100  125  150
Scale in miles

———— CMStP&P, October 1948

▬▬▬▬ Routes of the Hiawathas

CHIPPEWA HIAWATHA
Chicago-Ontonagon

MIDWEST HIAWATHA
Chicago-Omaha-Sioux Falls

NORTH WOODS HIAWATHA
New Lisbon-Star Lake

OLYMPIAN HIAWATHA
Chicago-Tacoma

TWIN CITIES HIAWATHA
Chicago-Minneapolis

CHICAGO
MILWAUKEE
ST. PAUL
AND PACIFIC

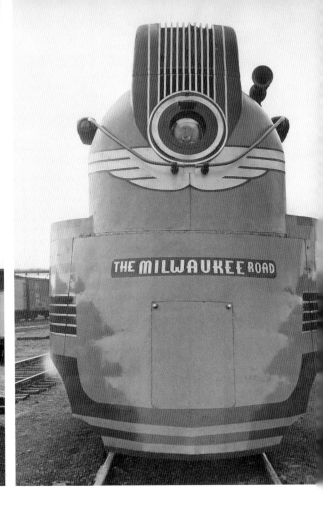

# LOCOMOTIVES

THE Milwaukee's most famous steam power, and certainly among the best known of all North American steam locomotives, was the Class A *Hiawatha* Atlantics. They were built to include all the latest in steam locomotive design in 1935. The A's were constructed with speed in mind, and they were the first locomotives that were shrouded at birth. Built to meet the challenge of the upstart diesel-electric, they surpassed it. They were designed to handle six cars,

and they maintained increasingly tightened schedules with nine cars. Eventually they were replaced, not because of any failures but simply because of the greatly increased train lengths during World War II and the subsequent economies of diesels which could double the A's daily mileage. Although the fact was not publicly known at the time, industrial designer Otto Kuhler was primarily responsible for the exteriors of the sleek 4-4-2's. As is often the case, though, the finished locomotive was not exactly as he had envisioned it in his studio.

The Atlantics were featured for many years in a Lionel trainset, but the cars they pulled did not resemble the prototype. The image of the A's is so enduring that they were favored with a color illus-

224

Distinctive motive power for distinctive trains was a hallmark of the *Hiawatha* era. Five series of steam locomotives displayed novel streamlining. From left to right, front-end styling is illustrated by: Alco-built Class A 4-4-2 No. 2; Alco-built Class F-7 4-6-4 No. 101, with the Mars signal-light modification; home-shrouded Class F-2 4-6-2 No. 812; home-shrouded Class F-1 4-6-2 No. 151; and home-shrouded Class G 4-6-0 No. 10. Credit for the majority of the Milwaukee Road photographs in this book belongs to Harvey Uecker, the road's official photographer during the steam era. — *All photos, Milwaukee Road.*

tration in a 1967 book by English rail author C. Hamilton Ellis. Moreover, in a hardly expected place, the July 1965 issue of the South African Railways employees' magazine states streamlining was considered for that system's Class 23 4-8-2's of 1938-1939 and that had it been carried out the shrouding of those 3-foot 6-inch-gauge Mountains would have been similar to that of the *Hiawatha*. Since the SAR engines preceded the Milwaukee F7's, the reference must have been to the 1-4.

Once this writer saw an A take 13 cars of *Hiawatha* No. 6 out of Milwaukee after the default of 6's regularly assigned diesel. The 4-4-2 had arrived on *Chippewa* 21, was hurriedly turned, and was attached to the *Hi*, which had been pulled west of the station by the depot's 600 h.p. EMD to the tangent west of Eighth Street. There the Atlantic was attached so that it could obtain a foothold, and it proceeded to churn through the depot curves with drivers spinning madly; but she kept her footing and got matters in hand up the elevation away from the Menomonee drawbridge. Another A once handled combined trains 56 and 2 between Milwaukee and Chicago with 20 cars (at the time, No. 2 was the *Copper Country Limited*); and No. 4 took combined *Hiawatha* 15 and *Milwaukee Express* 23 across the C&M: at least 17 cars, and losing only 20 minutes running time inclusive of a Sturtevant stop.

Although the F-7 Hudsons were introduced in the fall of 1938, the Atlantics continued taking turns on the *Afternoon Hi* for

225

## STEAM LOCOMOTIVES

| Class designation | Number built | Road numbers in Hiawatha service | Wheel arrangement | Driving wheel diameter (in.) | Cylinders (in.) | Boiler pressure (lbs.) | Tractive effort (lbs.) | Grate area (sq. ft.) |
|---|---|---|---|---|---|---|---|---|
| A | 4 | 1-4 | 4-4-2 | 84 | 19 x 28 | 300 | 30,700 | 69.0 |
| F-7 | 6 | 100-105 | 4-6-4 | 84 | 23½ x 30 | 300 | 50,300 | 96.5 |
| F-6 | 14 | 131, 132 | 4-6-4 | 80 | 26 x 28 | 225 | 45,250 | 80.0 |
| S-3 | 10 | 262, 263, 267, and 269 | 4-8-4 | 74 | 26 x 32 | 250 | 62,119 | 96.2 |
| G (Built as B-3) | 2 (69) | 10, 11 | 4-6-0 | 69 | 22 x 26 | 200 | 31,004 | 35.0 |
| F-2 (Built as F-5) | 2 (65) | 801, 812 | 4-6-2 | 73 (69) | 25 x 28 | 200 | 36,009 (43,120) | 48.8 |
| F-1 (Built as F-3) | 2 (70) | 151, 152 | 4-6-2 | 79 | 23½ x 28 (23 x 28) | 200 | 33,275 (31,870) | 48.8 |
| F-5 | 65 | 810 | 4-6-2 | 73 | 25 x 28 | 200 | 36,009 | 48.8 |

| Superheater heating surface (sq. ft.) | Total engine weight (lbs.) | Weight on drivers (lbs.) | Tender capacity | Builder | Date built | Date retired and comments |
|---|---|---|---|---|---|---|
| 1029 | 290,000 | 144,300 | 4000 gals. oil 13,000 gals. water | Alco | 1 — 5-4-35 | 11-9-51. This date conflicts with known fact No. 1 emerged at Alco on April 30. It may be acceptance date on CMStP&P, but this is stated to have been May 5. |
| | | | | | 2 — 5-8-35 | 11-9-51 |
| | | | | | 3 — 5-21-36 | 9-15-49 |
| | | | | | 4 — 4-20-37 | 6-8-51 |
| 1695 | 415,000 | 216,000 | 25 tons coal 20,000 gals. water | Alco | 100 — 8-13-38 | 10-11-49 |
| | | | | | 101 — 8-19-38 | 4-3-51 |
| | | | | | 102 — 8-26-38 | 8-2-50 |
| | | | | | 103 — 8-31-38 | 6-26-51 |
| | | | | | 104 — 9-9-38 | 6-13-51 |
| | | | | | 105 — 9-16-38 | 8-10-51 |
| 1815 | 375,850 | 189,720 | 20 tons coal 15,000 gals. water | Baldwin | 1929 and 1930 as Nos. 6400-6413 | 131 and 132 converted to oil and used between Avery and Othello. Other F-6's handled extra sections of Twin Cities, North Woods, and Chippewa Hiawathas. Class retired 1952-1954. |
| 1438 | 460,000 | 259,300 | 25 tons coal 20,000 gals. water | Alco | 1944 as Nos. 260-269 | 262, 263, 267, and 269 converted to oil and used between Avery and Othello. Class retired 1954-1956. |
| 504 | 187,600 | 138,600 | 12 tons coal 8500 gals. water | Baldwin | 10 — Oct 1900 as 315 | 5-3-51 as No. 1111 |
| | | | | | 11 — Sept 1900 as 306 | 10-29-51 as No. 1112 |
| 620 | 253,000 | 160,000 | 13 tons coal 8500 gals. water | Alco | 801 — Apr 1912 as 1523 | 3-24-50 |
| | | | | | 812 — May 1912 as 1542 | 6-16-50 |
| 620 | 247,300 | 157,200 | 13 tons coal 8500 gals. water | Alco | 151 — Feb 1910 as 1539 | 6-4-54 |
| | | | | | 152 — Mar 1910 as 1542 | 12-13-54. Renumbered 3240 in September 1910; as 6160 was converted to oil fuel, reclassified F-3-c-s, and painted to serve as Hiawatha relief power. |
| 620 | 253,000 | 160,000 | 13 tons coal 8500 gals. water | Alco | May 1912 as 1539 | 1-18-52 |

another three years until diesels arrived. The *Morning Hi*, particularly No. 5, was always a heavier train and always followed 4-6-4's. Until the *Midwest Hi* was dieselized, Nos. 1-4 regularly handled that train to Omaha. During the period of partial dieselization of the *Hi*'s, the A's also worked between Chicago and Milwaukee, Chicago and Madison, Milwaukee and Madison, and saw service too on the *North Woods Section* (Second or Third No. 5) from Chicago to New Lisbon, whence they returned on nothing less than heavy mail, express, and local passenger 58. This was sometimes a struggle for their 84-inch wheels.

At first these engines were designated as the "Milwaukee" type, but during the course of their careers the Atlantic name replaced the individualistic title. Of all steam locomotives associated with the *Hiawathas*, Nos. 1 and 2 were the only ones designed and constructed specially for *Hiawatha* service. Nos. 3 and 4 were acquired to handle extra sections and to work Chicago-Milwaukee "80-minute" trains. No. 3 was cannibalized upon retirement to keep the remaining A's operating a while longer.

The F-7 Hudsons that arrived in 1938 to meet the increased motive-power demands of longer *Hiawatha* consists were distinguished by a further development of the style of shrouding used to speedline the A's. Other than a modified livery pattern, the two most noticeable differences between the A's and F-7's were the Hudsons' full exposure of the drivers (to reduce shrouding weight) and a cab that featured a fishbowl-like expanse of glass. Notwithstanding his stated preference for "bullet-nosed" shrouding, Otto Kuhler designed this masterpiece of locomotive styling. At the approximate time the A was designed, Kuhler did a painting entitled "Steam Locomotives of the Future," in which one locomotive showed unmistakable characteristics of the *Hiawatha* Hudson. In production of the 4-6-4, the only deviation from his design was the omission of two additional headlights, one each at the forward end of the running boards. Chrome plates displaying the words "Speedlined by Otto Kuhler" were affixed to the black rectangular area on the cylinder covers of the F-7's. Originally Nos. 100-105 did not have Mars signal lights. These were installed, as accurately as can now be determined, coincident with the arrival of the first two passenger diesels.

Although the Hudsons could do more because of their size, they were not regarded as being as successful overall as were the Atlantics. The F-7's were slippery, stripped themselves, and developed

An artist's rendering (left) and a wood-block model (above) reveal early thought on *Hiawatha* design. Note that on the wood model the skirting is cut away to allow full access to the drivers. — *Both photos, collection of Earl Remmel.*

hot main pins. Of course, these things also happened to locomotives on other railroads. Unlike the A's, the cabs were hard riding at speed. Generally speaking, the 105 was considered the best of the class, doing a good job to the end.

Nevertheless, it was the F-7's that enabled train 6 to hold down what was, so far as can be determined, the fastest regularly scheduled run the world ever knew behind steam and the only known steam-powered run timed in excess of 80 mph: Sparta to Portage at a start-to-stop average speed of 81 mph. At that time there were speed restrictions of 50 mph west of, through, and east of Tunnel No. 1; 70 mph over the Omaha Railway crossing at Camp Douglas; and about 5 miles of "slow" (by *Hiawatha* standards) running in the vicinity of Wisconsin Dells — all of which meant that for the balance of the run the orange and gray speedsters would be running very close to the 100 mph allowed. It was not unknown for that maximum to be exceeded. In the *Milwaukee Magazine* of December 1938 C. H. Bilty stated that speed tapes indicated 120 mph had been reached.

It may be quite surprising, in view of the phenomenal success of the A's, to realize that years later a mechanical department official

of the road publicly mentioned that certain officers of the Milwaukee had favored adopting diesels in 1938 instead of continuing with the F-7's.[*]

As dieselization progressed, the 4-6-4's pulled Chicago-Milwaukee turns as well as through trains to Minneapolis, and sometimes propelled the *Arrow* between Chicago and Omaha. First to be retired was No. 100, which was withdrawn because of a cracked boiler. It was followed by No. 102, which threw its main rod on the right side at Edgebrook, Ill., while traveling 90 mph with a *North Woods Section* and was never repaired. As a class, Nos. 100-105 were survived by some of the A's and the nonstreamlined Hudsons.

For secondary *Hiawatha* service, where trains were light and track would not withstand the axle loadings of the A's and F-7's, elderly — even by steam standards — locomotives were spruced up externally through application of shrouds similar to those of the 4-4-2's and 4-6-4's. All such revamped power retained the small tenders of the unstreamlined members of their classes, and consequently seemed pushed together when compared to their proto-

*F. W. Bunce, Superintendent of Motive Power, before the Railroad Club of Chicago in April 1953.

types. This was particularly true of Pacifics 151 and 152, which had a noticeable decline in contour toward the front when viewed from some angles. This profile irregularity seemed to be characteristic of most locomotives streamlined late in life. However, their glamour blended with the cars of the trains they pulled.

Neither of the two Pacific classes ultimately used on the *Hiawathas* could be described as heavy. The F-5 was intended for use in mountain districts prior to electrification and the F-3 for flatland operation. After "motors" took over the Rocky Mountain and Coast divisions, some of the F-5 class locomotives were modified for gentler terrain by having extra tires shrunk over their drivers. Nos. 1523 and 1542, which ultimately were renumbered 801 and 812, underwent this modification.

After Nos. 801 and 812 received the shrouds in 1941, they were reclassified F-2. Following "bumping" from trains 132 and 133 by diesels, they handled trains 200 and 201 until April 1947.

Of the two *Chippewa* engines, the 152 deserves special recognition. As No. 6160 it was converted to oil and classed F-3-c-s coincident with the inauguration of the original *Hiawatha*. It was given a modernistic gray, orange, and maroon dressup with ornamentation on the running boards, and was used to substitute (rarely required) for Nos. 1 and 2 and to handle additional sections until No. 3 was received. Returned to coal as fuel, it powered the first *Chippewa*, and then was renumbered and shrouded. To differentiate them from their unshrouded kin, No. 151 was redesignated F-1 from F-3-a and No. 152 was changed from F-3 to F-1.

The 6160 occasionally was pressed into mainline *Hiawatha* service when the regularly assigned locomotives broke down. The author recalls watching on several occasions a late-running train 101 going like the wind through Pewaukee behind the "old" engines. The F-3, in fact, was more or less officially regarded as being the best passenger engine the Milwaukee owned — one that "didn't owe the railroad a cent." As recently as 1950, enginemen stated they could get "a little over 90 mph" by "pounding the living daylights out of them."

F-3's 6139 and 6168 (new numbers 177 and 197) were assigned at various times to the *Chippewa*. They were decorated with the same flashy paint work that adorned the 6160. Since these locomotives worked the *Chippewa* before the train actually became the *Chippewa–Hiawatha*, they cannot strictly be considered *Hiawatha* locomotives, and therefore they are not listed in the roster of steam locomotives in this chapter. A standard locomotive in a flashy paint scheme that does qualify as a *Hiawatha* locomotive is number 810, an F-5 that pulled the *Midwest Hiawatha*'s Manilla-Sioux Falls section before the advent of the shrouded 801 and 812.

Following dieselization of the *Chip*, No. 151 saw service out of Milwaukee, sometimes handling *Cannonball* commuter trains 12 and 23 as late as 1952. The 152 was the protection engine at Green Bay. The two F-1's outlasted all other shrouded power on the road.

Two Ten-Wheelers were streamlined for service on the *North Woods Hiawatha* — No. 10 in 1936 and No. 11 in 1937. With the exception of two conventional F-6 Hudsons on the Idaho division, they were the only Baldwin-built power regularly assigned to *Hiawatha* service. Built as compounds, they were renumbered twice before being rebuilt as "simple" and renumbered a third time. Nos. 2769 and 2765 received their fourth numbers — 10 and 11 — when they were streamlined. The 11 was deshrouded by February 1947, and was used in Chicago suburban service.

Two other classes of steam locomotives were used with some regularity in *Hiawatha* service across the nonelectrified Idaho division. They were Class F-6, 4-6-4 wheel arrangement, and S-3, 4-8-4 wheel arrangement. Chicago, Milwaukee & St. Paul had plans for a 4-6-4 locomotive drawn before New York Central produced theirs; but Central had the first of the breed on rails, and what might have been the Milwaukee type became the Hudson. When the road first had its 4-6-4's they were often referred to as Baltics, but this was not a correct application of the name because true Baltics were 4-6-4 tank engines. To cope with increased wartime traffic, Nos. 131 and 132 were converted to burn oil fuel and were sent to the Idaho division in 1944. They finished their careers on that division and commencing late in 1949 regularly hauled the *Olympian Hiawatha*. They were joined by four Class S-3 Northerns and, as mentioned in Chapter 11, trains 15 and 16 were steam powered between Avery and Othello for approximately three years. These 4-8-4's also pulled the *Columbian* (trains 17 and 18), occasional extras, and freight trains.

Class S-3 was built by American in 1944. Owing to wartime restrictions on totally new designs, the 4-8-4's were hybrid locomotives, combining a Delaware & Hudson boiler on a Rock Island frame and trailing a Union Pacific tender. The S-3 was the last class of steam locomotive constructed for the road. In January 1955, steam operation officially ceased on the Milwaukee.

Air rushing through the A's grilles (left) was expelled behind the stack, lifting the smoke. Tender (above) had oil-fuel hatch and contoured water-compartment doors. — *Both photos, Milwaukee Road.*

When they were new, all four of the Class A 4-4-2's posed for official portraits. The A's sported identical gray-and-orange-with-maroon-stripes color schemes; differences in tones on these black-and-white prints are due to film sensitivity. — *Above left, above right, and below, Milwaukee Road; bottom, American Locomotive Company.*

The shrouding of the upper half of the front end comprised large swinging doors offering easy access to the smokebox and to equipment mounted on top of the engine bed. Smaller doors concealed the bell and drop coupler. Tender had a platform to facilitate watering. — *All photos, Milwaukee Road.*

The smooth shrouding was only slightly ruffled by the handles of doors placed opposite washout plugs, sand traps, boiler checks, and other apparatus. The main rod was connected to the lead driver. — *All photos, Milwaukee Road.*

The Hiawatha Indian emblem did not appear on the tenders of Nos. 1 and 2 when they were built. However, the ovals were soon added, and 3 and 4 carried the emblems right from the factory. — *Both photos, Milwaukee Road.*

Designer Otto Kuhler was able to see his sketch of the streamlined 4-6-4 (above) develop into the famous F-7, which he posed beside (below) at the Alco plant. — *Above, collection of Earl Remmel; below, collection of Otto Kuhler.*

Fore and aft top views of No. 100 show how the black-painted cowling over the stack, sandbox, and dome ended in a fishtail on the cab. Tender's rear end had a dummy vestibule. — *Both photos, Milwaukee Road.*

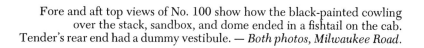

Hudson streamlining followed the Atlantic theme; but the skirting was contoured for a full view of the drivers, and the throttle linkage and some piping were placed outside the shrouding. — *All photos these pages, Milwaukee Road.*

Front-end shrouding (above) opened to provide access to the smokebox and the top of air pumps mounted behind the pilot beam. Hinged panel (right) also permitted air pump and cylinder servicing. These coal-fired engines had Standard stokers (far right) and Franklin Butterfly fire doors (below).

The all-welded tender tank was built up on a Commonwealth water-bottom cast-steel underframe. Equalized Commonwealth tender trucks had 38-inch wheels.

Before 801 and 812 were shrouded, No. 810 hauled the *Midwest Hi*'s Sioux Falls section. — *Collection of Earl Remmel*.

Hudson-styled streamlined power for the *Midwest Hi*'s Manilla-Sioux Falls section: 4-6-2 812. — *Milwaukee Road*.

F-5's 812 (shown in 1941) and 801, previously modified with 79-inch drivers, became F-2's. — *Milwaukee Road.*

F-3-a 4-6-2's 151 (above) and 152 emerged from the Milwaukee Shops shrouded for the *Chippewa.* — *Milwaukee Road.*

The many-faceted career of *Hiawatha* locomotive No. 152 began in March 1910 when it was delivered from Alco as No. 1542. Six months later it was renumbered 6160 (left above), a number that was retained through a 1935 shopping which prepared it for *Hiawatha* relief-engine service. It received a gray, orange, and maroon livery, "flower-box" running boards, roller-bearing pony and trailing trucks, oil-burning apparatus, and an oil-fuel tender (left below). Two years later it was reconverted to coal and assigned to the *Chippewa* (right top). Then, in 1939, it was photographed with a new number, 152 (right center). Finally, in 1941, the Milwaukee Road Shops gave it a shroud for the *Chippewa*, which in the fall of 1948 became the *Chippewa-Hiawatha* (right bottom). — *Left above and below, and right top, Milwaukee Road; right center, Henry J. McCord; right bottom, Jim Scribbins.*

For the *Hiawatha — North Woods Section*, the Milwaukee Road Shops took two 4-6-0's built in 1900 and encased them in stream-lined shrouding patterned after that of the Class A 4-4-2's. No. 10 (left) was photo-graphed on September 18, 1936, and No. 11 (below) posed for the company photographer on May 19, 1937. — *All photos these pages, Milwaukee Road.*

Skirting was later cut away around the drivers, and the pattern of the striping was revised.

Despite the sleek look of its shroud and the tender, No. 11 was a hand-fired coal-burner.

The running boards supported the ribbing for the shroud.

243

No. 269 (above) was one of four S-3's and No. 132 (below) was one of two F-6's converted from coal to oil fuel for Western service. — *Both photos, J. F. Larison.*

*Hiawathas* normally were entrusted only to certain classes of locomotives, but occasionally a breakdown or an emergency would find the roundhouse empty and an alien locomotive would be pressed into operation. On May 30, 1949, an S-2 4-8-4 freight locomotive (above) rushes the *Morning Hiawatha* through Truesdell, Wis. In a similar vein, the gray-orange-and-maroon paint scheme generally was accorded only to *Hiawatha* locomotives, but there were exceptions. Pacifics 177 and 152 (right) — both in the decorative colors — team up to move a prewar *Chippewa* out of Milwaukee.
— *Above, Donald H. Kotz; right, Henry J. McCord.*

# ELECTRIC LOCOMOTIVES

| Class | Number built | Builder and date | Road numbers in Hiawatha service | Wheel arrangement | Number of motors | Total weight (lbs.) | Weight on drivers (lbs.) | Diameter of drivers (in.) |
|---|---|---|---|---|---|---|---|---|
| EP-1 | 12 | General Electric, 1916 | E-22, E-23 | 2-B-B/B-B-2 | 8 GE 253 | 662,000 | 566,000 | 52 |
| EP-2 | 5 | General Electric, 1919-1920 | E-1 — E-5 | 1-B-D/D-B-1 | 12 GE 100 | 521,000 | 458,000 | 44 |
| EP-3 | 10 | Westinghouse, 1919-1920 | E-10 — E-12, E-14 — E-18 | 2-C-1/1-C-2 | 6 Westinghouse 348 DC | 620,000 | 420,000 | 68 |
| EP-4 | 2 | General Electric, 1949 | E-20, E-21 | 2-D/D-2 | 8 GE 750 | 586,600 | 443,000 | 47¼ |

Four types of electric locomotives handled the *Olympian Hiawatha* across the Rocky Mountain and Coast divisions. The first to be used were the Westinghouse Class EP-3 motors, which saw service from late 1949 until December 1950 over the Rocky Mountain division. Eight of the original 10 EP-3's were in operation when the *Hi* was electrified.

General Electric bi-polar motors, Class EP-2, were used from late 1949 to 1956 on the Coast division and from 1956 until 1958 on the Rocky Mountain division.

The armatures of these gearless locomotives were mounted on the axles. The contoured hood styling helped make them the best known of CMStP&P electrics — at least until the advent of the "Little Joes." Indeed, they were likely the most familiar "juice jacks" in the United States with the obvious exception of the Pennsylvania's Class GG1. A Lionel tinplate version was seen beneath Christmas trees for years, and they were associated with the Milwaukee Road in the public consciousness almost as much as the A's. The EP-2's rivaled the diesels in number of livery changes. After many years in solid black, Nos. E-1 and E-3 appeared in

striking combinations of orange, maroon, and silver during the late Forties (before their *Hiawatha* duty).

The E-3 also displayed wraparound striping on each end similar to the fluting applied to the *Olympian Hiawatha*'s Fairbanks-Morse diesels. With electrification of the streamliner in 1950, the same black, orange, and maroon color scheme that was used on "Little Joes" E-20 and E-21 was applied to all EP-2's, and the windows in the doors at the extreme ends of the hoods were removed. The general appearance of the locomotives was cleaned up early in 1955 when the ends were contoured to cover the sandboxes, headlights and classification lamps were partially recessed, and the central portion of the cab (which was, incidentally, an articulated affair uniting the three segments of the locomotive) emerged with one window instead of two. When virtually everything in the way of passenger equipment "went yellow," the bi-polars followed suit.

Between December 1950 and 1956 General Electric-streamlined motors E-20 and E-21 pulled the *Hi* in the Rocky Mountain trolley zone.

Originally destined for export to the Soviet Union, the "Little

246

| Tractive effort (lbs.) | | | Horsepower | | Speed | | | Comments |
|---|---|---|---|---|---|---|---|---|
| Continuous | 1-hr. rating | At 25% adh. | Continuous | 1-hr. rating | Continuous | 1-hr. rating | Maximum | |
| 43,200 | 60,000 | 141,500 | 3340 | 4100 | 29.0 mph | 26.5 mph | 70 mph | 30 EF-1's (no steam generator) also built for freight service; some of both original classes still in freight service. |
| 42,000 | 48,500 | 114,450 | 3180 | 4120 | 28.2 mph | 24.9 mph | 70 mph | Scrapped after 1960; E-2 donated to National Museum of Transport, St. Louis, Mo. |
| 49,000 | 66,000 | 105,000 | 3400 | 4200 | 26.0 mph | 23.8 mph | 65 mph | E-13 and E-19 scrapped (1947 and 1942 respectively) before advent of Olympian Hiawatha; all engines scrapped by 1957. |
| 77,000 | 85,500 | 110,750 | 5110 | 5530 | 25.2 mph | 24.5 mph | 84 mph | 10 EF-4's also purchased for freight service; EP-4's later converted to EF-4. All 12 still in service. |

Joes" — as they came to be known — remained at home because of Cold War tensions. The Milwaukee purchased 12 of them (three went to the Chicago South Shore & South Bend Railroad), converted them from 5-foot to standard gauge, and installed steam generators in the rear cabs of the two slated for use in passenger service, making them, in effect, single ended. After 1956 the boilers in E-20 and E-21 were removed, and the engines were reclassified as EF-4 for freight service.

As mentioned in Chapter 11, the EP-1's are part of the original electric locomotive order. They served in freight service from the time of delivery of the Quills until they were upgraded in 1953 for *Columbian* service. Specifications shown are for a two-unit locomotive, although at times after May 1955 the E-23 was operated as a three-unit machine. E-22 and E-23 received the yellow Union Pacific colors, but by the spring of 1964 they were back in black, orange, and maroon freight colors. Since that time the maroon bands have slowly disappeared from freight power, replaced by extension of the orange paint. The use of electric power on the *Olympian Hi* ended in September 1958.

In 1949, EP-3's (including the E-17, shown detouring on NP at Missoula in 1945) began hauling *Olympian Hiawathas*. — *Bamford J. Dodge.*

Two of the famous "Little Joes" were regularly assigned in passenger service over the Rocky Mountain electrified zone. E-20, as well as sister E-21, had a steam generator in the rear cab. — *Richard Steinheimer.*

The bi-polars first pulled *Olympian Hi*'s over the Coast division in orange-and-maroon garb (above left); later over the Rockies in yellow dress (left). — *Above left, Stuart B. Hertz; left, Philip C. Johnson.*

Two GE box-motors, E-22 and E-23, were modified with streamlined cabs for the *Columbian*, but they also were used on the *Olympian Hi.* — *Above, Wade Stevenson; far left and left, Richard Steinheimer.*

249

# DIESEL LOCOMOTIVES

| Class | Builder and date | Road numbers in Hiawatha service | Total number of units, combinations | Wheel arrangement | Total horsepower | Comments |
|-------|-----------------|----------------------------------|-------------------------------------|-------------------|------------------|----------|
| **DL-109** | Alco, 1941 | 14 | 2 (A-A) | A1A-A1A/A1A-A1A | 4000 | Scrapped. |
| **E6** | Electro-Motive, 1941 | 15 | 2 (A-A) | A1A-A1A/A1A-A1A | 4000 | Turned in to Electro-Motive in 1961 as a trade-in on an order for E9's destined for Chicago suburban service. |
| **E7** | Electro-Motive, 1946 | 16-20 | 10 (A-A) | A1A-A1A/A1A-A1A | 4000 | Nos. 16, 19A, and 20A turned in for E9's in 1961. 20B scrapped in 1964. Others out of service by the end of 1969. |
| **Erie** | Fairbanks-Morse, 1946-1947 | 5-9 | 15 (A-B-A) | A1A-A1A/A1A-A1A/A1A-A1A | 6000 | An additional booster unit was purchased in 1948. All are now scrapped. |
| **Erie** | Fairbanks-Morse, 1947 | 21, 22 | 4 (A-A) | A1A-A1A/A1A-A1A | 4000 | Scrapped. |
| **RSC-2** | Alco, 1947 | 989-992 | 4 (road-switcher) | A1A-A1A | 1500 | Removed from passenger service in 1968. All have been renumbered at least once. No. 991 ultimately became chopnose rebuild 576. |
| **FP7** | Electro-Motive, 1950-1951 | 90-105 | 48 (A-B-A) | B-B/B-B/B-B | 4500 | Nos. 90-94 renumbered 60-64, painted orange, and assigned to freight service in 1959. Others recently used in freight service. |
| **GP9** | Electro-Motive, 1954 | 201, 203, 205 | 3 (road-switcher) | B-B | 1750 | Originally numbered 2427, 2429, and 2431. Part of an order for 10 passenger Geeps. Assigned to Chicago commuter service in 1960; currently in freight service. |
| **E9** | Electro-Motive, 1956 | 200-205 | 18 (A-B-A) | A1A-A1A/A1A-A1A/A1A-A1A | 7200 | Present numbers are 30-35. |
| **FP45** | Electro-Motive, 1968-1969 | 1-5 | 5 (cowl-type) | C-C | 3600 | Nos. 1, 3, 4, and 5 transferred to freight service in early 1970. |

Two classes of steam first powered the *Hi's*, but in 1941 EMD 15 and Alco 14 (above) introduced the diesel age. — *Alco.*

Before the present mating of various models and makes of diesel units as one "locomotive," the *Hiawathas* were pulled by six designs of diesel power from three builders: Alco DL-109 No. 14; EMD E6 No. 15; EMD E7's 16-20; FM Erie-builts 5-9 and 21-22; EMD FP7's 90-105; and EMD E9's 200-205.

No. 14, except for occasional *Chippewa* or *North Woods* mainline usage, ceased to pull *Hiawathas* after delivery of the 10 units comprising locomotives 16-20. In 1953 Alco-built No. 14 was extensively renovated, receiving a new nose similar to EMD styling, and was relegated to secondary services. Both in its original and rebuilt form, it was undoubtedly the most individual *Hiawatha* diesel locomotive in appearance. By 1959 it was retired from service and removed from the roster. Nos. 15, 16, 19A, and 20A were returned to EMD in 1961 in exchange for new E9's equipped with Cummins auxiliary power for use with bi-level push-pull cars in Chicago commuter service.

In 1946 and 1947, Milwaukee received five locomotives of three units each from Fairbanks-Morse. In 1948 an additional single unit, 10B, was acquired, and the "C" cab units of the first five FM's were rearranged and renumbered to provide six sets of two-unit (cab-booster) 4000 h.p. engines. Nos. 5-10 were assigned to *Olympian Hiawatha* service while the two "new" locomotives, 11 and 12, both consisting of two cab units, went into other mainline service.

Meanwhile, in the fall of 1947, the first Erie-builts were joined by Nos. 21 and 22, 4000 h.p. locomotives consisting of two cab units. They were graced with a larger but less rectangular windshield that was a pleasant esthetic improvement. However, they did not sport the chrome nose grill. Intended only for Chicago-Twin Cities and Kansas City line trains, they ultimately worked the *Midwest* and *Chippewa Hi's*, and even reached Harlowton on the *Olympian*. In the renumbering of 1959, Nos. 21 and 22 became Nos. 13 and 14. All FM passenger units were retired and scrapped in 1963.

Although the *North Woods Hi* ceased to exist in 1956, the classic RSC-2 road-switchers remained in passenger service until 1968 after renumbering and uprating to 1600 h.p.

Fresh diesel horses — 4500 of them per locomotive — arrived from La Grange in 1950 and 1951 in the form of cab-booster-cab FP7's numbered 90-105. In 1959 Nos. 90-94 were renumbered 60-64 and assigned to freight service. Technically, there is no such thing as an FP7 booster. All cabless units are F7's; but the road commonly refers to all units capable of passenger service as FP7. With the continued curtailment of passenger trains, more FP7 booster units have been converted to freight service.

The EMD E9's came to the *Hiawatha* indirectly, having been intended as Milwaukee's contribution to the motive-power pool for the *City* streamliners. Reduction of those services has gradually

251

released more and more E9's for use on the road's other services. With consolidation of the *Olympian* and Twin Cities *Hi's* in 1957, full three-unit E9's often were assigned to the combined trains east of Minneapolis. Nos. 200-205 have been renumbered 30-35.

During 1957, the Milwaukee began operating various combinations of units together. Since that time, a multiple passenger locomotive is seldom seen with all its units bearing the same numerical prefix, or even with all units being of the same model. However, streamlined passenger units now are exclusively Electro-Motive. FP45 3600 h.p. "cowl" passenger units were placed in service during the 1968-1969 New Year holiday, and were run Chicago-Twin Cities and Chicago-Omaha. When on Minneapolis trains, the 1-5 are most often used in combination with a single FP7 or a single E9. A *Hiawatha* is rarely pulled by two FP45's.

Close-up view of No. 14 shows Otto Kuhler's needle-nose styling as well as the prevailing Milwaukee Road passenger livery of 1949. — *Jim Scribbins.*

Workmen at Milwaukee Shops rebuilt No. 14-B with an Electro-Motive-style nose during the summer of 1953. — *Jim Scribbins.*

In 1945 No. 14 displayed a two-tone orange-and-gray color scheme. — *Kenneth L. Zurn, collection of Harold A. Edmonson.*

Famous 15 (above) preceded 14 onto the roster in 1941 and established a herculean performance record. EMD E7's (below) came in 1946 to supplement 14 and 15 on the *Hi's. — Above, Milwaukee Road; below, Jim Scribbins.*

The bright-gray roof and orange-and-maroon sides — plus the chrome nose plate on A units — made the 15 Fairbanks-Morse units that were delivered for *Olympian Hi* service among the most eye-arresting diesels ever built. — *Rail Photo Service: B. F. Cutler.*

254    FM's 5 (left), shown in a rare livery, and 21 (right) illustrate the two different windshield shapes. — *Left, Jim Scribbins; right, Carl Bachmann.*

(Above) In orange paint separated from a gray roof by a maroon stripe, 1500 h.p. Alco RSC-2's 989-992 began pulling the *North Woods Hiawatha* in 1947. They left passenger operation in 1968. — *Jim Scribbins*.

(Above right) Electro-Motive FP7's were delivered in A-B-A combinations in 1950 and 1951, although almost immediately they also were operated in two-unit sets. — *Henry J. McCord*.

(Right) GP9 No. 2427 and sisters 2429 and 2431 saw passenger service in Washington and Idaho (with at least one other Geep) before they were assigned to the *Chippewa* in 1958. — *Jim Scribbins*.

Passenger service mainstays today are Nos. 30-35, E9's built by EMD in 1956 as Nos. 200-205. Some units have been modified — e.g., No. 32A (below) lost its portholes. — *Both photos, Jim Scribbins.*

Newest passenger power: 3600 h.p. FP45's. Following discontinuance of the *Afternoon Hiawatha*, four of the five units began showing up on freight trains more often than on passenger trains. — TRAINS, *Harold A. Edmonson.*

What passenger trains in America besides the *Hiawatha* fleet locked couplers with such a variety of power — either over the span of many years or during the course of a single run? From fleet Atlantics to powerful Hudsons to needle-nosed Alcos to chrome-faced FM's to bi-polar electrics to low-nose FP45's, the evolution was a classic of railroading. Fortunately for photographers in the Northwest, that evolution often could be depicted on a single negative, when examples from different eras in the Milwaukee's locomotive chronology posed side by side during power changes on the fringes of electrified territories. Thus we find a 1919 Westinghouse Quill electric waiting to relieve 1950 FP7's at Harlowton (top right), a 1919 bi-polar ready to take over from a 1944 S-3 at Othello (center right), and a 1916 box-cab and 1954 Geeps at Othello (bottom right).
— *Top right, Bob Stacy; center and bottom right, Wade Stevenson.*

257

Original 1934 *Hiawatha* cars, including Beaver Tail *Wenonah*, at the Shops in Milwaukee. — *Milwaukee Road.*

# ROLLING STOCK

This roster includes only cars constructed for *Hiawatha* trains. The Milwaukee Road built a number of other streamlined passenger cars and acquired some from outside builders for trains other than the *Hiawathas*, but these are not listed here, even though a few of them worked at some time or other on the *Hiawathas*. Notes on the conversion or disposition of the cars are included. Rolling stock for which no conversion or disposition is shown existed in its original form at the time of writing. Figures shown for the seating capacity of coaches refer to the number of revenue seats in the body of the car. Seats in the smoking rooms are not included; nor are smoking room seats of the 1934 Beaver Tails and straight parlors, nor of the 1936 straight parlors that were equipped with them.

| Numbers and/or names | Date built | Original service | Subsequent service | Remarks, conversion and/or disposition |
|---|---|---|---|---|

## PARLOR-OBSERVATION

### Beaver Tail — 24 seats

| Numbers and/or names | Date built | Original service | Subsequent service | Remarks, conversion and/or disposition |
|---|---|---|---|---|
| Nokomis (4449)* | 1934 | Hiawatha | North Woods, Chippewa Hiawathas | Converted to storage car No. 1955 in 1952. |
| Wenonah (4450) | 1934 | Hiawatha | North Woods, Chippewa Hiawathas | Converted to storage car No. 1956 in 1952. |

* Early source material refers to the cars by the numbers given in parentheses, but no evidence can be found that these numbers were actually applied to the cars in operation.

### Beaver Tail — 26 seats, plus 12 seats in the solarium

| Numbers and/or names | Date built | Original service | Subsequent service | Remarks, conversion and/or disposition |
|---|---|---|---|---|
| Omeme | 1936 | Hiawatha | Midwest Hiawatha, Chicago-Milwaukee pool | In 1948 the rear ends of these cars were altered with fins and large rear windows similar to those of the 1938 cars, and the last row of seats was turned to face the rear. Omeme converted to storage car 1957 after 1952; Opeche to storage car 1958 after 1952. |
| Opeche | 1936 | Hiawatha | Midwest Hiawatha, Chicago-Milwaukee pool | |

### Beaver Tail — 28 seats, plus 17 seats in the solarium

| Numbers and/or names | Date built | Original service | Subsequent service | Remarks, conversion and/or disposition |
|---|---|---|---|---|
| Earling | 1938 | Twin Cities Hiawatha | Midwest Hiawatha | Converted to storage car 1959. |
| Merrill | 1938 | Twin Cities Hiawatha | Midwest Hiawatha | Converted to storage car 1960. |
| Miller | 1938 | Twin Cities Hiawatha | Morning, Midwest, and Chippewa Hiawathas | The Miller and Mitchell were modified in 1941 to 21 seats and a drawing room and were placed in Morning Hiawatha service. Both cars were scrapped in 1961. |
| Mitchell | 1938 | Twin Cities Hiawatha | Morning, Midwest, and Chippewa Hiawathas | |

### Skytop Lounge — 12 solarium seats, 24 seats, drawing room

| Numbers and/or names | Date built | Original service | Subsequent service | Remarks, conversion and/or disposition |
|---|---|---|---|---|
| 186 Cedar Rapids | 1948 | Twin Cities Hiawatha | | Withdrawn from revenue service in 1970. |
| 187 Coon Rapids | 1948 | Twin Cities Hiawatha | | Withdrawn from revenue service in 1970. |
| 188 Dell Rapids | 1948 | Twin Cities Hiawatha | | Withdrawn from revenue service in 1970. |
| 189 Priest Rapids | 1948 | Twin Cities Hiawatha | | Scrapped in 1970. |

## PARLOR CAR

### 22 seats

| Numbers and/or names | Date built | Original service | Subsequent service | Remarks, conversion and/or disposition |
|---|---|---|---|---|
| Ishkoodah | 1934 | Hiawatha | Passenger pool | Converted to storage car 1953. |
| Minnewawa | 1934 | Hiawatha | Passenger pool | Converted to storage car 1954. |

### 28 seats

| Numbers and/or names | Date built | Original service | Subsequent service | Remarks, conversion and/or disposition |
|---|---|---|---|---|
| Iagoo | 1936 | Hiawatha | Passenger pool | Converted to storage car 1950. |
| Sahwa | 1936 | Hiawatha | Passenger pool | Converted to coach 566. |

### 22 seats, drawing room

| Numbers and/or names | Date built | Original service | Subsequent service | Remarks, conversion and/or disposition |
|---|---|---|---|---|
| Shada | 1936 | Hiawatha | Passenger pool | Converted to storage car 1951. |
| Wawa | 1936 | Hiawatha | Passenger pool | Converted to storage car 1952. |

### 24 seats, drawing room

| Numbers and/or names | Date built | Original service | Subsequent service | Remarks, conversion and/or disposition |
|---|---|---|---|---|
| Chandler | 1938 | Twin Cities Hiawatha | Passenger pool | Converted to coach 562. |

| Numbers and/or names | Date built | Original service | Subsequent service | Remarks, conversion and/or disposition |
|---|---|---|---|---|
| Hiland | 1938 | Twin Cities Hiawatha | Passenger pool | Converted to coach 565. |
| Sewall | 1938 | Twin Cities Hiawatha | Passenger pool | Converted to coach 561; scrapped in 1965. |
| Whittemore | 1938 | Twin Cities Hiawatha | Passenger pool | Converted to coach 560; scrapped in 1963. |
| Hanson | 1938 | Twin Cities Hiawatha | Passenger pool | The Hanson and Manchester were converted to parlor-buffet cars; later to coach-vending machine cars Nos. 563 and 564 for Chippewa Hiawatha service. Both cars were scrapped in 1964. |
| Manchester | 1938 | Twin Cities Hiawatha | Passenger pool | |

### 30 seats, drawing room

| | | | | |
|---|---|---|---|---|
| 190 Maple Valley | 1948 | Twin Cities, Midwest Hiawathas | Pass. pool, Morning Hiawatha | |
| 191 Wisconsin Valley | 1948 | Twin Cities, Midwest Hiawathas | Pass. pool, Morning Hiawatha | |
| 192 Gallatin Valley | 1948 | Twin Cities, Midwest Hiawathas | Pass. pool, Morning Hiawatha | |
| 193 Fox River Valley | 1948 | Twin Cities, Midwest Hiawathas | Pass. pool, Morning Hiawatha | |
| 194 Red River Valley | 1948 | Twin Cities, Midwest Hiawathas | Pass. pool, Morning Hiawatha | |
| 195 Pleasant Valley | 1948 | Twin Cities, Midwest Hiawathas | Pass. pool, Morning Hiawatha | |
| 196 Rock Valley | 1948 | Twin Cities, Midwest Hiawathas | Pass. pool, Morning Hiawatha | |
| 197 Spring Valley | 1948 | Twin Cities, Midwest Hiawathas | Pass. pool, Morning Hiawatha | |

## SLEEPING CAR

### Skytop Lounge — 8 bedrooms

| | | | | |
|---|---|---|---|---|
| 12 Alder Creek | 1948* | Olympian Hiawatha | | CN 1900 Mahone* |
| (No. 13 was omitted) | | | | |
| 14 Arrow Creek | 1948 | Olympian Hiawatha | | CN 1901 Malpeque |
| 15 Coffee Creek | 1948 | Olympian Hiawatha | | CN 1902 Fundy |
| 16 Gold Creek | 1948 | Olympian Hiawatha | | CN 1903 Trinity |
| 17 Marble Creek | 1949 | Olympian Hiawatha | | CN 1904 Baddeck |
| 18 Spanish Creek | 1949 | Olympian Hiawatha | | CN 1905 Gaspe |

* All six cars were built by Pullman-Standard; they were sold to the Canadian National in 1964 and renumbered and renamed.

### 10 roomettes, 6 bedrooms

| | | | | |
|---|---|---|---|---|
| 2 Lake Coeur d'Alene | 1948* | These cars were built for Olympian Hiawatha service, which normally required six of the cars. Four cars were used in the extra pool. | Effective October 1955 two cars were assigned to the Arrow for two years. From October 1957 through April 1960, two cars were used in Chicago-Austin (Minn.) service. From April 1962 through October 1965, two cars were assigned to Chicago-Sioux Falls (S. Dak.) service. | CN 2142 Wanapitei River* |
| 3 Lake Keechelus | 1948 | | | CN 2143 Warpath River |
| 4 Lake Pepin | 1948 | | | CN 2144 Vermillion River |
| 5 Lake Oconomowoc | 1948 | | | |
| 6 Lake Pend Oreille | 1948 | | | CN 2145 Dauphin River |
| 7 Lake Chatcolet | 1948 | | | |
| 8 Lake Pewaukee | 1948 | | | CN 2146 Torch River |
| 9 Lake Nashotah | 1948 | | | |
| 10 Lake Kapowsin | 1948 | | | |
| 11 Lake Crescent | 1948 | | | |

* All ten cars were built by Pullman-Standard; five cars were sold to the Canadian National in 1967 and renumbered and renamed.

| Numbers and/or names | Date built | Original service | Subsequent service | Remarks, conversion and/or disposition |
|---|---|---|---|---|

## Touralux — 14 sections

| Numbers and/or names | Date built | Original service | Subsequent service | Remarks, conversion and/or disposition |
|---|---|---|---|---|
| 5740 Mount Spokane | 1947 | Olympian Hiawatha | In addition to Olympian Hiawatha service, some of these cars were used on the Columbian in 1953-1955 during the last months this train operated. | Converted to storage car 2017. |
| 5741 Mount Washington | 1947 | Olympian Hiawatha | | Converted to baggage-dormitory 1354; later to express car 1340. |
| 5742 Mount McKinley | 1947 | Olympian Hiawatha | | |
| 5743 Mount Bosley | 1947 | Olympian Hiawatha | | |
| 5744 Mount Rainier | 1947 | Olympian Hiawatha | | Converted to wrecker car X-423. |
| 5745 Mount Rushmore | 1947 | Olympian Hiawatha | | |
| 5746 Mount St. Helens | 1947 | Olympian Hiawatha | | Converted to wrecker car X-422. |
| 5747 Mount Wilson | 1947 | Olympian Hiawatha | | |
| 5748 Mount Hope | 1947 | Olympian Hiawatha | | |
| 5749 Mount Stuart | 1947 | Olympian Hiawatha | | Converted to baggage-dormitory 1351. |
| 5750 Mount Harold | 1947 | Olympian Hiawatha | | Converted to storage car 2015. |
| 5751 Mount Angeles | 1947 | Olympian Hiawatha | | Converted to baggage-dormitory 1350. |
| 5752 Mount Chittenden | 1947 | Olympian Hiawatha | | Converted from Touralux-coach Sioux Falls. |
| 5753 Mount Jupiter | 1947 | Olympian Hiawatha | | Converted from Touralux-coach Chippewa Falls; converted to storage car 2016. |
| 5754 Mount Tacoma | 1947 | Olympian Hiawatha | | Converted from Touralux-coach Crystal Falls; converted to storage car 2014. |

## TOURALUX-COACH

### 8 sections, 32 coach seats

| Numbers and/or names | Date built | Original service | Subsequent service | Remarks, conversion and/or disposition |
|---|---|---|---|---|
| 5770 Sioux Falls | 1947 | Olympian Hiawatha | | Converted to Touralux Mount Chittenden. |
| 5771 Chippewa Falls | 1947 | Olympian Hiawatha | | Converted to Touralux Mount Jupiter; later converted to storage car 2016. |
| 5772 Granite Falls | 1947 | Olympian Hiawatha | | Converted to leg-rest coach 552. This car, as well as 5774 and 5775, were among the first leg-rest coaches; see coach description for later renumbering into 600 series. |
| 5773 Crystal Falls | 1947 | Olympian Hiawatha | | Converted to Touralux Mount Tacoma; later converted to storage car 2014. |
| 5774 Metaline Falls | 1947 | Olympian Hiawatha | | Converted to leg-rest coach 553. |
| 5775 Cannon Falls | 1947 | Olympian Hiawatha | | Converted to leg-rest coach 554. |

## DINING CAR

### 48 seats

| Numbers and/or names | Date built | Original service | Subsequent service | Remarks, conversion and/or disposition |
|---|---|---|---|---|
| 100-101 | 1936 | Hiawatha | Passenger pool | Both cars scrapped in 1952. |
| 109-112 | 1938 | Twin Cities Hiawatha | Passenger pool | All four cars scrapped in 1961. |
| 113 | 1942 | Afternoon Hiawatha | Passenger pool | Scrapped in 1964. |
| 114 | 1942 | Afternoon Hiawatha | Passenger pool | Converted to storage car 2007. |

### 40 seats

| Numbers and/or names | Date built | Original service | Subsequent service | Remarks, conversion and/or disposition |
|---|---|---|---|---|
| 115 | 1947 | Olympian Hiawatha | | Converted to storage car 2010. |

| Numbers and/or names | Date built | Original service | Subsequent service | Remarks, conversion and/or disposition |
|---|---|---|---|---|
| 116 | 1947 | Olympian Hiawatha | | Converted to storage car 2011. |
| 117 | 1947 | Olympian Hiawatha | | Converted to storage car 2013. |
| 118 | 1947 | Olympian Hiawatha | | Converted to storage car 2012. |
| 119 | 1947 | Olympian Hiawatha | | Converted to storage car 2009. |
| 120 | 1947 | Olympian Hiawatha | | |

**48 seats**

| | | | | |
|---|---|---|---|---|
| 121-126 | 1948 | Twin Cities, Chippewa Hiawathas | Two of the cars were assigned to the Midwest Hiawatha. | Nos. 124, 125, and 126 were converted to Buffeteria cars. |

## DINER-LOUNGE

**32 dining seats, 16 lounge seats**

| | | | | |
|---|---|---|---|---|
| 170-171 | 1948 | Midwest Hiawatha | Extra service | |

## TAP-CAFE

**24 tap seats, 24 cafe seats**

| | | | | |
|---|---|---|---|---|
| 5251 | 1935 | Hiawatha | North Woods and Midwest Hiawathas, passenger pool | Rebuilt during World War II for midtrain use; later converted to express car 1123. |
| 5252 | 1935 | Hiawatha | North Woods and Midwest Hiawathas, passenger pool | Rebuilt during World War II for midtrain use; later converted to storage car 2000. |

## TAP-DINER

**19 tap seats, 32 dining seats**

| | | | | |
|---|---|---|---|---|
| 151 | 1936 | Midwest Hiawatha (see express-tap listing) | North Woods Hiawatha | Scrapped in 1961. |
| 152 | 1936 | | North Woods Hiawatha | Converted to storage car 1953. |

## EXPRESS-TAP

**40 seats in the tap room**

| | | | | |
|---|---|---|---|---|
| 151 | 1936 | Hiawatha | | Both cars converted in 1942 to tap-diner for Midwest Hiawatha service. |
| 152 | 1936 | Hiawatha | | |

**44 seats in the tap room**

| | | | | |
|---|---|---|---|---|
| 153 | 1938 | Twin Cities Hiawatha | Passenger pool | Converted to express car 1308. |
| 154-156 | 1938 | Twin Cities Hiawatha | Passenger pool | Converted to express cars 1337-1339. |

## TAP-LOUNGE

**12 tap seats, 40 lounge seats**

| | | | | |
|---|---|---|---|---|
| 160-161 | 1942 | Afternoon Hiawatha | Morning Hiawatha (May 1948) | Both cars scrapped in 1961. |

**26 tap seats, 18 lunch (cafe) seats**

| | | | | |
|---|---|---|---|---|
| 162 | 1947 | Olympian Hiawatha | | Converted to business car Montana. |

| Numbers and/or names | Date built | Original service | Subsequent service | Remarks, conversion and/or disposition |
|---|---|---|---|---|
| 163 | 1947 | Olympian Hiawatha | | Converted to baggage-dormitory 1355. |
| 164 | 1947 | Olympian Hiawatha | | |
| 165 | 1947 | Olympian Hiawatha | | |
| 166 | 1947 | Olympian Hiawatha | | Converted to baggage-dormitory 1353. |
| 167 | 1947 | Olympian Hiawatha | | Lounge later changed to 34 seats. |
| 172-173 | 1948 | Afternoon Hiawatha | Passenger pool | |

## SUPER DOME

### 68 dome seats, tap room with 28 seats on lower level

| Numbers and/or names | Date built | Original service | Subsequent service | Remarks, conversion and/or disposition |
|---|---|---|---|---|
| 50 | 1952* | Olympian, Twin Cities Hiawathas | After the termination of the Olympian Hiawatha, a pair of the cars ran in the Chicago-Madison and Chicago-Milwaukee service. In addition, the cars were used on the City of Denver between Chicago and Denver, and between Cheyenne (Wyo.) and Ogden (Utah) on the Union Pacific for one summer. | CN 2400 Jasper* |
| 51 | 1952 | Olympian, Twin Cities Hiawathas | | CN 2404 Qu'Appelle |
| 52 | 1952 | Olympian, Twin Cities Hiawathas | | CN 2405 Columbia |
| 53 | 1952 | Olympian, Twin Cities Hiawathas | | CN 2401 Athabaska |
| 54 | 1952 | Olympian, Twin Cities Hiawathas | | CN 2402 Yellowhead |
| 55 | 1952 | Olympian, Twin Cities Hiawathas | | |
| 56 | 1952 | Olympian, Twin Cities Hiawathas | | CN 2403 Fraser |
| 57 | 1952 | Olympian, Twin Cities Hiawathas | | |
| 58 | 1952 | Olympian, Twin Cities Hiawathas | | |
| 59 | 1952 | Olympian, Twin Cities Hiawathas | | |

* All ten Super Domes were built by Pullman-Standard; six were sold to the Canadian National in 1964 and renumbered and renamed.

## BAGGAGE-DORMITORY

| Numbers and/or names | Date built | Original service | Subsequent service | Remarks, conversion and/or disposition |
|---|---|---|---|---|
| 1309-1314 | 1947 | Olympian Hiawatha | Milwaukee Road-Union Pacific City streamliners | |

## RAILWAY POST OFFICE

| Numbers and/or names | Date built | Original service | Subsequent service | Remarks, conversion and/or disposition |
|---|---|---|---|---|
| 2150-2151 | 1938 | Morning Hiawatha | Pool service | |
| 2152-2153 | 1947 | Morning Hiawatha | Pool service | |

## RPO-EXPRESS

| Numbers and/or names | Date built | Original service | Subsequent service | Remarks, conversion and/or disposition |
|---|---|---|---|---|
| 1205 | 1937 | North Woods Hiawatha | Pool service | |
| 1208-1213 | 1947 | Olympian Hiawatha | Chippewa Hiawatha and other trains | 1208 converted to RPO 2160; 1211 converted to RPO 2155. |

## EXPRESS

| Numbers and/or names | Date built | Original service | Subsequent service | Remarks, conversion and/or disposition |
|---|---|---|---|---|
| 1305-1307 | 1938 | Morning Hiawatha | Pool service | |
| 1330-1336 | 1947 | Twin Cities, Midwest Hiawathas | Pool service | Built with conductor's office room for Hiawatha use; later room was removed. |

| Numbers | Seats | Date built | Service | Remarks, conversion and/or disposition |
|---|---|---|---|---|

## COACHES

As subsequent groups of coaches were built for *Hiawatha* service, each preceding group
was transferred to other trains or to the general passenger pool.

| Numbers | Seats | Date built | Service | Remarks, conversion and/or disposition |
|---|---|---|---|---|
| 4401-4440 | 48 | 1934 | The original Hiawathas received coaches from a group of 40 constructed for systemwide service in 1934. | Thirty-one were sold to National Railways of Mexico and 2 to the Chicago Great Western; 7 were scrapped. |
| 400-416 | 52 | 1936 | Hiawatha | 400, 402-403, 405, 409-410, 413-416 were sold to Edwards International in 1965-1966; 407 was donated to the city of Tomah, Wis.; the others were scrapped by the road in 1965-1966. |
| 417-435 | 52 | 1937 | Hiawatha | 417, 419, 428, 432, 435 were sold to Edwards International; the others were scrapped by the road in 1965-1966. |
| 437-452 | 56 | 1938 | Twin Cities Hiawatha | 437-438, 440-442, 444, 451 were sold to Edwards International in 1965; the others were scrapped by the railroad, primarily in 1963-1967. |
| 454-478 | 56 | 1942 | Twin Cities Hiawatha | 457 was converted to commuter lounge 4570 in 1963. 469, 454, 455, and 459 were converted to commuter coaches 4571-4574. 458, 461, 464-466, 476 were scrapped by the road, primarily in 1965-1967. |
| 480-497 | 52 | 1947 | Olympian Hiawatha | Selected cars converted to leg-rest. |
| 535-536 | 52 | 1947 | Olympian Hiawatha | Converted to leg-rest. |
| 543-549 | 52 | 1947 | Olympian Hiawatha | Selected cars converted to leg-rest. |
| 552-554 | 40 | 1947 | Olympian Hiawatha | Converted from Touralux-coach. |
| 498-514 | 52 | 1948 | Twin Cities, Midwest, and Chippewa Hiawathas | 514 converted to leg-rest. |
| 515-534 | 48 | 1948 | Olympian Hiawatha | These cars omitted the backward-riding seats at the forward bulkhead. |
| 537-542 | 48 | 1948 | Passenger pool | |
| 550-551 | 48 | 1948 | Passenger pool | |

## EXPRESS-COACH

| Numbers | Seats | Date built | Service | Remarks, conversion and/or disposition |
|---|---|---|---|---|
| 206-207 | 40 | 1942 | Afternoon Hiawatha | |

## ———— LEG-REST COACHES ————

Beginning in the last half of 1955, the following coaches were given leg-rest-style seats
and reduced to 40-seat capacity; all leg-rest cars were renumbered into the 600 series.

| Orig. No. | Leg-rest No. | Orig. No. | Leg-rest No. | Orig. No. | Leg-rest No. |
|---|---|---|---|---|---|
| 481 | 608 | 508 | 635 | 525 | 627 |
| 483 | 637 | 509 | 633 | 527 | 615 |
| 485 | 606 | 510 | 638 | 528 | 628 |
| 488-489 | 603-604 | 511 | 630 | 529-530 | 610-611 |
| 490 | 601 | 512 | 639 | 531 | 618 |
| 492 | 632 | 513 | 636 | 532 | 617 |

| Orig. No. | Leg-rest No. | Orig. No. | Leg-rest No. | Orig. No. | Leg-rest No. |
|---|---|---|---|---|---|
| 493 | 605 | 514 | 619 | 533 | 629 |
| 495 | 607 | 515-518 | 620-623 | 534 | 614 |
| 496 | 634 | 519 | 616 | 535-536 | 652-653 |
| 497 | 600 | 520 | 624 | 537-538 | 654-655 |
| 504 | 631 | 521 | 609 | 546-549 | 656-659 |
| 505 | 640 | 522-523 | 625-626 | 550-551 | 660-661 |
| 506 | 602 | 524 | 612 | 552-554 | 649-651 |

Summary: Non-leg-rest coaches — 480, 482, 484, 486-487, 491, 494, 498-503, 507, 526, 539-545. Leg-rest coaches—600-612, (613 omitted), 614-640, 649-661.

Parlor-observation car *Mitchell* poses for the company photographer on August 30, 1938. — *Milwaukee Road.*

# INDEX

## A

Aberdeen, S. Dak., 159, 163, 174, 178, 181, 187
Accidents, 175, 199
Africa, South:
South African Railways, 225
Akron, Ia., 150
Allen, Cecil J., 70
American Locomotive Company:
Advertisements, 14, 15
**DL-109 No. 14,** 72, 75, 83, 84, 90, 106, 251
**4-4-2 No. 1,** 22, 23, 62, 228
**4-4-2 No. 2,** 11, 16, 23, 40, 54, 225, 228
**4-4-2 No. 3,** 38, 46, 54, 144, 145, 150, 228
**4-6-4 No. 101,** 83, 106, 107, 225
**4-6-4 No. 102,** 61, 63, 229
Role in choosing *Hiawatha* name, 22
RS-2's perform road work on freight, 137
RSC-2's in passenger service, 137, 138, 139, 251, 255
Anderson, O. R., 124
Anderson, Mrs. William S., 38
*Arrow,* 13, 62, 229
Atlantics:
Appearance before shrouding, 12
**No. 1,** 22, 23, 62, 228
**No. 2,** 11, 16, 23, 40, 54, 225, 228
**No. 3,** 38, 46, 54, 144, 145, 150, 228
**No. 4,** 43, 140, 144, 146, 150, 228
Official portraits, 232
Performance, 62, 63, 72, 84
Avery, Ida., 163, 175, 178, 230

## B

Babcock, Wis., 128
Baker, Mont., 176, 178
Baldwin Locomotive Works, 128, 221
Baltimore & Ohio, 175, 186
Bearmouth, Mont., 165
Beaver Tails:
Parlors:
*Earling,* 150, 151, 200
*Merrill,* 150, 151, 200
*Miller,* 72, 74, 151, 199, 200
*Mitchell,* 72, 74, 151, 199, 200, 265
Name first used, 22
*Nokomis,* 194
No. 101 with car, 21, 46, 58
Replaced, 93, 139, 200
Sioux Falls section carries, 148, 149
*Wenonah,* 194, 258
Sleepers, 156
Beerman, O. H., 150
Beloit, Wis., 23, 159
Bensenville, Ill., 26, 144, 151, 153, 204, 207
Bertil, Prince of Sweden, 62
Beverly, Wash., 166

Bilty, C. H., 22, 62, 72, 84, 229
Black River, Wash., 173
Blackbird Junction, Minn., 67
Bock, Sandra, 140
Bowman, N. Dak., 176, 178
Brokaw, Wis., 135, 137
Brookfield, Wis., 36, 61, 209
Brophy, Clarence E., 22
Budd Company, 163
Buffeteria diners, 126
Buffet-parlor cars, 139, 151, 194
Buford, C. H., 90
Butte, Mont., 159, 161, 163, 169, 174, 178, 181, 187

## C

Caledonia, Wis., 66, 71
Camp Douglas, Wis., 66, 123, 212, 219, 229
Camp McCoy, Wis., 66, 81, 120
Canadian National, 111, 112, 115, 186
Canton, S. Dak., 149, 150
Cedar Falls, Wash., 171
Cedar Rapids, Ia., 140
Champion, Mich., 200
Channing, Mich., 188, 194, 196, 199, 200
Charter Oak, Ia., 150, 155
*Chicago Arrow* (PRR), 188
Chicago, Ill.:
Century of Progress Exposition, 13
*Chippewa* discontinued, 199, 201
*Hiawatha* equipment exhibited, 23, 40, 43
Mont Clare station, 146
*Olympian Hiawatha,* final departure, 187
Railroad Fair, 1948, 106
Union Station, 10, 20, 36, 38, 46, 58, 63, 70, 83, 87, 124, 139, 165, 188, 205
Chicago & North Western:
*400's,* 22, 24, 31, 36, 43, 74, 126, 127, 196, 210
Milwaukee (Wis.) passenger station (1965), 209
North Western Terminal (Chicago), 58, 205
Omaha Railway, 212, 229
Overpass at Techny, Ill., 26
Proviso (Ill.)-Butler (Wis.) freight line, 111
Speed restrictions, 71
UP's streamliners switched to Milwaukee Road, 155
Chicago, Burlington & Quincy:
*Exposition Flyer,* 140
Routes, 67, 100, 118, 119, 126, 178, 222
*Zephyrs,* 13, 16, 22, 23, 24, 36, 43, 62, 63, 127, 140, 181
Chicago North Shore & Milwaukee, 162, 207, 209
Chicago, Rock Island & Pacific, 140, 221, 222
Chicago South Shore & South Bend, 247
Chilton, Wis., 188

*Chippewa:*
Beaver Tails carried, 35, 131
Equipment, 125
**4-6-2 No. 152,** 230, 239, 241, 245
GP9 Nos. 2427 and 2429, 170
**No. 21,** 131, 199, 201, 225
Speed schedule, 64
*City of Los Angeles* (UP), 125, 155, 163
*City of San Francisco* (UP), 116, 125
Cle Elum, Wash., 174
Coach 477, 79, 81
Coach 4000, 10, 13, 16, 150
Coach 4400, 10, 13
*Coast Daylight* (SP), 72
Cocktail bar (first on a train), 28
Coleman, Wis., 188, 191, 200
*Columbian:*
Discontinued, 178
EP-1's upgraded for service, 247
First train to arrive at new Tacoma (Wash.) station, 176
4-8-4's supply power, 230
GE box-motors E-22 and E-23 used, 249
Name and numbers transferred from *Olympian Hi* schedule, 162
Remnants, 181
Train 18 leaves Spokane, Wash., 169
Columbus, Wis., 59, 95, 125, 215
Consolidation of trains, 116, 125, 151, 153, 155, 179, 200
Consolidations, 131, 199
Coon Rapids, Ia., 155
*Copper Country Limited,* 6, 196, 200, 225
Copper Range Railroad, 199
Council Bluffs, Ia., 116, 140, 150, 151, 178
Crippen, Curtiss E., 127
Crivitz, Wis., 188, 199
Crouse, C. H., 10

## D

Dakota, Minn., 123
Davis Junction, Ill., 150, 153
*Day Express,* 13, 59
Daybreak, Chief, 124
Deer Lodge, Mont., 159, 163, 174, 175
Deerfield, Ill., 54, 66, 188
Delaney, Edward, 93
Delmar, Ia., 150, 155
Dempsey, William, 13
Des Moines, Ia., 115, 140, 142, 150, 154, 155
Dickerman, William, 22
Dining car (Buffeteria), 126
Dixon, Jeannie, 10
Dixon, W. B., 36
Donahue, Ed, 23
Donald, L. F., 140
Dubuque, Ia., 140, 150, 153, 155
Dugan, Larry H., 176
Duluth, South Shore & Atlantic, 194
Duplainville, Wis., 36, 175, 209, 214

## E

East Rio, Wis., 66
East Wye Switch, S. Dak., 154, 155
Eau Claire, Wis., 125, 126
Edgebrook, Ill., 71, 229
Electrics:
Bi-polars, 170, 175, 246, 248, 257
EP-4's, 165, 166, 175, 179
Quills, 175, 247, 257
Elgin, Ill., 150, 155
Elgin, Joliet & Eastern, 71, 89, 162, 204, 207
Elk Point, S. Dak., 155
Elkhart Lake, Wis., 188, 197, 199
Ellensburg, Wash., 163
Ellis, C. Hamilton, 225
Elm Grove, Wis., 36, 204
Elmwood Park, Ill., 146
*Empire Builder* (GN), 127, 156, 159, 174, 176
Ennis, J. B., 22
*Exposition Flyer* (CB&Q), 140

## F

Fairbanks-Morse:
EMD units spliced with FM's, 118, 124, 125
Milwaukee Road receives units for *Olympian Hi* service, 162, 251, 254
**No. 5,** 157, 159, 251, 254
**Nos. 12-A and 12-B,** 153
**No. 21A,** 106
**Nos. 21 and 22,** 97, 251
Power pool entered, 84
Six-axle units replaced, 102
Fastest steam runs in America, 66, 71
*Fast Mail,* 13, 72
Final dates of operation:
*Afternoon Hiawatha,* 127
*Chippewa,* 200
*Midwest Hiawatha,* 155
Milwaukee-Madison trains, 116
*North Woods Hiawatha,* 139
*Olympian Hiawatha,* 185, 187
Finke, Walter, 93
Florida East Coast, 178
Fordson Junction, Minn., 67
*400's* (C&NW), 22, 24, 31, 36, 43, 74, 126, 127, 196, 210
Franksville, Wis., 71
Frederick, Crown Prince of Denmark, 62
Fredonia, Wis., 197
Frontenac, Minn., 67

## G

Galewood, Ill., 42
Gas-electric, 199
General Electric, 175, 246, 247, 249
General Motors:
Electro-Motive Division:
**E6 No. 15,** 72, 84, 87, 89, 94, 95, 170, 181, 251, 253
**E7's,** 84, 90, 97, 98, 99, 101, 124, 125, 135, 150, 151, 153, 162, 253
**E9's,** 46, 118, 124, 125, 179, 180, 182, 215, 218, 251, 252, 256

**FP7's,** 46, 102, 106, 114, 118, 124, 125, 137, 139, 153, 170, 179, 182, 199, 216, 218, 251, 255, 256
**FP45's,** 46, 124, 215, 252
**GP9's,** 170, 199, 200, 255
Gessaman, John, 150
Gillick, J. T., 22
Glenview, Ill., 42, 70, 125
Grandy, Al, 83, 162
Grant, L. E., 23
Grayland, Ill., 70, 71, 86, 204
Great Britain:
Allen, Cecil J., 70
Great Western, 13
London & North Eastern, 26
*Great Falls,* sleeper, 10, 16
Great Northern, 156, 176, 218
Green Bay, Wis., 115, 188, 196, 199, 200
Green, Dwight H., 90
Green Island, Ia., 150, 155
Grey, Nancy, 62
Greyhound, 215
Gurnee, Ill., 66, 71

## H

Haddock, Ernie, 62, 83
Hampl, Edward, 90
Harlowton, Mont., 138, 159, 163, 175, 179, 251, 257
Harrington, Russ, 124
Hartland, Wis., 57, 68
Hastings, Minn., 26, 67, 119, 204, 220, 222
Hawarden, Ia., 150
Haynes, George B., 36
Hettinger, N. Dak., 159, 163
Hicks, F. N., 59, 156
Hilbert, Wis., 188, 196, 199
Hoard, A. C., 66, 67
Hudsons:
**E7's replace,** 84, 90
**No. 100,** 64, 67, 70, 77, 229, 235
**No. 101,** 83, 106, 107, 225
**No. 102,** 61, 63, 229
**No. 103,** 58
**No. 104,** 76
**No. 131,** 72, 175
**No. 132,** 175
**No. 6402,** 12, 13
Performance, 62
Hyak, Wash., 178

## I

Ianelli (sculptor), 114
Illinois Central, 186
Inaugural dates:
*Afternoon Hiawatha,* 26
*Chippewa,* 188
*Midwest Hiawatha,* 140
*Morning Hiawatha,* 59
*North Woods Hiawatha,* 128, 131
*Olympian Hiawatha,* 162
Ingrid, Princess of Denmark, 62
Iron Mountain, Mich., 188, 199
Iron River, Mich., 188, 194, 200
Ishpeming, Mich., 196
Island Siding, Minn., 67

**J**

Janesville, Wis., 23, 204, 209
Johnson, Carrie, 36

**K**

Kansas City, Mo., 115, 204, 221
Kellogg, Minn., 67
Kelly, Edward J., 10, 59
Kiley, Jane, 115
Kiley, John P., 115
Kinnickinnic drawbridge
   (Milwaukee), 70, 204, 208
Kittitas, Wash., 175
Knowlton, H. B., 66, 67
Kuhler, Otto, 44, 46, 75, 224, 228, 235, 252

**L**

La Crosse, Wis., 23, 66, 67, 111, 120, 125, 163, 204, 222
Ladies' and children's coach-
   Touralux car, 163, 174
Lake, Wis., 13, 54, 64, 66, 70, 71, 87, 89
Lake City, Minn., 67, 114
Lamoille, Minn., 97
Leg-rest coach seats, 176
Lehman, Herbert, 22
Lemmon, S. Dak., 174
Lionel, 63, 224, 246
Longfellow, Henry Wadsworth, 22, 38
Lunch coaches, 200

**M**

Madison, Wis., 23, 36, 43, 116, 125, 204, 209, 215
Madrid, Ia., 140, 142, 150
Manilla, Ia., 138, 140, 144, 149, 150, 151, 153, 154, 155
Mannheim, Ill., 140
Maple Valley, Wash., 181
Mapleton, Ia., 150
Marinette, Wis., 194
Marion, Ia., 140, 144, 150, 153, 155
Marks, Jerry, 140
Marmarth, N. Dak., 159, 163, 178
Marshall Field & Company, 10
Mass, Mich., 199
Mathers, Lloyd W., 62
Mauston, Wis., 36, 66, 217
Mayfair, Ill., 64, 70, 71, 204, 206
McKeever, Mich., 199
McManus, Hugh, 63, 83
McPherson, W. R., 124
Menominee, Mich., 194, 200
Menomonee drawbridge
   (Milwaukee), 175, 211, 225
*Mercury* (NYC), 93
Merriam Park, Minn., 67
Merrill, Wis., 128
Meyer, Betty, 163
*Midwest Hiawatha*, 35, 131, 135, 188, 194, 200
Mikados, 110, 194
Milbank, S. Dak., 181, 187
Miles City, Mont., 163, 165

Milwaukee, Wis.:
   Depot (1886), 12, 61, 83, 86, 123, 192
   *Hiawatha* equipment exhibited, 23, 40, 43, 115
   Passenger station (1965), 126, 209, 210
   Skytops stored, 202
Milwaukee & Mississippi, 209
*Milwaukee Magazine*, 229
Minneapolis, Minn., 97, 116, 176, 179, 187, 221, 222
Minnesota Transfer Railway, 222
Minocqua, Wis., 36, 66, 128, 131
Missoula, Mont., 163, 247
Mobridge, S. Dak., 138, 159, 163
Montana Canyon (Sixteen Mile
   Canyon), 157, 163
Montevideo, Minn., 163
*Morning Hiawatha* (inaugural date), 59
Mount Carroll, Ill., 155

**N**

National Railway Historical
   Society, 62, 124
Necedah, Wis., 138
Netherlands, 93
New Lisbon, Wis., 36, 59, 128, 131, 202
New York Central, 62, 93
Newport, Minn., 67, 118, 222
*North Coast Limited* (NP), 127, 176
*North Woods Hiawatha*, 35, 38, 66, 144, 194
Northbrook, Ill., 66, 70
Northern Pacific, 126, 127, 156, 165, 176, 187, 247
Northerns, 169, 175, 230
Nystrom, Karl F., 13, 44, 74, 90

**O**

Oakdale, Wis., 66, 107
Oakland, Minn., 67
Oakwood, Wis., 13, 66, 87
Oconomowoc, Wis., 74, 116, 128
Okauchee, Wis., 128
Olivia, Minn., 176
*Olympian Hiawatha*, 13, 48, 53, 62, 156, 159
Omaha, Nebr., 62, 140, 149, 150, 151, 153, 155
Omaha Railway (C&NW), 212, 229
Ontonagon, Mich., 194, 199
Ortonville, Minn., 181
Othello, Wash., 163, 170, 230, 257

**P**

Pacific Coast Railroad, 181
Pacific Junction, Ill., 71
Pacifics:
   **F-3's**, 188, 191, 192
   **No. 150**, 196
   **No. 151**, 194, 196, 197, 199, 225, 230, 239
   **No. 152**, 193, 194, 196, 197, 199, 230, 239, 241, 245
   **No. 184**, 94

No. 801, 144, 149, 230, 238, 239
No. 812, 135, 136, 137, 144, 149, 225, 230, 238, 239
No. 6160, 36, 37, 230, 241
Passenger stations (new):
   Butte, Mont., 178
   Milwaukee, Wis., 126, 209, 210
   Tacoma, Wash., 176
Pembine, Wis., 188
Penn Central, 64
Pennsylvania Railroad, 178, 188, 218, 246
Perlick, B. H., 114
Permacel train, 210
Perry, Ia., 140, 150, 153, 154, 155
Peterson, Audrey, 163
Pewaukee, Wis., 57, 68, 123, 209, 214
*Pioneer Hiawatha*, 90
*Pioneer Limited*, 7, 13, 23, 36, 62, 90, 163, 171
Plymouth, Wis., 188, 197
Pollock, Dr. and Mrs. Lewis J., 59
Portage, Wis., 36, 63, 66, 84, 89, 181
Poss, Ellen, 140
Powerton, Wis., 92
Pullman Company, 174
Pullman-Standard, 90, 112, 114, 159, 160, 162, 163, 170, 174

**R**

Racine, Wis., 204
*Railroad Magazine*, 64
Railroad Society of Milwaukee, 90, 162, 170, 207
*Railway Reminiscences of Three
   Continents*, 63
Ranney, Wis., 66, 87, 89
Rapid City, S. Dak., 149, 150
Raymore, Wis., 66
Red Wing, Minn., 23, 31, 59, 67, 222
Re-equipping dates:
   *Chippewa*, 199
   *Midwest*, 150
   *Twin Cities*, 40, 43, 74, 90
Renslow, Wash., 175
Renton, Wash., 163, 185
Rhame, N. Dak., 159
Ringling, Mont., 178
River Junction, Minn., 67
Rockford, Ill., 23, 140, 150
*Rocky Mountain Rocket* (CRI&P), 140
Rondout, Ill., 66, 70, 71, 87, 89, 162, 204, 207
Roundup, Mont., 163
Ryan, N. A., 13

**S**

St. Paul, Minn., 13, 59, 63, 64, 76, 118, 220
Saukville, Wis., 197, 199
Savanna, Ill., 115, 126, 140, 150, 153, 155
Scandrett, H. A., 10, 22, 38, 59, 83
Schofield, Wis., 135, 136
Seattle, Wash., 156, 159, 173, 174, 181, 185, 186

Section operation of trains, 12, 13, 36, 38, 63, 74, 86, 95, 116, 118, 120, 128, 131, 134, 139, 179, 199
Sidnaw, Mich., 194
Signaling, 26, 150, 155, 195, 199, 207
*Sioux*, 13, 149
Sioux City, Ia., 115, 140, 150, 151, 155
Sioux Falls, S. Dak., 115, 138, 140, 150, 153, 155
Skytop Lounge cars:
   Parlors:
      Advertisements, 106
      Beaver Tails replaced, 93
      *Coon Rapids*, 104, 202
      *Dell Rapids*, 202
      *Priest Rapids*, 123
      Schedule change, 187
      Slogan, 90
      Straight parlors replace, 120
   Sleepers:
      Advertisements, 159, 170, 176
      Milwaukee Road takes delivery, 163, 170
Snoqualmie Pass, Wash., 182
Soo Line, 36, 126, 209, 211
Southern Pacific, 72, 126, 251
*Southwest Limited*, 13
Sparta, Wis., 59, 63, 66, 81, 84, 89
Speed logs, 67, 68, 87
Spokane, Wash., 163, 169, 174, 181, 186, 187
Star Lake, Wis., 128, 131, 132, 139
Stassen, Harold, 59
Stephens, W. E., 64, 67
Stevens, Brooks, 90, 91, 158, 160, 162, 163, 170
Still Day, Chief, 124
Sturgeon Bay, Wis., 194
Sturtevant, Wis., 13, 42, 66, 70, 87, 164, 177, 204
Summit, S. Dak., 181
Super Domes, 110, 111, 112, 114, 115, 123, 125, 176, 200, 202
Superior, Mont., 178
Swanson, Cliff, 93

**T**

Tacoma, Wash., 159, 174, 176, 178, 179, 187
Tama, Ia., 150
Techny, Ill., 13, 26, 64, 66, 71
Ten-Wheelers, 128, 130, 131, 133, 199, 225, 230, 242
Thompson, E. L., 64
Three Forks, Mont., 163
Tip Top Tap cars:
   Exterior design, 74, 151
   Interior design, 28, 33, 43, 44, 53, 58, 79, 93, 100, 105, 150, 151
   Profits, 36
Tomah, Wis., 36, 66, 116, 120, 176, 181
Tomahawk, Wis., 128
Touralux (intermediate) sleepers, 159, 163, 176, 186
Towers:
   A-5 (Pacific Junction, Ill.), 71, 204

A-20 (Techny, Ill.), 13, 26, 64, 66, 71, 204, 207
A-68 (Caledonia, Wis.), 66, 70, 87
CK (Winona, Minn.), 67, 222
G (Merriam Park, Minn.), 67
Grand Crossing (La Crosse, Wis.), 66, 222
Medary (La Crosse, Wis.), 66, 222
North Milwaukee, 195
St. Croix (Hastings, Minn.), 119, 178, 202, 204, 220, 222
Transportation Act of 1958, 200
Travel-Dine-Sleep plan, 186, 187
Truesdell, Wis., 245
Tunnel City, Wis., 66, 74, 180, 218, 222
*20th Century Limited* (NYC), 62
25th anniversary *(Afternoon
   Hiawatha)*, 124

**U**

Uecker, Harvey, 225
Union Pacific:
   *City of Los Angeles*, 125, 155, 163
   *City of San Francisco*, 116, 125
   Streamliners, 10, 116, 125, 126, 151, 153, 155, 173, 178
   *Train of Tomorrow*, dome-diner, 172, 173

**V**

Vending machine coach, 197
Vendome, Mont., 166
Vuillet, Baron Gérard, 63

**W**

Wabash, 188
Wabasha, Minn., 67, 125, 126
Wadsworth, Ill., 13, 66, 87
Wallace, William, 124
Warden, Wash., 178
Watertown, S. Dak., 181
Watertown, Wis., 23, 66, 101, 116, 125, 212, 215
Wausau, Wis., 128, 131, 135, 137, 138, 139, 212
Wausaukee, Wis., 188
Wauwatosa, Wis., 66, 102, 103, 109
Weaver, Minn., 67, 219, 222
Webster, S. Dak., 181, 187
West Lake Forest, Ill., 55, 66, 87
West Salem, Wis., 66, 222
Westinghouse, 246, 257
Whitman, Minn., 99, 123, 219
Wilson, Ill., 66, 71
Winona, Minn., 22, 23, 67, 125, 174, 222
Wisconsin Dells, Wis., 36, 44, 99, 112, 124, 125, 181, 212, 217
Wisconsin Rapids, Wis., 128
Wolf, J. W., 176
Woodruff, Wis., 128, 131, 139, 212
World's fastest diesel run, 181
World's fastest steam run, 63, 186

**Z**

Zackon, Walter, 62
*Zephyrs* (CB&Q), 13, 16, 22, 23, 24, 36, 43, 62, 63, 127, 140, 181

**Jim Scribbins** is a retired Milwaukee Road executive. He lives in West Bend, Wisconsin. He is also the author of *The 400 Story: Chicago & Northwestern's Premier Passenger Trains.*

———

**Also Published by the University of Minnesota Press**

*The Great Northern Railway* by Ralph W. Hidy, Muriel E. Hidy, Roy V. Scott, and Don L. Hofsommer

*The Hook & Eye: A History of the Iowa Central Railway* by Don L. Hofsommer

*The Tootin' Louie: A History of the Minneapolis & St. Louis Railway* by Don L. Hofsommer

*Minneapolis and the Age of Railways* by Don L. Hofsommer

*Minnesota Logging Railroads* by Frank A. King

*The Missabe Road: The Duluth, Missabe and Iron Range Railway* by Frank A. King

*Dining Car to the Pacific: The "Famously Good" Food of the Northern Pacific Railway* by William A. McKenzie

*Union Pacific: Volume I, 1862–1893* by Maury Klein

*Union Pacific: Volume II, 1894–1969* by Maury Klein

*Twin Cities by Trolley: The Streetcar Era in Minneapolis and St. Paul* by John W. Diers and Aaron Isaacs

*The Boomer: A Story of the Rails* by Harry Bedwell